Quality in eBusiness
The New DNA

Edited By

Professor Mohamed Zairi

European Centre for Best Practice Management
PUBLISHING HOUSE

Quality in eBusiness
The New DNA

1st Edition 2009

ISBN 978-1-906993-06-1

9 781906 993061 >

Published by:

European Centre for Best Practice Management

1, Carriage Fold
Cullingworth
Keighley. West Yorkshire
BD13 5DW
UK
Tel: +44-1535-275030
www.ECBPM.com

Cover Design

UpStart Design & Media

25 Aireville Crescent
Bradford
BD9 4EU
UK

"We are just starting to witness the beginning of a new and exciting Quality Revolution in the 21st century".

"Intrinsic is the belief that quality does not happen by accident, it must be Planned"!

Dr. Joseph Juran

Contents

List of figures

List of tables

List of co-contributors

Dr Saad Al Wabel	(Chapters 2, 3 and 4)
Dr Turki Al Tameem	(Chapter 5)
Miss Wafa' Abu Snieneh	(Chapter 6)
Peter Massey, David Naylor, Marion Howard-Healy and Tony Bruno	(Chapter 7)[i]
Sam Huang	(Chapter 1)[ii]

---

[i] Report produced with special permission (granted 8th October 2007) – All rights reserved to Limebridge Global Alliance, 2005.

[ii] Report produced with special permission (granted 15th October 2007) – All rights reserved to GCCRM.

Acknowledgements

No book is ever written alone and no research endeavour is ever carried out in solitude.

First and foremost, my greatest appreciation has to go to my research teams past and present, and in particular, the individuals involved in these compilations and whose research projects I have enjoyed leading and closely supervising. In particular, my sincere thanks and deep appreciation go to my co-contributors: **Dr Saad Al Wabel, Dr Turki Al Tameem, Miss Wafa' Abu Snieneh** and in particular to **Mr Sam Huang** from **GCCRM** and **Mr Tony Bruno** from **Limebridge Global Alliance** for contributing chapters 1 and 7, respectively. Thank you to all for making the book on *Quality in the New Digital Age,* possible.

My sincere thanks also go to my support teams, past and present, who make our work possible every day of the week, all months of the year and who have helped sustain our focus and our determination to continue pioneering.

Lastly, my thanks and appreciation go to my wife Alweena and my children Adel, Bilal and Nadir for their unconditional love and unwavering support.

Dedication

But when I searched, I found no work so meritorious as the discovery and development of the arts and inventions that tend to civilise the life of man. (Francis Bacon)

This book is dedicated to all the men and women whose mission in life is to pioneer, validate and enlighten others with knowledge and the discovery of facts and the truth. It is also dedicated to all those who can help by developing solutions to problems and finding answers to enquiries. Dr Joseph Juran once said: 'My job of contributing to the welfare of my fellow man is the great unfinished business.'

It is therefore hoped that the content of this book will help move forward the human thinking capacity, will assist in the development of the enquiry mind and will support future quests for knowledge and advancement of theory and practice in the field of Total Quality Management and related topics.

Our biggest thrill would be to see that the content of this book is used, the knowledge presented consumed and the various ideas applied. It may of course be wishful thinking but we remain hopeful that the efforts made in putting this text together are not futile and that there will be some positive use of the various concepts presented.

As Rita C. Richey (October, 1999) wrote:

Ideas often take a substantial amount of time to be appreciated, and even for those few that attract attention quickly, there is an assumption that one needs the perspective of hindsight to determine their lasting value. Consequently, an intellectual inheritance is usually determined by the survivors rather than by the donor, and the labels that describe the merit of one's ideas are affixed by subsequent generations.

Introduction

Talking about quality in a digital environment is perhaps a very challenging consideration, since we are faced with a multitude of challenges that have never been experienced before. Quality in the conventional sense, being implemented in a brick and mortar environment, has been a daunting experience for most businesses in the vast majority of industrial sectors. Indeed, for the last 100 years or so companies have wrestled with aspects of quality control, quality assurance, bringing consistency across the value chain and delivering reliably and dependably to their customers. The tools and the techniques of Total Quality Management that have helped to drive industrial growth and development East and West have been extremely valuable and demonstrate that overall, customer value has increased. The levels of reliability, consistency and dependability have significantly improved in most industries. Here, however, stops the net value of what can be referred to as conventional quality and this marks the start of a new set of challenges and questions that need to be asked for an e-based business environment.

The main questions about quality in an e-based environment are as follows:

- How do we define the criteria of total quality management that drives an e-based business environment?
- What are the critical elements that shape an e-based business environment for which we can design the processes, systems and methods that we can control throughout the value chain of a business?
- What are the technical parameters that need to be optimised and made right first time so that a business can perform 24/7 and in a consistent and reliable manner?

- How do we ensure that the human element interfaces in the right way with an IT based environment so that the customer is not ignored or neglected at the other end?
- How do we maintain constant, continuous and positive interaction with the customer if the new ethos of an e-based environment is a customer 'pull' mentality driven by a self service business practice?
- How do we respond with flexibility, with speed and with innovation and empathy to customer needs if the customer is in the driving seat?

There are, of course, additional questions that lead us to redefine quality in a suitable manner as we engage more and more with the advent of new technology and start to make e-business a normal practice across the board. These questions are to do with defining the real value of customer experience and would also entail redefining the real purpose of the modern business environment.

A useful white paper, published by Strativity (2006), asked the question about the paradigm shift in terms of servicing customers and also presented many useful and challenging questions to be considered in terms of the discovery of what has been referred to as the 'tribal customer'. The white paper states that:

> *Despite their best efforts to delight customers through the web, companies have rarely succeeded in elevating their web experiences beyond experience parity to a point of competitive differentiation. These sites have optimized business processes, solved problems, and presented requisite information but have done little else. Customers do not generally flock to websites that look similar to the next website, requiring companies to compensate by lowering prices to drive traffic and increase sales. Although recent effort to improve the self service experience is a positive step forward, attempts to satisfy a time starved, price sensitive*

customer, who does not seek any emotional engagement remains highly unlikely.

Indeed, the feasibility of making the web experience more fulfilling and beyond transactional efficiencies, as argued in the white paper, remains elusive. Most e-commerce sites are driven by internal motives to create bigger transactional efficiencies and to drive internal requirements, rather than to acknowledge the paradigm shift in what has been referred to as a shift from a utilitarian to a tribal customer breed. Emotional interactivity and the individualisation or personalisation of the service to allow customers to conduct their own self expressions remains under question.

It is clear that the challenges for online customer interactions are going to be pervasive, not just in terms of tackling the urgent technical quality aspects of creating seamlessness in the e-business value chain, and making technology a true enabler for customers to indulge in their own individual experiences, but also the biggest challenge is to change the business mindset and create a focus or a centric approach that considers the customer a 'tribal customer' and moves away from the utilitarian mindset. It has already been acknowledged that by focusing on internal optimisation and the design of traditional processes, and on the provision of self service sites that only reinforce the practice, commoditisation is now becoming more common. Most sites are designed in the same way and most approaches to customer service are conducted in the right way and therefore this is blurring the competitive differences between various organisations in various industries.

E-businesses that have been naïve enough or complacent enough to consider the customer from a utilitarian perspective have actually created several challenges for their future. At the basic level, by negating the importance of the customer and the importance of the individualisation or personalisation of customer experience, businesses have developed websites that are as big as their smallest competitors. Visually, of course, the customer sees a business on a computer screen and cannot therefore be in a position to distinguish or differentiate the size, the quality, the capability or the uniqueness of the providers. The commoditisation principle referred to earlier means that the customers sees that they are being offered something with 'one size fits all' and that the approach adopted by the e-business provider is transactionally driven. In a sense, focusing on website design strips organisations from their competitive differentiations and enables inferior businesses to eliminate their competitive disadvantages. By reaching a parity level between various businesses, the quality challenge for the future is going to be whether those businesses can rise to the challenge and acknowledge that a customer paradigm shift has taken place and that the ethos of their business has to move from a transactionally based product or service 'push' mentality, to a relationship based, or customer engagement and empowerment base. The approach to self service therefore has to be redefined so that the move is to redefine the value from a price driven perspective to a customer value definition basis. This will enable e-businesses to reposition and truly differentiate themselves by creating close identification with the tribal customer, who is driven by emotional engagement and who craves emotional interactivity and personal expression – as opposed to the utilitarian customer, who is emotionless and wants what can be referred to as 'the convenient in and out' transaction.

There are, however, growing experiences and changes across the board that indicate the importance of the tribal customer. Businesses are starting to acknowledge that quality in a digital environment has to be totally redefined and that the new parameters for designing the infrastructure, to allow customer engagement and interaction, have to be right first time. Also, by putting the customer in the driving seat, the focus in the future is going to be more on redefinition across the board and a new mindset of engagement for the customer as a plc and as a complete partner, working upstream and downstream the value chain creating value for all parties concerned. The white paper by Strativity concludes that many firms have now started to transform the parity based experiences into emotionally engaging and passionate experiences because they have started to acknowledge several principles, including:

- Emotionally engaging: this is to allow customers to really feel that they are valued and to ignite their passion and create their connection.
- Interactive: this means that customers upstream and downstream are co-creators of products and services. For instance, Nike allows customers to design their own shoes. This experience is reflected in other industries too, for example, Ikea allows their customers to design their own kitchens, and some paint manufacturers allow customers to choose and make their own paint.
- Personal: personalised experiences designed with a specific individual in mind and crafted by the individuals themselves, where there is an emotional attachment.
- Expressive: customers are able to express their emotions in a unique and exciting way, for example, in social networking sites, which allow customers to create their own identities with the association of their favourite brands.
- Authentic: this means that the customer experience cannot be for others as well. It is unique and is an individual customer's own experience. The authenticity matters to emotionally attached customers. For example, Amazon's inclusion of customer ranking systems for its books authenticates the experience for their customers. Chevrolet, for example, introduced a website allowing visitors to personalise and create their own commercial vehicles (Strativity, 2006).

The question is, are we ready to face the digital business environment, where the customer is king, and where customer demands have shifted from transactional purposes to emotional fulfilment purposes? A survey conducted by Forrester (2005) targeted 176 decision makers of large North American companies with annual turnovers exceeding $500 million, and was related to an evaluation of customer experience practices. The survey revealed that companies are still struggling to fulfil their customer needs using the web as one of the main channels.

Figure 0.1 indicates that there is still extensive reliance on other touch points and other channels to fulfil customer needs and requirements; the web was rated as the most useful means by only 25% of respondents.

Figure 0.1 Fulfilment of customer needs in various channels

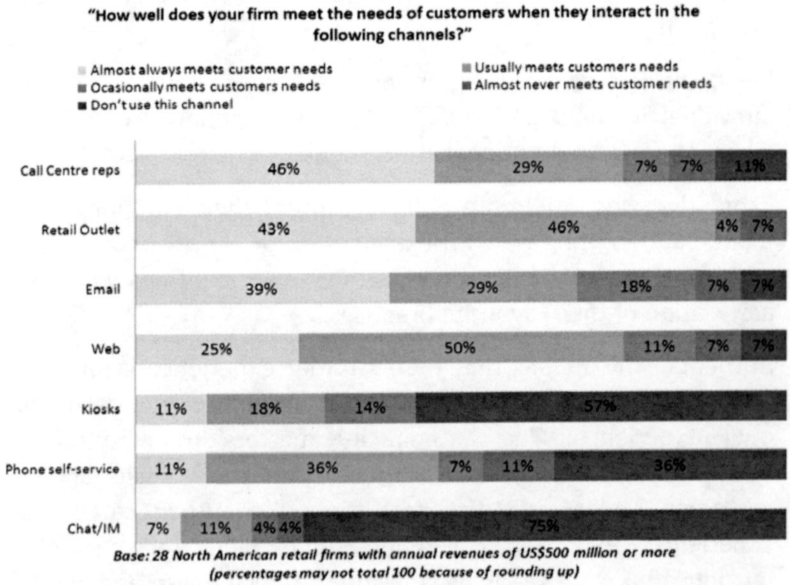

Source: Forrester Research, Inc (2005)

Figure 2 does, however, indicate that the respondents acknowledge that in the future the internet is going to grow significantly and will allow them to interact with their customers in a more pervasive manner.

Figure 0.2 Retailers anticipate a large increase in volume in online channels

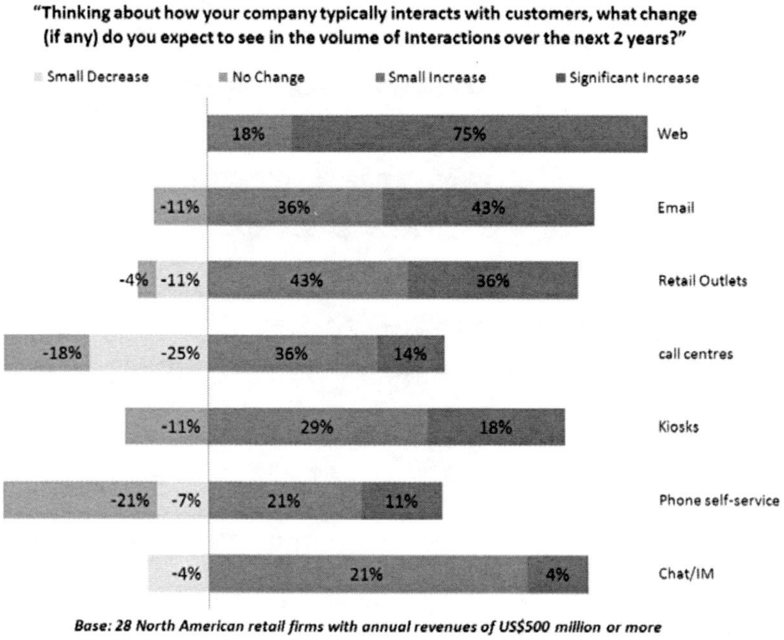

Source: Forrester Research, Inc (2005)

Figure 0.3 indicates that the survey has an interesting finding in relation to the challenges that hinder customer experience improvement. It is not surprising that they see that trying to change employee behaviour is perhaps the highest priority and the biggest challenge, in addition to managing technology and the related quality issues. There is, however, a big challenge in defining customer experience and putting effective strategies for that alongside measurement of the individualised customer experiences discussed earlier.

Figure 0.3 Internal challenges hinder customer experience improvements

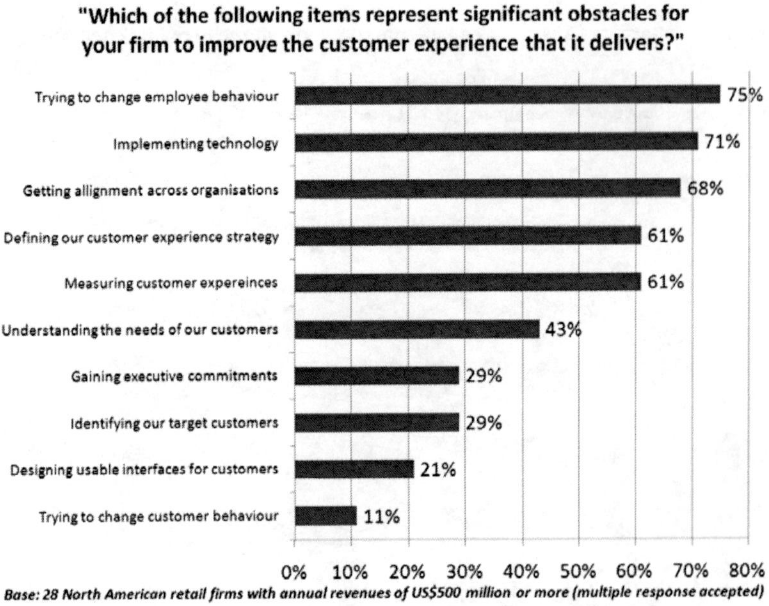

Source: Forrester Research, Inc (2005)

This manuscript attempts to put together the aspects of quality that will help govern an e-based working environment, by going back to basics and understanding evolution and development of the internet phenomenon and how it works in practice, together with a critical analysis of quality factors that impinge on the management of an e-business organisation effectively, reliably, consistently and with high levels of dependability. This will be useful in managing quality in online business. There is also a chapter which refers to the practice of e-commerce in a non-profit context; this is particularly suitable for the e-Government context. Furthermore, there is comprehensive analysis and evaluation of the growth and development of online shopping behaviour and the associated quality issues and quality challenges involved in this context.

We hope you find this compilation useful as we continue to face the reality of the digital world and the changes brought about by the internet.

Professor Mohamed Zairi

Editor

References

Root, N. L., Johnson, C. A. and Amato, M (2005) *Survey of NA Firms Reveals Retail Customer Experience Trends*, Forrester Research Inc.

Strativity White Paper (2006) Redefining Customer Self Service - From Utilitarian to the Tribal Customer, RCV WP 0708, Strativity Group Inc.

Chapter 1

Love it or hate it – The internet is here to stay: The GCCRM Online Customer Experience Research Report (2007)

Objective

With the boom of the internet in China, surfing has become a part of people's lives. In order to better understand customers' online experience so as to modify or fine-tune the experience process for China's users, the 'Online Customer Experience Survey in Mainland China' was conducted. The survey was jointly organised by Web Analytics Association (US) and GCCRM, and aimed to reveal the online experience from an experience-centric perspective rather than the traditional process-centric or efficiency-centric angle.

Methodology

This survey appeared in the form of an online questionnaire (from which it was divided into an e-commerce section and non-e-commerce section). A sample of 10,000 active online members was selected and all respondents were asked a series of questions. After choosing their most loved/hated sites, they had to rate their satisfaction and importance level of 22 sub-processes throughout a typical online experience. The survey began on November 20, 2006 and ended on December 1, 2006. A total of 2,013 valid responses were obtained. 1,386 were from e-commerce websites. 627 were from non-e-commerce websites.

Sub-process

We divided e-commerce into 22 sub-processes and non-e-commerce into 13 sub-processes, as follows:

Table 1.1 Division of sub-processes

E-commerce section	Non e-commerce section
• S1: Loading speed • S2: Visual design • S3: Site navigation • S4: Functionality • S5: Search • S6: Categorisation • S7: Visual aid • S8: Comprehensiveness of information • S9: Customer review column • S10: Product variety • S11: Products are of good value for money • S12: Product quality and reliability • S13: Enquiry column • S14: Purchasing history review • S15: Customised webpage • S16: Customised promotion information • S17: Choices of payment • S18: Freight calculator • S19: Choices of delivery • S20: Confirmation by e-mail or SMS • S21: Goods return or exchange policy • S22: Customer complaint/ feedback system	• S1: Loading speed • S2: Visual design • S3: Site navigation • S4: Functionality • S5: Search • S6: Categorisation • S7: Visual aid • S8: Comprehensiveness of information • S9: Customer review column • S10: Enquiry column • S11: Customised webpage • S12: Customised promotion information • S13: BBS

E-commerce section (N=1386)

Figure 1.1 Ranking of 'love most' e-commerce websites

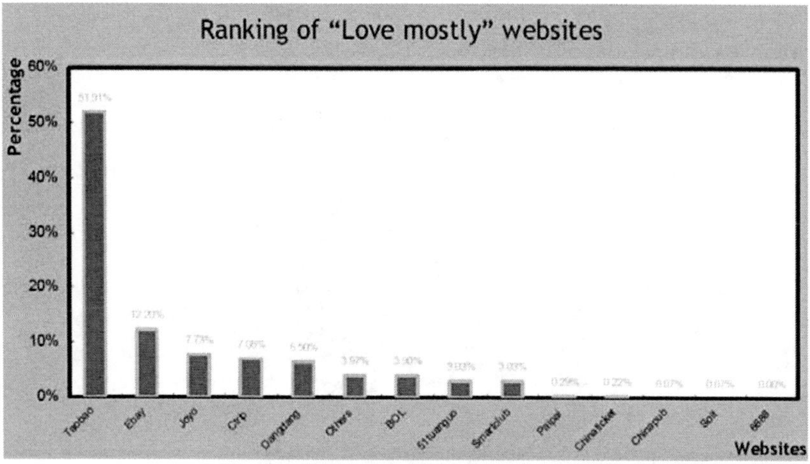

In terms of most loved websites, Taobao was the champion. When asked which e-commerce website they liked most, 51.91% of participants chose Taobao. On the contrary, eBay, the US e-commerce giant, was not so popular in mainland China; only 12.20% of participants chose it. Other followers were Joyo, Ctrip and Dangdang with respective percentages of 7.73%, 7.08% and 6.50%.

Websites with low rankings were not so popular. They included Paiapi, Chinaticket, Chinapub, Soit and 6688; none of the participants chose 6688 as their 'love most' website. These websites all have a low awareness and reputation in the market.

Macoxlane (m18.com) and Orient CJ (ocj.com.cn) performed outstandingly. When participants were asked to write down any other websites, not in the list, which they liked, 27.3% chose Macoxlane (www.m18.com) while 21.8% chose Orient CJ (www.ocj.com.cn).

As shown in the following chart, 29% of participants put convenience as the number one reason to like a website, while 26% chose the variety of products. A third reason to love a website is information security. It is important to point out is that price was not a top reason for customers to like a website. Only 11% thought price was a key reason.

Figure 1.2 Reasons for liking an e-commerce website

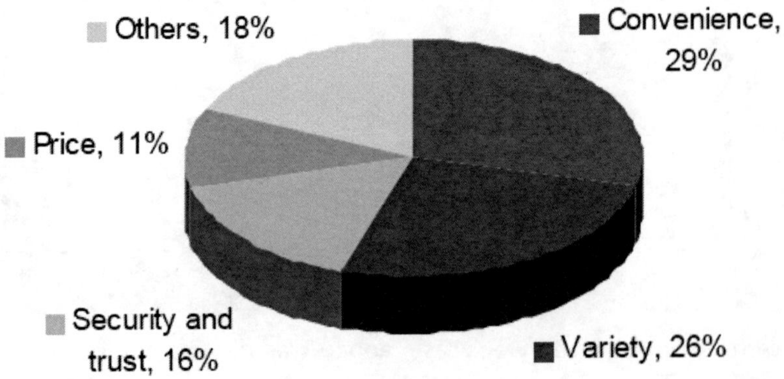

As can be seen from Figure 1.3, eBay China and BOL ranked as the 'most hated' websites, eBay China (19.77%) and BOL (18.4%) were much higher than the others. Although Taobao was the number one 'love most' website, 8.08% of participants chose it as their 'hate most' website. Dangdang followed with 7.79%.

As shown in Figure 1.4, 18% of participants hated a website because of price while 18% hated it because of the design. Top reasons to like a website, such as convenience, product variety, etc. were not top reasons to hate a website.

Figure 1.3 Ranking of 'most hated' e-commerce websites

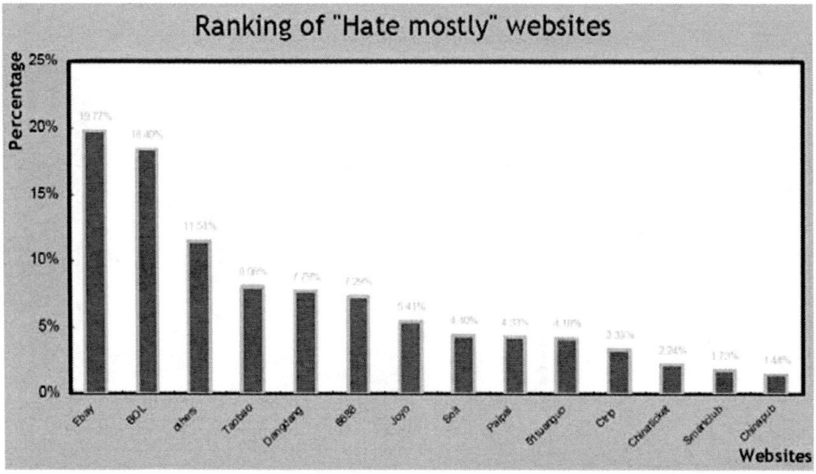

Figure 1.4 Reasons for hating an e-commerce website

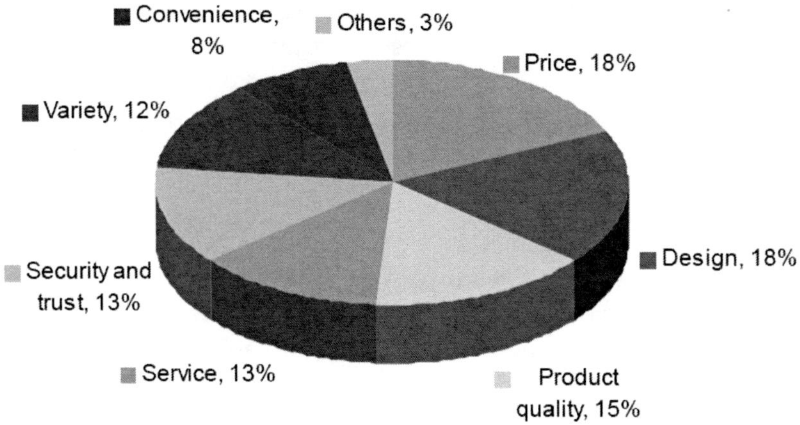

Figure 1.5 Gap analysis – e-commerce websites

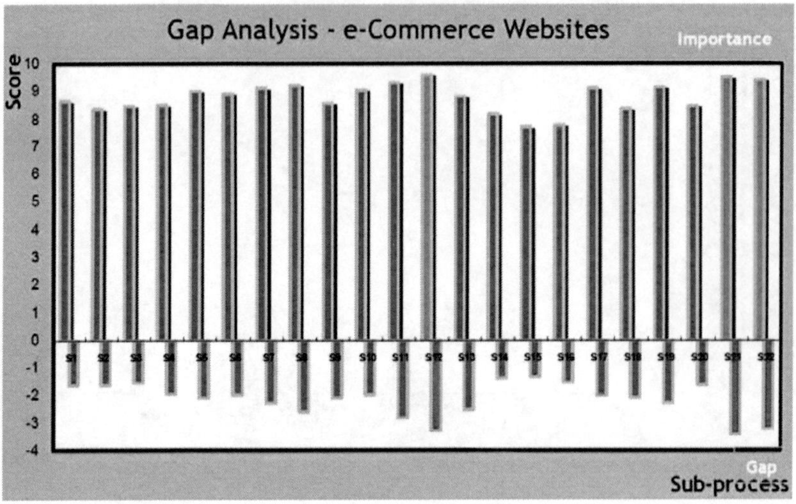

Importance: Among the 22 sub-processes, S12 (product quality), S21 (goods return or exchange) and S22 (customer complaint and feedback) were the top three most important processes (See the X axis in Figure 1.5). When customers purchased online, they cared a lot about the good quality of products, a convenient process for return or exchange, and a good service for handling customer complaints.

Gap analysis: The second part of the X axis calculates the gap between importance and satisfaction (satisfaction is the average value of 'like most' websites and 'hate most' websites). One interesting finding is that top three biggest gaps occur on the top three most important sub-processes: S12 (Product quality), S21 (goods return or exchange) and S22 (customer complaint and feedback).

The smallest gaps occurred on S14 (review purchasing history), S15 (customised web pages) and S16 (customised promotion

Reproduced with special permission from GCCRM – 'Online Customer Experience Research Report', February 2007.

information). Though these processes are not very important, customers get good experience from them.

Case analysis - Taobao vs. eBay China

Figure 1.6 Love most website – Taobao

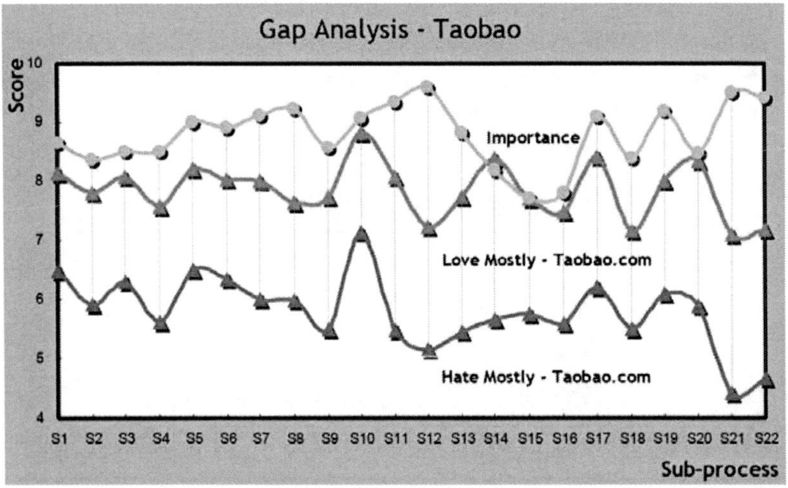

As mentioned before, Taobao is the number one 'love most' website (51.91%). However, 8.08% of participants chose it as the 'hate most' website. The two satisfaction curves have the same pattern. As shown in Figure 1.6, the satisfaction curve of customers who like Taobao largely has the same pattern as the curve of customers who hate Taobao most. Their peaks and troughs occur on the same sub-processes.

Processes leading to a good experience: By comparing the importance curve and the satisfaction curve from customers who like Taobao, it is evident that Taobao provides them with a very good experience on S14 (review of purchasing history). In this sub-process, the value of satisfaction is higher than that of importance.

Need to improve important sub-processes: As mentioned before, even though Taobao is the number one 'love most' website, there are still some customers who chose it as their 'hate most' website. The three biggest gaps between importance and satisfaction happen on S21 (goods return or exchange), S12 (product quality) and S22 (customer complaint and feedback). Detailed numbers are 2.44, 2.38 and 2.22, respectively. These three sub-processes are considered the most important, however, Taobao does not give customers good experiences on these processes.

Figure 1.7 Hate most website – eBay China

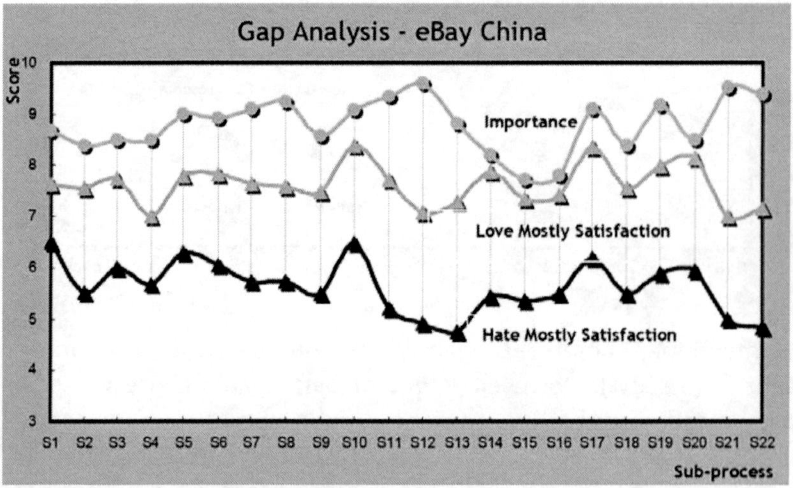

As mentioned earlier, eBay China is the number one 'hate most' website. What follows is an in-depth analysis for the satisfaction curve and importance curve.

The two satisfaction curves have the same pattern. As shown in Figure 1.7, the satisfaction curve of customers who like eBay China and the curve of customers who hate eBay China most, have their peaks and troughs on the same sub-processes.

Does not provide a good experience on important processes: Although eBay China is the number one 'hate most' website, it still gives customers good satisfaction on S1 (loading speed), S16 (customised promotion information) and S15 (customised webpage). However, the three biggest gaps between importance and satisfaction occur on the three most important processes: S21 (goods return or exchange), S12 (product quality) and S22 (customer complaint and feedback). eBay China does not give customers good experience on those processes.

Most of the customers who hate eBay China do so because they think that it is not convenient to use and feel webpage design is poor and has a limited variety of products. Some customers also complained about the information security of eBay China.

Non-e-commerce section (N=627)

As can be seen from Figure 1.8, below, PC-Online took the lead in the 'love most' category. The two most favourable websites were pconline.com.cn (platform/portal of IT information and services) and 51job.com (platform/portal of hiring and recruiting). They were far ahead of the remaining nominated websites, receiving 20.19% and 18.76% of the votes, respectively. In addition, chinamobile.com and tianya.cn are quite popular, receiving 7.15% and 6.84%, respectively.

Figure 1.8 Ratings for 'love most' non-e-commerce websites

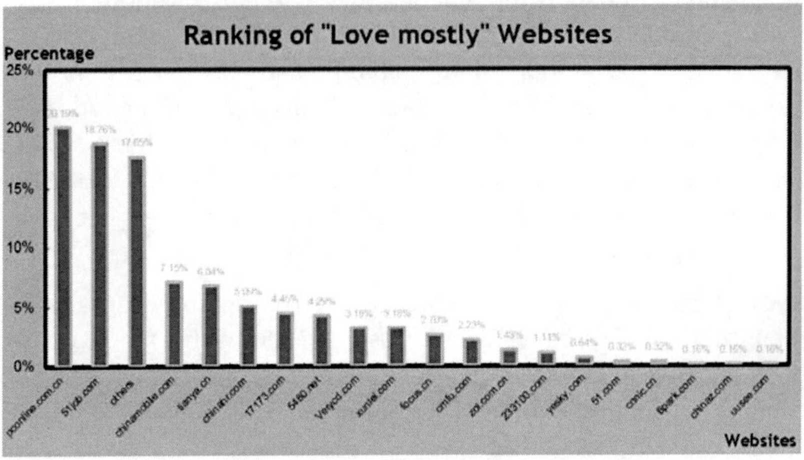

Figure 1.9 Reasons for liking a non-e-commerce website

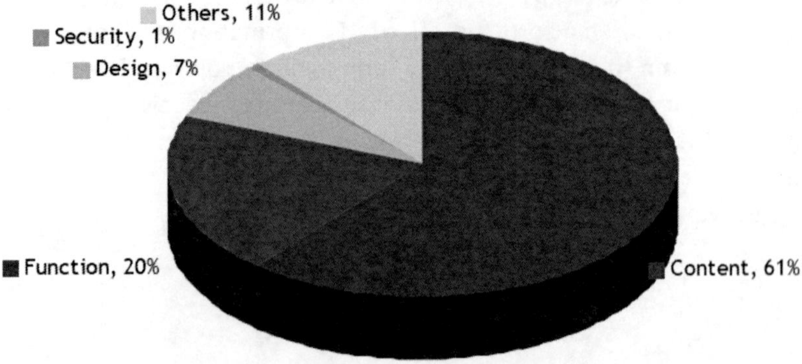

Sixty-one percent of respondents named content as the major reason for them to love the websites that they voted for, while only 20% of respondents named functionality.

Good customer experience of non-e-commerce websites relies more on the concrete content and material provided. Whereas, safety and convenience, two important factors for good online sales websites, are not the key points which customers pay attention to for non-sales websites.

Figure 1.10 Ranking of 'hate most' non-e-commerce websites

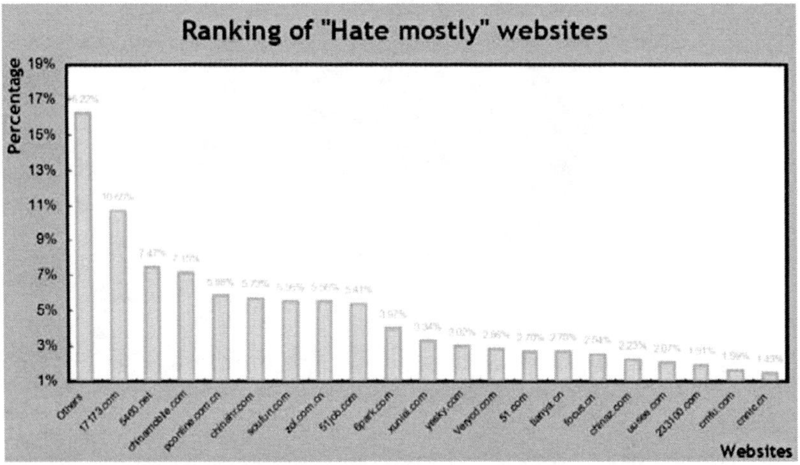

17173 (web portal of online games) was the most disliked non-e-commerce website. A large number of respondents (16.22%) did not choose from the listed websites but chose the option 'others, please specify'. As a result, that option shows no convergence, and most respondents actually answered 'don't hate or dislike any particular website'. Many mentioned that they don't like malicious websites, such as 'strange websites that pop-up by themselves', 'websites with many not working links', and 'websites hidden behind the search result'.

17173.com was the most disliked non-e-commerce website, as voted by 10.65% of respondents.

Webpage layout and the first impression on entering the website, received 26% of respondents' votes as the major reason to dislike a certain website. Only 20% of respondents named functionality. The second tier reasons were 'safety', 'functionality' and 'content', with a relatively equal vote rate of 20%, 19% and 17%, respectively.

Figure 1.11 Reasons for disliking a non-e-commerce website

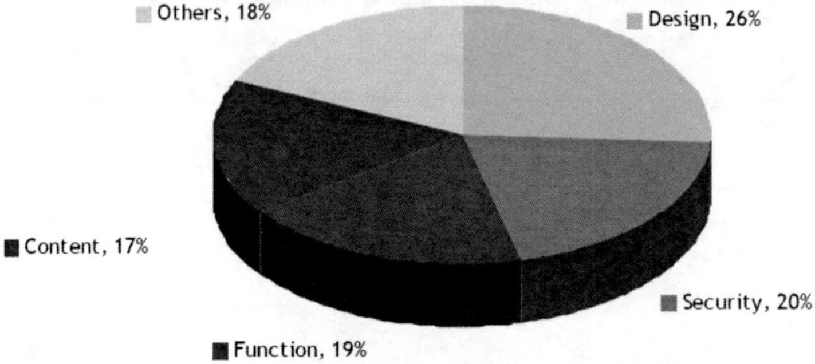

Figure 1.12 Gap analysis-non-e-commerce websites

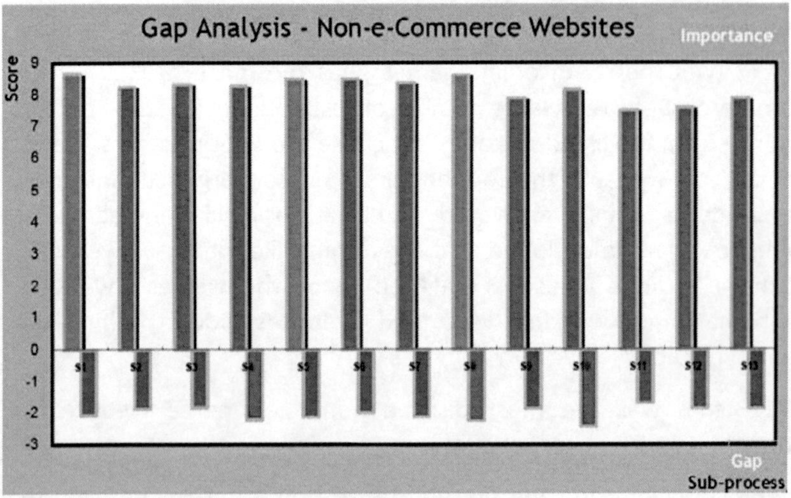

Importance/expectation: Figure 1.12 shows us the importance rating (reflection of expectation) for each of the 13 sub-processes (refer to the positive quadrant above the x axis).

S1 (loading speed), S8 (information abundance) and S5 (searching) rated in the top three positions in terms of importance. Unlike customers of online sales websites, who put more emphasis on product quality, convenient goods return or exchange and customer complaint/feedback, customers of non-sales websites put greater emphasis on convenient online exploring factors, such as loading speed, content abundance and convenient searching.

Gap analysis: The negative quadrant of Figure 1.12 (below the x axis) tells us the average satisfaction rate of all nominated websites (including the most favourable and most disliked websites) in terms of each of the 13 sub-processes. The biggest gaps (difference between importance/expectation and actual satisfaction rate of a certain sub-process) lie in three sub-processes, namely S10 (convenient online query), S8 (complete information) and S4 (no bad links). In other words, on average, non-sales websites did not do well in these sub-processes.

However, the section on e-commerce websites showed a different pattern: S8 (complete information) had one of the greatest gaps, but S5 (searching) and S1 (loading speed) had relatively lower gaps, ranked sixth and seventh respectively. Unlike e-commerce websites, in which the worst customer experiences came from the top three important sub-processes, non-e-commerce websites had definite divergence between worst experience (top three gaps) and importance.

Appendix – Questionnaire

Have you bought anything from a website before?

☐ Yes (Go to e-commercial section)

☐ No (Go to non-e-commercial section)

E-commerce section

Q1: Which online e-commerce website do you like the most? (Brand or company) (Choose one only)?

- 51tuanguo
- 6688
- BOL
- Chinapub
- Chinaticket
- Ctrip
- Dangdang
- Ebay
- Joyo
- Paipai
- Smartclub
- Soit
- Taobao
- Others (please specify)______________________________

Q2: Why do you like this website most?

Q3: Please rate your satisfaction level of the above website from 10-most satisfied to 1-least satisfied

Loading speed	10/9/8/7/6/5/4/3/2/1/N.A
Visual design	10/9/8/7/6/5/4/3/2/1/N.A
Site navigation	10/9/8/7/6/5/4/3/2/1/N.A
Functionality	10/9/8/7/6/5/4/3/2/1/N.A
Search	10/9/8/7/6/5/4/3/2/1/N.A

Categorisation	10/9/8/7/6/5/4/3/2/1/N.A
Visual aid	10/9/8/7/6/5/4/3/2/1/N.A
Comprehensiveness of information	10/9/8/7/6/5/4/3/2/1/N.A
Customer review column	10/9/8/7/6/5/4/3/2/1/N.A
Product variety	10/9/8/7/6/5/4/3/2/1/N.A
Products are of good value for money	10/9/8/7/6/5/4/3/2/1/N.A
Product quality & reliability	10/9/8/7/6/5/4/3/2/1/N.A
Enquiry column	10/9/8/7/6/5/4/3/2/1/N.A
Purchasing history review	10/9/8/7/6/5/4/3/2/1/N.A
Customised webpage	10/9/8/7/6/5/4/3/2/1/N.A
Customised promotion information	10/9/8/7/6/5/4/3/2/1/N.A
Choices of payment	10/9/8/7/6/5/4/3/2/1/N.A
Freight calculator	10/9/8/7/6/5/4/3/2/1/N.A
Choices of delivery	10/9/8/7/6/5/4/3/2/1/N.A
Confirmation by e-mail or SMS	10/9/8/7/6/5/4/3/2/1/N.A
Goods return or exchange policy	10/9/8/7/6/5/4/3/2/1/N.A
Customer complaint/feedback system	10/9/8/7/6/5/4/3/2/1/N.A

Q4: Which online e-commerce website do you like least? (Brand or company) (Choose one only)?

- 51tuanguo
- 6688
- BOL
- Chinapub
- Chinaticket
- Ctrip
- Dangdang
- Ebay
- Joyo
- Paipai

- Smartclub
- Soit
- Taobao
- Others (please specify)____

Q5: Why do you like this website the least?

Q6: Please rate your satisfaction level of the above website from 10-most satisfied to 1-least satisfied

Loading speed	10/9/8/7/6/5/4/3/2/1/N.A
Visual design	10/9/8/7/6/5/4/3/2/1/N.A
Site navigation	10/9/8/7/6/5/4/3/2/1/N.A
Functionality	10/9/8/7/6/5/4/3/2/1/N.A
Search	10/9/8/7/6/5/4/3/2/1/N.A
Categorisation	10/9/8/7/6/5/4/3/2/1/N.A
Visual aid	10/9/8/7/6/5/4/3/2/1/N.A
Comprehensiveness of information	10/9/8/7/6/5/4/3/2/1/N.A
Customer review column	10/9/8/7/6/5/4/3/2/1/N.A
Product variety	10/9/8/7/6/5/4/3/2/1/N.A
Products are of good value for money	10/9/8/7/6/5/4/3/2/1/N.A
Product quality & reliability	10/9/8/7/6/5/4/3/2/1/N.A
Enquiry column	10/9/8/7/6/5/4/3/2/1/N.A
Purchasing history review	10/9/8/7/6/5/4/3/2/1/N.A
Customised webpage	10/9/8/7/6/5/4/3/2/1/N.A
Customised promotion information	10/9/8/7/6/5/4/3/2/1/N.A
Choices of payment	10/9/8/7/6/5/4/3/2/1/N.A
Freight calculator	10/9/8/7/6/5/4/3/2/1/N.A

Choices of delivery	10/9/8/7/6/5/4/3/2/1/N.A
Confirmation by e-mail or SMS	10/9/8/7/6/5/4/3/2/1/N.A
Goods return or change policy	10/9/8/7/6/5/4/3/2/1/N.A
Customer complaint/feedback system	10/9/8/7/6/5/4/3/2/1/N.A

Q7: As a customer of online sales, please rate the below factors according to their importance to your online experience from 10-most important to 1-least important

Loading speed	10/9/8/7/6/5/4/3/2/1/N.A
Visual design	10/9/8/7/6/5/4/3/2/1/N.A
Site navigation	10/9/8/7/6/5/4/3/2/1/N.A
Functionality	10/9/8/7/6/5/4/3/2/1/N.A
Search	10/9/8/7/6/5/4/3/2/1/N.A
Categorisation	10/9/8/7/6/5/4/3/2/1/N.A
Visual aid	10/9/8/7/6/5/4/3/2/1/N.A
Comprehensiveness of information	10/9/8/7/6/5/4/3/2/1/N.A
Customer review column	10/9/8/7/6/5/4/3/2/1/N.A
Product variety	10/9/8/7/6/5/4/3/2/1/N.A
Products are of good value for money	10/9/8/7/6/5/4/3/2/1/N.A
Product quality & reliability	10/9/8/7/6/5/4/3/2/1/N.A
Enquiry column	10/9/8/7/6/5/4/3/2/1/N.A
Purchasing history review	10/9/8/7/6/5/4/3/2/1/N.A
Customised webpage	10/9/8/7/6/5/4/3/2/1/N.A
Customised promotion information	10/9/8/7/6/5/4/3/2/1/N.A
Choices of payment	10/9/8/7/6/5/4/3/2/1/N.A
Freight calculator	10/9/8/7/6/5/4/3/2/1/N.A
Choices of delivery	10/9/8/7/6/5/4/3/2/1/N.A

Confirmation by e-mail or SMS	10/9/8/7/6/5/4/3/2/1/N.A
Goods return or change policy	10/9/8/7/6/5/4/3/2/1/N.A
Customer complaint/feedback system	10/9/8/7/6/5/4/3/2/1/N.A

General information

Sex: Male / Female

Age: <20 / 20-30 / 30-40 / 40-50 / >50

Education: High school / Middle school/ University / College/ Undergraduate and above

Monthly Salary (RMB): <2,000 / 2,000-5,000 / 5,000-10,000 / 10,000-20,000 / >20,000

Location: (Drop-down)

Email: ____

Online purchase frequency:

Once per month/ once per quarter/ once per half-year/ once per year/ once per week

Non e-commerce section

Q1: Which non-e-commercial website do you like the most?

- 17173.com 17173
- 233100.com
- 51.com
- 51job.com
- 5460.net
- 6park.com
- chinahr.com
- chinamobile.com
- chinaz.com
- cmfu.com
- cnnic.cn
- focus.cn
- pconline.com.cn
- soufun.com

- tianya.cn
- uusee.com
- Verycd.com
- xunlei.com
- yesky.com
- zol.com.cn
- Others (please specify)____

Q2: Why do you like this website most?

Q3: Please rate your satisfaction level of the above website from 10-most satisfied to 1-least satisfied

Loading speed	10/9/8/7/6/5/4/3/2/1/N.A
Visual design	10/9/8/7/6/5/4/3/2/1/N.A
Site navigation	10/9/8/7/6/5/4/3/2/1/N.A
Functionality	10/9/8/7/6/5/4/3/2/1/N.A
Search	10/9/8/7/6/5/4/3/2/1/N.A
Categorisation	10/9/8/7/6/5/4/3/2/1/N.A
Visual aid	10/9/8/7/6/5/4/3/2/1/N.A
Comprehensiveness of information	10/9/8/7/6/5/4/3/2/1/N.A
Customer review column	10/9/8/7/6/5/4/3/2/1/N.A
Enquiry column	10/9/8/7/6/5/4/3/2/1/N.A
Customised webpage	10/9/8/7/6/5/4/3/2/1/N.A
Customised promotion information	10/9/8/7/6/5/4/3/2/1/N.A
BBS	10/9/8/7/6/5/4/3/2/1/N.A

Q4: Which non-e-commercial website do you like the least?

- 17173.com 17173
- 233100.com
- 51.com
- 51job.com
- 5460.net
- 6park.com
- chinahr.com
- chinamobile.com
- chinaz.com
- cmfu.com
- cnnic.cn
- focus.cn
- pconline.com.cn
- soufun.com
- tianya.cn
- uusee.com
- Verycd.com
- xunlei.com
- yesky.com
- zol.com.cn
- Others (please specify)____

Q5: Why you like the website the least?

Q6: Please rate your satisfaction level of the above website from 10-most satisfied to 1-least satisfied

Loading speed	10/9/8/7/6/5/4/3/2/1/N.A
Visual design	10/9/8/7/6/5/4/3/2/1/N.A
Site navigation	10/9/8/7/6/5/4/3/2/1/N.A
Functionality	10/9/8/7/6/5/4/3/2/1/N.A
Search	10/9/8/7/6/5/4/3/2/1/N.A
Categorisation	10/9/8/7/6/5/4/3/2/1/N.A
Visual aid	10/9/8/7/6/5/4/3/2/1/N.A

Comprehensiveness of information	10/9/8/7/6/5/4/3/2/1/N.A
Customer review column	10/9/8/7/6/5/4/3/2/1/N.A
Enquiry column	10/9/8/7/6/5/4/3/2/1/N.A
Customised webpage	10/9/8/7/6/5/4/3/2/1/N.A
Customised promotion information	10/9/8/7/6/5/4/3/2/1/N.A
BBS	10/9/8/7/6/5/4/3/2/1/N.A

Q7: To the non-e-commerce websites, please rate the below factors according to their importance to your online experience from 10-most important to 1-least important

Loading speed	10/9/8/7/6/5/4/3/2/1/N.A
Visual design	10/9/8/7/6/5/4/3/2/1/N.A
Site navigation	10/9/8/7/6/5/4/3/2/1/N.A
Functionality	10/9/8/7/6/5/4/3/2/1/N.A
Search	10/9/8/7/6/5/4/3/2/1/N.A
Categorisation	10/9/8/7/6/5/4/3/2/1/N.A
Visual aid	10/9/8/7/6/5/4/3/2/1/N.A
Comprehensiveness of information	10/9/8/7/6/5/4/3/2/1/N.A
Customer review column	10/9/8/7/6/5/4/3/2/1/N.A
Enquiry column	10/9/8/7/6/5/4/3/2/1/N.A
Customised webpage	10/9/8/7/6/5/4/3/2/1/N.A
Customised promotion information	10/9/8/7/6/5/4/3/2/1/N.A
BBS	10/9/8/7/6/5/4/3/2/1/N.A

General information

Sex: Male / Female

Age: <20 / 20-30 / 30-40 / 40-50 / >50

Education: High school / Middle school/ University / College/ Undergraduate and above

Monthly Salary (RMB): <2,000 / 2,000-5,000 / 5,000-10,000 / 10,000-20,000 / >20,000

Location: (Drop-down)

Email: ____

Chapter 2

E-commerce: the new competitive force

E-commerce: an emerging concept

The popularity of e-commerce has made the world change faster than ever before and has removed, to some extent, geographical and physical boundaries by enabling people from different countries to communicate electronically with each other and distribute information rapidly and straightforwardly (Gattiker *et al.*, 2000). The rapid development and wide adoption of e-commerce technology has brought new business opportunities. In February 2000, a Forrester Research report heralded that e-marketplaces would lead to $2.7 trillion US business in 2004 (Forrester Research, 2000a), and in June 2000 another report claimed that: '900 billion Euros will flow via EU e-marketplaces by 2005' (Forrester Research, 2000b), while the Asia Pacific region will have e-commerce revenue of US$992 billion (Gartner Group, 2000). The trend of market globalisation and an increasing emphasis on knowledge management have accelerated the business and economic process worldwide. The change in global information and communication technologies (ICT) to internet-based activity has many implications for the management of financial services industries. Furthermore, e-commerce creates some unprecedented opportunities for almost all industries to increase their trade directly and punctually by eliminating the role of middlemen, and increasing collaboration with suppliers and other business partners without the need for full integration with other businesses.

The origins of e-commerce

The rapid growth of ICT such as the internet and e-commerce has forced or encouraged society, and the organisations within, to adapt to the innovative technology. This technological change has driven the development of e-commerce technologies and activities, as they allow companies to experiment with new goods, services and processes and so conduct business activities more efficiently and effectively. Subjectivity in the interpretation of the term 'e-commerce' has been noted in the literature (Malone *et al.*, 1987; Banaghan and Bryant, 1998) and is reflected in widely varying statistics on current and predicted e-commerce activity (for example, OECD, 2000). However, a firm still cannot evaluate the need for e-commerce strategies or for associated changes in business strategy without a clear notion of what e-commerce is all about. Schneider and Perry (2000) argue that:

> *... e-commerce includes so many activities that it can be difficult for managers to decide where and how to use it in their businesses.*

This difficulty is complicated by many authors' failure to define their usage of the term 'e-commerce' (Plant, 2000; Maddox and Blankenhorn, 1998). Sometimes the term is described rather than defined, e.g. 'e-commerce covers the range of on-line business activities for products and services, both business-to-business and business-to-consumer, through the internet' (Rosen, 2000). Internet e-commerce includes electronic trading of physical goods and of intangibles such as information. This encompasses all the trading steps such as online marketing, ordering, payment and delivery support as well as the electronic provision of services such as after-sales support (Timmers, 1999). According to Westland and Clark (1999) e-commerce can be defined as '.... the automation of commercial transactions using computer and communication technologies'. Yet Malone *et al.* (1987) define e-commerce as an electronic intermediary over which multiple customers and suppliers perform business. They hereby focus more on the intermediary nature of a market and its role as an operation facilitator.

However, Kalakota and Whinston (1997) go further and define e-commerce from the following four perspectives:

- *Communication perspective*: e-commerce is the delivery of information, products and/or services, or payments via telephone lines, computer networks, or any other electronic means.
- *Business process perspective*: the application of technology towards the automation of business transactions and workflows.
- *Service perspective*: with the help of e-commerce the quality of the goods can be improved while the speed of service delivery can be increased.
- *Online perspective*: the buying and selling of products and information online.

However, another definition is given by Rowley (2002) e-business is a wider concept that embraces all aspects of the use of IT in business. It includes not only buying and selling, but also servicing customers and collaborating with business partners, and often involves integration across business processes and communication within the organisation. This definition shows that, although technology provides the opportunity for new business approaches, the technology needs to be driven by business goals and business processes. Thus, Ahmed *et al.* (2003) go further and define e-commerce as a shorthand term that embraces a complex mixture of technologies, infrastructures, processes and products which brings together whole industries and narrow applications, producers and users, information exchange and economic activity into a global marketplace called 'the internet'. Similarly, Kalakota and Robinson

(1999) maintain that 'e-business is about redefining old business models, with the aid of technology, to maximise customer value'.

Consequently, there is some confusion over the terms e-commerce and e-business. For many, e-commerce is seen as online transactions (ordering and/or settling payments) conducted purely between business partners whereas e-business is seen as the entire process of conducting commerce online, whether between businesses (B2B) or between the business and consumer (B2C). Turban *et al.* (2000) present a good point regarding the dimensions of e-commerce, since they distinguish between pure and partial e-commerce, where pure e-commerce infers all dimensions are digital and partial e-commerce includes a mix of digital and physical dimensions, as illustrated in Figure 2.1. They created a model that assists in understanding the different forms of e-commerce that companies can take. There are three dimensions in this model which present the degree of digitisation: (1) the product sold; (2) the process; and (3) the delivery agent.

Figure 2.1 The dimensions of e-commerce

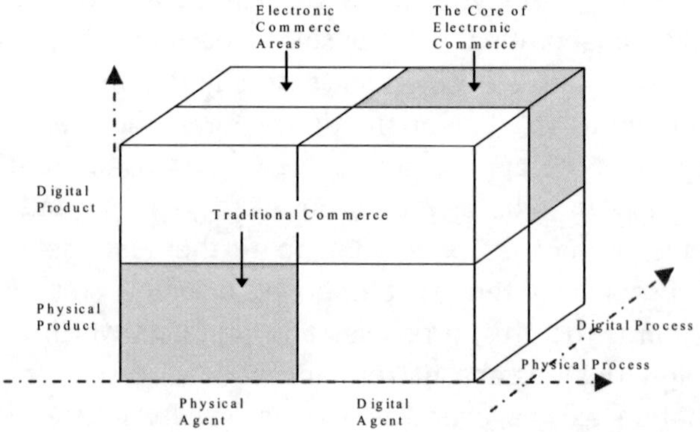

Source: Turban *et al.* (2000)

As can be seen from the Figure 2.1, in conventional commerce all three dimensions are physical (lower-left cube), whereas in pure e-commerce companies all three dimensions are digital (upper-right cube). A pure e-commerce organisation would have a digitised product, e.g. a music album, which would be sold and delivered through the internet.

Thus, there is not likely to be a unique definition of e-business and e-commerce; as Ahmed *et al.* (2003) state, there is no universal definition of e-commerce because the internet as a marketplace and its participants are frequent and their intricate relationships are evolving rapidly. The terms 'e-business' and 'e-commerce' will be used interchangeably to mean 'the utilisation of IT which enables the functions of a company's business processes to be conducted electronically to achieve customer value and to exploit opportunities offered to companies by e-commerce technology' (Alwabel and Zairi, 2005c). This stance has been taken because many of the authors cited in this thesis are themselves still unsure of which term has become the *de facto* 'standard'.

Business processes in this case can be defined as the essential activities that every business must perform to succeed in acquiring resources, producing a good or service, and selling the product or service (Walker and Black, 2000). The extension of the business processes, according to Rooyen (2002), refers to extra services that can be offered to customers through the internet. In this case both internal processes such as customer order entry systems as well as external processes facilitating inter-organisational information networks are part of e-business.

Development of the concept

The past three decades have seen wonderful developments in software for manufacture and operations management. This has been an express result of developments in computers and IT, and also of the techniques used by companies to run their businesses. There has been a separate trend of increased relationship building amongst trading partners over the years. The traditional technique of doing business with specific lines of isolation between roles and responsibilities of individual units is fast giving way to shared information and responsibilities amongst trading partners. The growth of software applications over the years reflects these trends.

Although the internet seems to be new, early versions of the net have been around since the 1960s. However, only after the mid-1990s did it begin to have a serious open impact. Thus, the attitudes toward e-commerce have rapidly evolved. Although the business press was initially dominated by stories of new B2C firms on the web, the more important global development was the movement of large B2B revenues to web-enabled systems. Since internet purchase transactions replaced paper, telephone, fax and private electronic data interchange (EDI) systems, the reported figures on business procurement via the internet have grown rapidly.

Historically, exchanges of information and collaboration between organisations have taken place for many years by phone, fax, mail or email. Computer systems in various forms have been used for some time to get better production efficiency in organisations. In the last decades, IT and its applications in organisations have changed considerably. The evolution of e-commerce has become linked to evolution of the IT, as can be seen in Table 2.1 below; however a full explanation of e-commerce evolution phases will be examined in the following sections.

Table 2.1 E-commerce evolution

Periods	Phases	Function
Future of e-commerce 2004-onward	A multiplicity of trends will drive the growth and development of e-commerce in the future. The more the people learn about e-commerce the greater the e-commerce expansion will be (Turban *et al.*, 2000).	The following will be achieved: integration, increased connectivity and digitisation, wireless media, smaller devices and intermediaries.
1990s-present	**Extended business system** CRM and SCM 'Supply chain dimension of e-commerce', totally integrated supply chain, confident that technology will be able to support the scalability, breadth of functions.	Multiple directionality will be achieved through entire supply chain community.
1990s-present	**Holistic organisational system** Organisation culture and change, organisation structural systems, business process re-engineering, 'The sequence for integrated IT requires a strong push from the top' (Keen, 1986).	Dealing with both soft and hard issues, by utilising IT, organisations can structure their operations in better ways. E-commerce does not bring competitive advantages by itself (Alwabel and Zairi, 2005b).
1975-1990s	**Integrated upstream and downstream system 'integration and planning'** MRP, MRP II and ERP. Cover: human resources, finance, product design, communication systems, operation and projects management etc.	Connecting all processes of the firm, capturing both financial and non-financial data to facilitate access and *ad hoc* analysis.
1965-1975	**Integrated downstream system** IOSs and the sub-set EDI, Computer-to-computer exchange of commercial documents.	Limited, expensive, inflexible; only one-to-one relations.

1958-1965	**IT mainframes** Automation of the paperwork, accounting and record-keeping functions.	Limited to large organisations and inflexible.

Consequently, in order to understand the evolution of e-commerce it is useful to begin by looking briefly at the technological developments that make e-commerce possible and desirable. New information technologies have greatly reduced both the time and cost of communicating information, just as the telegraph did when it was introduced (Malone *et al.*, 1987). IT has evolved from a mere supporting role in the back-office to a competitive advantage in the marketplace (Ives and Learmoth, 1984; Porter and Millar, 1985). The combination of increased capabilities to process information and declining costs of this technology has resulted in a broader range of computer functions in organisations. The first phase, in the late 1950s and early 1960s was characterised by experimentation with the newly developed computing technology. Operating in a batch processing mode initially, large repetitive jobs were automated to support public programmes, such as motor vehicle registration and tax processing, as well as internal operations like payroll (Argyris, 1971).

The success of those early applications in addition to the rapid growth of the computer industry as a whole, led to the second phase, the integrated downstream system, in the mid-1960s to mid-1970s. This phase of applications was focused on decision support systems. These systems provided decision-makers with powerful models for analysing information, and getting better decision quality (Flores *et al.*, 1988). The development of networks made possible the arrival of a new type of system such as the inter-organisational systems (IOSs). They enabled organisations to communicate more easily and cheaply across time or geographic locations, to communicate more rapidly and with more accuracy to targeted groups, and to keep track of the content and nature of the communication (Hiltz and Turoff, 1993).

Thus, the 1970s and the 1980s were driven by dramatic technological change – micro-electronic circuitry and the development of microchips. As the underlying hardware became more capable, the software that ran on it was able to accomplish more, thus this led to the third phase, an integrated downstream and upstream system. This phase focused on material requirement planning (MRP), which was introduced and proposed by Joseph Orlicky, who is regarded as the father of MRP (1970) in the USA (Vollmann *et al.*, 1992). During the 1970s MRP packages were extended and further applications were added (Chung and Snyder, 2000), which resulted in the introduction of manufacturing resource planning (MRP II) systems; this development has continued (Koh *et al.*, 2000). These systems later evolved into enterprise resource planning (ERP) systems, a term coined by Gartner Research Group in 1992 and the name can probably be derived from the MRP and MRPII systems (Klaus *et al.*, 2000).

However, running business electronically does not deliver real benefits when applied to the wrong organisational areas; where it is superimposed upon existing procedures there is only superficial change in company functions. Implemented in this way, e-commerce opportunities will not really be exploited. According to Rockart and Scott Morton (1984) there will be few changes as a result of only changing the way the paperwork is done. Moreover, using IT for the manual output would have a huge impact on the organisation's productivity. Essential changes would then occur beyond existing business strategies (Rockart and Scott Morton, 1984). Therefore, the combination of IT and organisational redesign was introduced and described (Davenport and Short, 1990; Hammer, 1990). Thus, this led to the fourth phase, the holistic organisational system.

The way organisations collect and manage information is a key component of any customer-centric business model, and one which enables organisations to be effective, profitable and sustainable. Thus, a customer-centric business model is needed (Kalakota and Robinson, 2001). In a rapidly changing business environment, companies are realising that the best and most effective way to deliver dramatic business benefits is to bridge the information divide between customers, back office operations and the supply chain. According to Kalakota and Robinson (2001), e-business design is about integrating the complicated set of business processes that occur along the value chain so they work together to manage, organise, and transform information. Therefore, this leads into the fifth and last phase, extended business systems.

Transformational thinking in e-commerce evolution

To understand the evolution of e-commerce and web-based systems that are mostly likely to be successful, it is necessary to consider power relationships in the supply chain and cooperative partnership arrangements of many kinds. Before one can begin to understand e-commerce, evolutionary stages of e-commerce history must first be presented.

Phase 1 – information technology 'mainframes' (1958-1965)

IT mainframes represented the first phase of e-commerce, which started as early as 1958. The term IT was first used by Leavitt and Whisler (1958) to highlight the role of computers to support decision making and organisational information processing. This term integrates not only the data processing capabilities of the computer, but also the human and executive abilities involved in their use. The evolution of IT has been a very vital enabler of change in most industries. The technological advances in both hardware and software have made it possible to collect, manage, distribute and utilise information to achieve much stronger integration of the channel. Strategic and well-coordinated IT planning across the organisation, considered within the information technology infrastructure, will maximise the resources and effectiveness of the organisation (Ernst and Segall, 1995). Most importantly, using IT to enable and fundamentally change the administrative business of an organisation will create more opportunities and enhance competitive advantage.

In the 1960s, mainframe computers were introduced in large organisations to take over many operational and everyday tasks. Their role was to automate the paperwork, particularly in accounting and record-keeping functions, in order to perform tasks more efficiently and effectively than traditional manual methods. These tasks were previously performed entirely by book-keeping personnel. In this period, the computer was like a heavy-duty calculator entirely controlled by computer professionals.

Information technology: schools of thought

Technology has always been a central variable in organisational theory, information research and practice. Despite years of research there is little agreement on the definition of technology (Macdonald *et al.*, 1983). In the literature, IT is described in various ways. This variety of definitions resulted in conflicting measures for IT (Markus and Robey, 1988). However, two schools of definitions can be distinguished:

- *The technological definitions*: the tools for the automation of information services are described, such as hardware and software. Examples of this are: Stegwee (1992) uses the term IT as a term for hardware, software and services relating to the processing, storage and communication of information, using mainly optic-electronic means. Scarbrough and Corbett (1992) defined technology as machinery, hardware and software. However, this definition concentrates purely on technical matters and lacks attention to databases, procedures and people.

- *The knowledge definitions*: IT is viewed as the body of knowledge and skills within the organisation contributing to the information services. Examples of this are: Flores *et al.* (1988) state that, IT involves not only processors and related artefacts, but also the plan of new practices and possibilities for new realms of practice. Scott (1992) stated that: 'Technology includes not only the hardware used in performing work but also the skills and knowledge of the workers, and even the characteristics of the objects on which work is performed'. Flores *et al.* (1988) added that technology is more than just machinery. It also encompasses the design of practices and possibilities to be realised through artefacts. They go on to define IT as the interaction between artefacts (hardware, software and networks) and the practices to be realised through these artefacts.

Information services on the other hand concern the input, storage, processing and distribution of information for the execution, planning and control, and the support of the primary processes of organisations (Cecil and Hall, 1988). The performance of these primary processes determines the functioning of the organisation and the resulting competitive position (Porter and Millar, 1985). By means of the automation of the information services, IT contributes to the performance of the primary processes and therefore to the success of the organisation. Some authors even consider information to be of such significance to our society that they regard it as a new production factor, in addition to the traditional macro production factors (Wilkes, 1991). This idea supports the importance of IT as a strategic means of production for organisations.

In the knowledge definition, reference is made to all kinds of optic-electronic, computer tools. The inclusion of knowledge in the definition of IT makes it possible to explain an important aspect of IT, its ability to innovate work processes in organisations. Knowledge can be seen as a resource in organisations. According to Penrose (1959), innovation of processes or products is the result of the re-organising of resources in organisations.

Phase 2 – integrated downstream systems (1965-1975)

Integrated downstream systems represented the second phase of e-commerce. The evolution of information technologies and communications, the necessity of relationship marketing, and the nature of competition forced enterprises to rethink business strategic options. Business processes shifted from adversarial to more co-operative practices. Traditionally, organisations have used paper forms to exchange information which created problems of slow transactions and extensive human handling. Hence, the importance of finding a more effective way to communicate and process data was realised, and resulted in inter-organisational information systems (IOS) being introduced in the 1960s (Alt and Fleisch, 2001). IOSs use telecommunication technology to couple machine agents that are usually geographically dispersed but always belong to different organisations. This boundary-spanning aspect implies a level of cooperation and coordination well beyond that of the traditional arms length relationship that exists between organisations in a totally free market (Ives and Learmoth, 1984). IOSs are not a new phenomenon; mail and telephone networks can be considered long-standing examples of inter-organisational systems.

Inter-organisational information systems (IOSs)

IOSs are usually encountered between two stages in a linear value-added chain, and thus can be thought as having two primary types of participants (sellers and buyers). Ives and Learmoth (1984) define

IOSs as computer based information systems shared by two or more companies that automate the flow of information among them. Barrett and Konsynski (1982) go further and define an IOS as a system 'that involves resources shared between two or more organisations'. Therefore, IOS systems support the relationships between organisations, attempt to strengthen existing business relationships and lock in partners by integrating the supplier into the buyer's value chain processes or through the supplier's ability to customise products or services (Steinfield *et al.*, 1995). This distinguishes it from an internal distributed information system such as an intranet, because an IOS system allows information to be transferred across the boundaries of organisations. It has become very obvious that IOS systems can bring significant competitive advantages to participants.

The integration between supplier-manufacturer-customer through an IOS system may establish a collaborative relationship and such integration can include just-in-time shipping and other supplier services, such as management of the customer's inventory as well as component quality functions (Archer and Yuan, 2000). One common form of IOS systems is electronic data interchange (EDI), linking suppliers and buyers through private value-added networks (VAN). EDIs were developed in the 1960s, being the first applications of e-commerce (Pawar and Driva, 2000), and were aimed at automating pre-existing relationships between suppliers and corporate customers, mostly in support of the procurement function of manufacturing industries (Fraser *et al.*, 2000).

EDI - subset of inter-organisational systems

The premise of EDI is to facilitate commerce by together tying business applications between trading partners (Pawar and Driva, 2000). Use of inter-organisational linkages such as EDI would enable new forms of organisations and reduce the coordination costs of increasingly market driven organisations (Johnson *et al.*, 1992).

Electronic linkages are becoming the necessary condition of doing businesses (Dornier, 1998). According to Fraser *et al.* (2000), EDI can be defined as:

> *... a particular sub-set of e-commerce that uses standardised, agreed formats for electronic messages to create extremely cost-efficient handling of transactions, such as product re-ordering between distributors and manufacturers who operate a build-to-order philosophy.*

Bamfield (1994) believes that EDI involves data communication between systems, usually two or more companies, by conforming to a common standard, defining the core information and where and how that information must become visible.

Currently the most widely used B2B communication method is EDI, which was established over three decades ago. EDI provides advantages compared to manual B2B communication methods. It has been shown that EDI between trading partners leads to faster transactions and cost savings (Pawar and Driva, 2000). As for the implementation of EDI, implementation ideally affects several organisational units, e.g. accounting, inventory and production. The implementation of EDI has been referred to as an administrative innovation (Drury and Farhoomand, 1996). This means that the implementation of EDI can lead to major perceived and actual changes in work procedures and tasks.

According to Johnson *et al.*'s (1992) survey, the key reasons for implementing EDI are: meeting a customer requirement; improving customer service; and gaining competitive advantage.

Although EDI is actually one of the foundation blocks for e-commerce, its wider-scale expansion has been limited. This is due to the cost involved and the inequity in power between companies in the hubs and the spokes. Yet, Angeles (2000) stated that the traditional role of EDI has been altered because of a new shape of internet-based EDI, which is more beneficial to companies, especially smaller ones with fewer resources. Moreover, even though IT is involved, EDI is more of a business issue than a technological one, since it needs a detailed review and re-engineering of intra- and inter-organisational business processes. Furthermore, it requires careful selection of business partners, continuous training and commitment of users, top management support and adequate funding.

Phase 3 – integrated upstream and downstream system 'integration and planning' (1975-1990)

The integrated upstream and downstream system represents the third phase of e-commerce evolution. The rapid change in technology and other skills, added to customers requiring highly specific and customised products, lead to the need for far greater cooperation within and between firms. This increasing pressure required companies to explore a reliable mechanism to make it easier to save, store and share useful information. Consequently, an accounting information system (AIS) was developed to offer a good foundation for controlling information and knowledge to contribute to a company's success (Wilkinson, 2000).

AIS can be, according to Romney and Steinbart (1999), referred to as a transaction processing system because it only deals with financial data and accounting transactions. It was mainly used as a reporting tool to perform functions such as payroll and invoicing. As the power and sophistication of IT continued to grow, the coverage potentials of AIS became gradually more inadequate, and not sufficient for business needs. With growing requirements for information other than financial data, organisations began to develop additional information systems. However, the existence of multiple systems creates various struggles and inadequacies (Romney and Steinbart, 1999). Very often, the same data, a sale record for instance, must be stored by more than one system.

Therefore, the term ERP (enterprise resource planning) appeared; this extends AIS to cover areas like human resources, finance, accounting, product design, communication systems, operation and project management. These areas are like jigsaw pieces, put together to form a complete picture of activities within any business enterprise.

As mentioned earlier, ERP originated from the packaged application software that has been widespread since the 1970s. However, ERP systems, like all information technologies, rapidly changed. During the 1980s this was abandoned and replaced by the client-server architectures and now newly released web-enabled versions have become more and more widespread (Markus and Tanis, 2000).

Materials requirement planning (MRP) systems

Materials requirements planning (MRP, or MRP-I) system was launched in the mid-1970s and quickly became popular for providing a logical, easily understood method for determining the number of parts, components and materials needed for the assembly of each end item in production. As computer power grew and demands for software applications increased, MRP systems evolved to consider other resources besides materials. Software modules were added to include functions such as scheduling, inventory control, finance, accounting and accounts payable.

The MRP-I system is a computer-based system for managing inventory and production schedules. This approach to materials management applies to large job-shop situations in which many products are manufactured in periodic lots in several processing steps (Bedworth and Bailey, 1987). MRP and push systems are often used interchangeably. Conceptually, MRP can be viewed as a method for the effective planning of all resources of a manufacturing organisation (Russell and Taylor, 1998). According to Daft (1991), MRP can be defined as a 'dependent demand inventory planning and control system that schedules the exact amount of all materials required to support the desired end product'. Torkzadeh and Sharma (1991) suggested an alternative definition for MRP as: 'an inventory ordering and time-phased scheduling technique, which uses bill of material, inventory data, and the master production schedule to calculate requirements for material and determine when to release the material replenishment order'. The following is a proposed MRP definition:

> *A computer based planning, scheduling, and control system that gives management a tool to plan and control its manufacturing activities and supporting operations to obtain a higher level of customer service while reducing costs.*

MRP is primarily used for scheduling high-value commissioned parts, materials and supplies when demand is reasonably well known (Ballou, 1999). Ballou further states that precise timing of material flows to meet production requirements is the principle behind MRP.

Problems with implementing MRP systems

Many authors state that the difficulties associated with MRP systems being implemented correctly are, to a certain extent, associated with organisational and behavioural factors (Chase and Aquilano, 1995). Yet, it seems to be generally agreed that failure of an MRP installation can be traced to problems such as: lack of top management commitment; intensive executive education being needed; and being too rigid.

MRP systems require a major commitment from top management in order for them to be successful. This means not only the commitment of resources, but also the commitment of top management's time to ensure the right coordination among the various functions. A well-functioning schedule can use the firm's assets effectively and efficiently, increasing the firm's profits. Thus, MRP should be acknowledged by top management as a planning tool with particular reference to profit results (Chase and Aquilano, 1995).

In nearly every study conducted, lack of proper training is considered a key barrier to MRP implementation. Raysman (1981) comments that lack of understanding about systems is frequently quoted as a reason for failure of companies' endeavours. Sum and Yang (1993) recognised that the lack of MRP expertise and training were main problems facing companies implementing MRP. In a desire to convert to the new system quickly, there is often an underperformance in the training of personnel at all levels. However, proper training is required from the technical perspective as well as from the users' perspective. Thus, the IT department within an organisation needs to understand entirely all of the technical characteristics of the system in order to provide proper support to the business functions that use it. Simultaneously, the business functions need to recognise the different procedures for entering data and producing reports.

The aims of the MRP system are to minimise inventory investment and maximise production operating efficiency, thus the accuracy of the recorded levels becomes significant. Chase and Aquilano (1995) state that: 'Perhaps one of the biggest complaints by users is that MRP is too rigid. When MRP develops a schedule, it is quite difficult to veer away from the schedule if need arises'.

Nevertheless, the MRP contains a method for planning and procuring the materials to support production. During years of using MRP, the need for other functions arose that would, together with MRP, create an integrated manufacturing management system. Thus, it was done by creating a large production control system named manufacturing resources planning (MRP II).

Manufacturing resource planning (MRP II) systems

Manufacturing resource planning (MRP II) is defined by the American Production and Inventory Control Society (APICS) as a system for the effective planning of all the resources of a manufacturing business (Higgins *et al.*, 1996). It is a direct successor of the material requirements planning (MRP). MRP II is concerned with managing the flow of material into, through and out of the organisation (Arnold, 1998). Thus, MRP II is a system in which the entire production environment is evaluated to allow master schedules to be adjusted and created based on feedback from current production/purchase conditions (Bedworth and Bailey, 1987).

Functions of the MRP II system

The operation and financial systems are the same as MRP. The functions of MRP II can be summarised as follows:

- It has simulation capabilities that enable predictions to be made beforehand.
- It involves every facet of business from planning to execution (Higgins *et al.*, 1996).

Disadvantages of the MRP II system

The inaccuracy of the bill of materials and inventory database is a common problem with MRP II systems (Toomey, 1996). Inaccurate bills of materials mean inaccurate material and capacity plans. Providing a management system that will facilitate data accuracy will likely require major adjustments in strategic management approaches (Kessler, 1991).

Nevertheless, MRP II is, as mentioned earlier, concerned with managing the flow of material into, through and out of the business (Arnold, 1998). During years of using MRP II, the need for other functions arose that would, together with MRP and MRP II, create an integrated manufacturing management system. Thus, it was done by creating a large production control system named enterprise resource planning (ERP) systems.

Enterprise resources planning (ERP) systems

ERP is the technological backbone of e-business in the back office. It was common during the 1990s to find that the computing software for the finance department was different from that used by the human resources or stores departments. According to Kalakota and Robinson (2001), ERP 'overcomes the integration challenges posed by disconnected, uncoordinated back office applications that have often outlived their usefulness'.

There are several ERP definitions that are all more or less similar (Hicks, 1997). ERP systems are defined as module-based integrated software packages that control all the personnel, material, monetary and information flows of a company (Granlund and Malmi, 2002). Gelinas *et al.*, (1999) suggest an alternative definition for ERP systems as:

> *... integrated software packages designed to provide complete integration of an organisation's business information processing systems and all related data. These systems are conceptually based on event-driven systems concepts, which include the capturing of both financial and non-financial data to facilitate access and ad hoc analysis.*

Yet another definition is given by Wallace and Kremzar (2001), who state that ERP systems are an enterprise-wide information system solution set of management tools that balance demand and supply, including the ability to link customers and suppliers into a complete supply chain, employing confirmed business processes for decision-making, and providing high degrees of cross-functional integration among sales, marketing, manufacturing, operations, logistics, purchasing, finance and human resources, thereby enabling people to run their businesses with high levels of customer service and productivity, and simultaneously lowering costs and inventories; and providing the foundation for effective e-commerce. Some ERP systems were developed out of administrative (financial and human resources) sides of the business (e.g. SAP and PeopleSoft), and others grew from materials resource planning in manufacturing (e.g. Baan) (Markus and Tanis, 2000).

According to Wallace and Kremzar (2001) ERP is far better than MRP II for three reasons:

- ERP applies a single set of resource planning tools across the entire enterprise;
- ERP provides real-time integration of sales, operating and financial data; and
- ERP connects resource planning approaches to the extended supply chain of customers and suppliers.

ERP systems implementation strategies

There are two characteristic ways of implementing an ERP found in the literature. These are termed the 'phased' implementation and the 'big bang' approach (O'Leary, 2000). Dependent on the organisational structure, the difficulty of the organisation, economical issues, strategic partners, time constraints and geographical locations (Markus and Tanis, 2000), the correct implementation approach should be selected. The big bang approach enables organisations to recycle all their legacy systems at once and implement a single ERP system across the entire organisation. This is the most ambitious and difficult of approaches to ERP implementation. On the other hand, a phased implementation consists of designing, developing, testing and installing different modules of the same ERP package. It suits large or diverse companies that do not share many common processes across business units. Independent ERP systems are installed in each unit, while linking common processes. Phased implementation is the most common way of implementing ERP and it allows the systems to link together only to share the information necessary for the corporation to get a big picture of performance across all business units.

Integrative framework for ERP implementation

ERP implementations have been well established in the private sector as well as manufacturing sector over the past decade; as a result there is an agreement that ERP benefits are maximised when a tight coupling is established between the implementation approach and project threads or business-wide performance measures. Common ERP implementation success factors include methods of addressing the challenges, such as managing change, developing training strategies, developing a project management plan, and obtaining senior management support and involvement throughout the project (Al-Mudimigh *et al.*, 2001; Al-Mashari *et al.*, 2003). Yet, ERP system implementation has been subdivided, according to Al-Mudimigh *et al.* (2001), into three levels: strategic, tactical and operational. Each level contains a number of critical factors. These levels of implementation, however, are not independent of each other, and each level should be applied to obtain the next level. Moreover, each level needs differing inputs; for example, there is a direct relationship between the implementation level at which a decision is being taken and the characteristics of the information required to support decision making, as illustrated in Figure 2.2.

Figure 2.2 Framework of ERP system project implementation

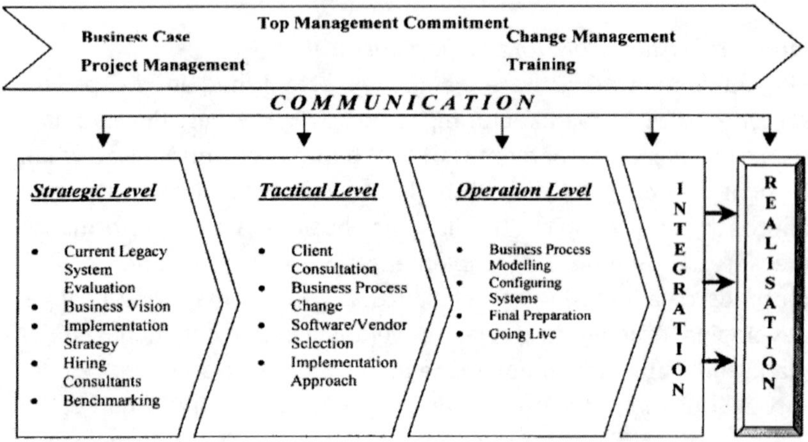

Source: adapted from Al-Mudimigh *et al.* (2001)

There are, according to Al-Mudimigh *et al.* (2001) major tangible and intangible benefits, see Table 2.2, to be achieved from successful ERP implementation in the manufacturing sector and beyond. To understand these benefits and to avoid implementation failure, organisations need to take in hand the critical issues that affect the implementation process of an ERP project. Sixteen critical factors were identified in Al-Mudimigh *et al's* (2001) study. All factors were classified analytically according to a common framework for ERP project implementation, as in Figure 2.2. The factor that showed as the most critical was top management commitment. Next in value was project vision. In addition, the following factors were found to be critical: business case, change management, project management, training, communication, current legacy system evaluation, hiring consultants, benchmarking, business process change, software/vendor selection, implementation approach, testing and integration. Whilst each factor is important on its own, they are also highly interdependent. Failure in just one area can affect the overall success of the ERP project implementation.

Table 2.2 Benefits of ERP implementation

Tangible	Intangible
• Reduced inventory • Reduced personnel • Increased productivity • Improved in order management • More rapid closing of financial cycles • Reduced IT costs • Reduced procurement costs • Improved cash management • Increased revenue and profits • Reduced transportation and logistics costs • Reduced need for system maintenance • Improved on-time delivery performance	• Increased visibility of corporate data • New or improved business processes • Improved responsiveness to customers • Unanticipated reduction in cost • Tighter integration between systems • Standardisation of computing platforms • Increased flexibility • Global sharing of information • Y2K compliance • Improved business performance • Improved visibility into SCM process

Source: adapted from Al-Mudimigh *et al.* (2001)

ERP systems and e-commerce

The internet continues to grow as a medium for commerce, allowing a company to conduct business everywhere, all the time. E-commerce and the internet eliminate the constraints of time and distance in operating a business and enable a multitude of connections between customers, suppliers and trading partners (Kalakota and Whinston, 1997). E-business according to Ahmed *et al.* (2003) can be defined as a shorthand term that embraces a complex mixture of technologies, infrastructures, processes and products, bringing together whole industries and narrow applications, producers and users, information exchange and economic activity into a global marketplace called 'the internet'.

The characteristics of the new economy have increased the level of competition in all industries and the internet presents an important opportunity for even small firms to launch new products or services because of the speed and low cost of doing business (Alwabel *et al.*, 2003). E-commerce also reduce inefficiencies caused by buyer search costs to obtain information about the price and product offerings as well as the cost of sellers to communicate information about their prices and product offerings (Kaplan and Sawhney, 2000). By assembling a network of partners that specialise and excel in the links of the value chain, it is possible for organisations to achieve new levels of quality, flexibility and cost savings. ERP and e-business are not competitive systems. Their greatest benefits can only be achieved when they are used in agreement, complementing each other. Thus, without a successful ERP system e-business systems would have little to present, as in today's new business environment power has shifted toward consumers who demand intelligent products that deliver new dimensions of value, time and content, in addition to the current ones of price and quality (Aldrich and Douglas, 1999).

The basic functionality of ERP and e-business are different. ERP is an integrated software package system that handles an organisation's internal information whereas e-business is fundamentally a distribution medium and does not involve a lot of processing. Although the information flowing through e-business is becoming more suited to processing all the time, it is still processed by applications, and the best business applications are still ERP and other enterprise packages from major vendors. According to a recent survey of e-business and ERP (Norris *et al.*, 2000), 66 % of IT managers viewed ERP as their most important and strategic platform because it provides a solid foundation and information backbone for e-business. When ERP and e-business are properly implemented, they supercharge each other. E-business is the best vehicle to share business information with partners for creating major B2B synergies (Norris *et al.*, 2000). A fully integrated ERP system will capture and create accurate, consistent and timely relevant data, and assist in intelligent business decision-making. E-business improves a company's business performance by connecting various stakeholders to the company's value chain and information systems, as illustrated in Figure 2.3. When any parts of the supply chain has access to other's business information, organisations can streamline their processes and automate data processing and business activities through the supply chain (Norris *et al.*, 2000).

Figure 2.3 E-business focuses on communication with external stakeholder

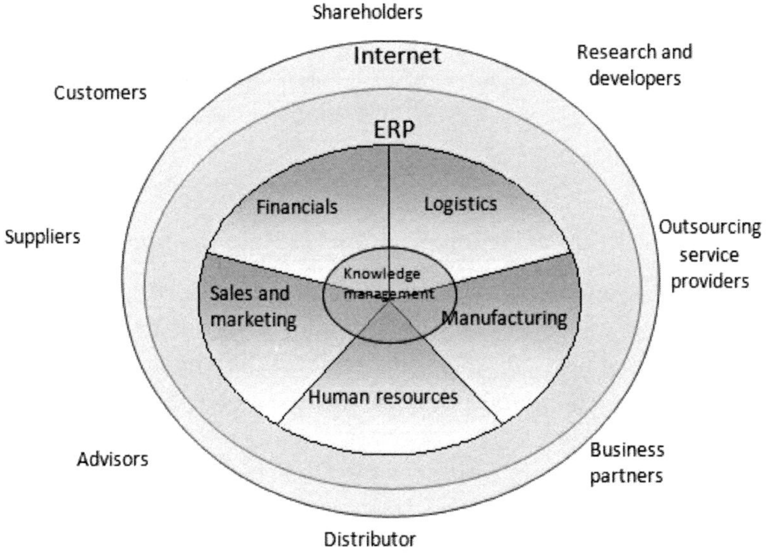

Source: adapted from Norris *et al.* (2000)

Furthermore, ERP systems according to Jaiswal (2002) can be organised to integrate smoothly various business functions and even can be extended to external business partners. It can also be organised as combined business models as shown in the Figure 2.4.

Figure 2.4 E-business scope of ERP systems

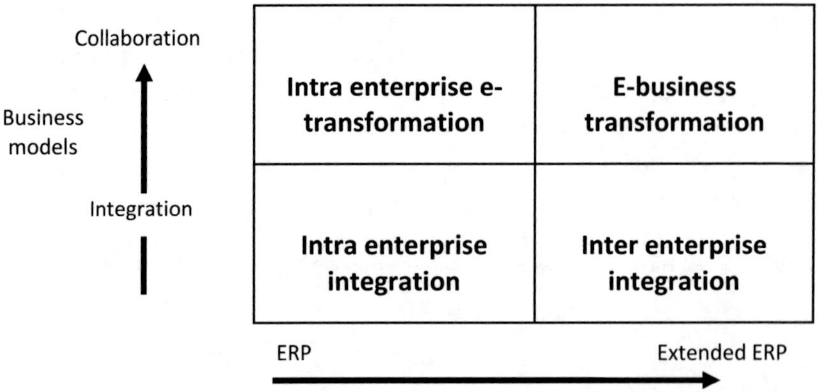

Source: adapted from Jaiswal (2002)

Phase 4 - holistic organisational system (1990-to the present day)

The holistic organisational system represents the fourth phase of e-commerce evolution. The existing literature sets out to prove that as a result of the new paradigm that exists within the organisational system, the e-commerce system needs new ideas, thought processes and structures to ensure that the full potential is realised. In order to maximise returns from the e-commerce business process, re-engineering and design will have to take place. Organisations must be willing and able to re-think and re-design radically the existing process. A paradigm shift is absolutely essential to obtain the maximum returns for the organisation. Emphasis is placed on the major components affecting the organisational system, including: organisational culture and change, structural systems and business process re-engineering (BPR). Each component of these will be examined in the following sections.

Organisational culture and change

One common thread that greatly affects many of the organisational aspects that enhance performance and increase productivity is the widely shared and strongly held values that underlie and define an organisation's culture. Moorman (1995) defined organisational culture as 'the pattern of shared values and beliefs that help individuals understand organisational functioning and provide norms for behaviour in the organisation'. Trice and Beyer (1993) defined organisational culture as:

> *... collective phenomena that embody people's responses to the uncertainties and chaos that are inevitable in human experience. These responses fall into two major categories. The first is the substance of culture shared, emotionally charged belief systems that we call ideologies. The second is cultural forms observable entities, including actions, through which members of a culture express, affirm, and communicate the substance of their culture to one another.*

Therefore, both definitions highlight the notion of sharing. However, it is significant to understand that 'culture depends upon both community and diversity. It allows for similarity, but also supports and relies upon difference. Sharing culture means that each member participates in and contributes to the broad patterns of culture, but the contributions and experiences of individual members of the culture are not identical' (Hatch, 1997).

Organisational structure systems

Organisational structure system describes the established systems, processes and exchange relationships within organisations. Size (number of employees), organisational structure (hierarchical versus network), roles and authorities (broadly defined versus narrow job descriptions), communication structures (formal or informal) and decision-making channels (top-down or participative), determine the flexibility of an organisation and, in turn, its ability to change. Rosetti and DeZoort (1989) stated that the shape, composition and degree of decentralisation are important structural factors that influence an organisation's capacity to change. The old model of organisational structure will not be suitable for the organisation in ten years time.

Informational strategies such as intellectual capital are a vital element to fully understand and appreciate the value of a company's assets, in order to be able to manage, protect and grow them. Knowledge and other intangible assets suddenly make up a large part of a company's value. Structural charge means that employees are required to have ever-higher qualifications. New technical aids, working materials and work processes are only useful and advantageous if the workers are put in a position where they can meet with the associated requirements and exploit the associated potential (Egan, 1998). Thus, in order for a company to achieve its aims there is a recognition that it must improve, in particular, management and supervisory skills at all levels, and provide more and better training (Alwabel *et al*, 2003).

Business process re-engineering (BPR)

It is true that IT does not bring real benefits when applied to the wrong organisational structures, where it is superimposed upon existing procedures and there is only superficial change in business functions. In that way, the IT opportunities are not really exploited. Rockart and Scott Morton (1984) expect few changes as a result of only changing the way the paperwork is done. In the 1970s in particular, most IT usage only speeded up the processing of paperwork. This did not produce really competitive advantages.

Hammer (1990) concludes that these disappointing results of IT were caused by mechanising old ways of doing business, leaving the existing processes untouched and using computers only to speed them up. This observation is very appropriate for the early use of IT in offices.

Therefore, organisational transformation was necessary in order to be able to use the potential of the IT for growing an organisation's productivity. IT is only an enabler and dramatic restructuring of an organisation is essential to yield increased returns on investment. Rockart and Scott Morton (1984) stated that using IT for the working productivity would have a huge impact on the organisation's productivity. Essential changes would then occur beyond existing business strategies, new products, services and markets, and cost structures of the firm. To clarify these changes, they offered a conceptual model of technology impact in which all the fundamentals of the organisation's functioning (IT, strategy, organisational structure and culture, individuals and their roles) must be in balance. The phenomenon of organisational changes through IT in fact arrived in 1990. Then, the combination of IT and organisational redesign was thoroughly described (Davenport and Short, 1990; Hammer, 1990). If organisations used IT as a critical factor and modelling tool for the redesign of organisational processes, actual improvement in the organisation's performance would be realised (Davenport and Short, 1990).

Hammer (1990) stated that 'we cannot achieve breakthroughs in performance by cutting fat or automating existing processes. Rather, we must challenge old assumptions and shed the old rules that made the business under perform in the first place'. Although there is no clear agreed upon definition of re-engineering, Hammer and Champy (1993) defined re-engineering as 'the fundamental rethinking and radical redesign of business processes to achieve dramatic improvements in critical contemporary measures of performance, such as cost, quality, service and speed'. Hammer and

Stanton (1994) stress focusing on processes instead of tasks: 'our problems lie not in the performance of individual tasks and activities, the units of work, but in the processes, how the units fit together into a whole'. Furthermore, the technique of re-engineering according to Davenport and Stoddard (1994) is based on several principles. Some of these fundamental principles are:

- An understandable strategic approach to organisational design and change.
- A direction to broad, cross-functional business processes.
- The need for radical change in process performance.
- IT as an enabler of change in how work is done; dramatic restructuring of organisations is essential.

Phase 5 - Extended enterprise systems (1990s-to present day)

Phase five of e-commerce evolution covers extended enterprise systems (ES) that include the management of inter-enterprise business processes like customer relationship management (CRM), web technology, analytical applications (data warehousing) and supply chain management (SCM). Over recent years it has been seen that the enterprise application focus has transferred from the cost-saving automation of the back office to revenue generating front office applications. Front office applications are often called CRM. According to Kalakota and Robinson (2001), putting a CRM system into practice requires developing a set of integrated applications to address all aspects of the front office, including automating customer service, field service, sales and marketing. This leads to more effective marketing, sales and customer service, 'enabling a customer experience that builds loyalty' (Kalakota and Robinson, 2001). Both CRM and SCM have been strongly affected and improved by e-commerce (Sterne, 2000). E-commerce can assist joining SCM and CRM into an entity, beneficial for the whole business network. Furthermore, firms should be encouraged to influence knowledge for competitive advantage by solving problems using special knowledge-based analytical systems (Hope and Hope, 1997). The knowledge-based organisation is able to monitor the performance of its value adding business units and teams. These extended enterprise systems will be discussed in the following sections.

Customer relationship management (CRM)

Customer relationship management (CRM) has been increasingly recognised as a business strategy to effectively understand, manage and sustain customer relationships with advanced information and communication technologies. Swift (2000) defined CRM as 'an enterprise approach to understanding and influencing customer behaviour through meaningful communication in order to improve customer acquisition, customer retention, customer loyalty, and customer profitability'. Todman (2001) gave an alternative definition of CRM as 'a strategy for optimising lifetime value of customers' by achieving two things: 'Getting to know your customer better and interacting appropriately with your customers'. CRM can also be defined as a method that integrates all business processes that contact customers, specifically sales, advertising and customer services, through advanced information technology.

Currently, in the e-business environment, companies are shifting their business strategies from product-oriented to customer-oriented. As a strategy to optimise lifetime-value of customers, CRM can assist companies to succeed in the world of e-business. Not only large, multi-national companies, but also SMEs are increasingly looking to implement CRM with the intention of finding a competitive advantage on which to base their business prospects for durability. The financial services industry is no exception. However, Kalakota and Robinson (1999) state that since CRM and data warehousing technologies are developed and implemented within and across organisations, products and services can be sold to customers on an individual, one-to-one basis. One-to-one selling is based on in-depth knowledge of the customer in addition to company flexibility to deliver highly customised products and services (Timmers, 1999); furthermore, it requires the firm to develop internal flexibility to respond to a potentially wide variety of customer needs, by customised development, production, and delivery. The aim of one-to-one selling is to sell to one customer at a time as many products or services as possible, over the duration of that customer's support (Peppers and Rogers, 1997). For this reason, companies need to move from a product-oriented to customer-oriented model, which serves customers with made-to-order products and services over the whole lifecycle based on the contact with these clients (Seybold and Marshak, 1998).

According to Tapscott *et al.*, (2000), the connectivity of the internet along with CRM technologies assist companies to get back detailed customer information and to make opportunities for dynamic, real-time feedback. However, technology is only an enabler of the process necessary to revolve strategy into business products (Greenberg, 2001). Consequently, the most important element of CRM according to Law *et al.* (2003) is the human aspects, the long-standing relationship between the customer and the corporation. Despite the wide publicity given to these new trends in marketing and CRM, these advance technologies have not yet really permeated the bulk of internet businesses (Timmers, 1999). Comparatively, companies face substantial challenges as they will need to change organisational structures, adapt established business processes, increase IT investments, and train employees (Alwabel *et al.*, 2003). Thus, clear awareness of strategic implications and implementation issues of CRM is key to the success of implementing CRM.

Web technology

The use of the internet over the past few years has grown rapidly. Access to information technology generally, and the web in particular, is extensive. Businesses, banks and schools have all been affected by the introduction of these new technologies. Individuals are currently utilising web technology for home banking, purchasing products, as a medium for educational studies and in many other areas of everyday life. Thus, a customer's skill set in relation to the use of web technology is also highly developed, reducing the learning curve in accessing information. There are three kinds of web technology, as discussed below.

Public internet

The internet is perhaps the most known and the largest implementation of networking, linking millions of individual networks all over the world. The internet is a global network of networks using transmission control protocol/internet protocol TCP/IP or interacting with networks via gateways, providing the users with electronic mail messaging, remote login, file transfer, network news, www and other related services and tools. The internet has a range of capabilities that organisations use to exchange information internally or to communicate externally with other organisations (Laudon and Laudon, 2000). The internet consists of thousands of related networks of computers all over the world operating on a standard protocol which allows data to be transferred between otherwise incompatible machines. The word itself means a 'network of networks' (Hamill, 1997).

The intranet

Companies can use this communicational technology both by showing web pages on the public internet and for internal use through an intranet. An intranet is a private network surrounded by a firewall constructed to keep out unwanted visitors (Curry and

Stancich, 2000). The firewall does not imply that authorised users are trapped inside their private network; they are still able to cross into the public internet. Moreover, the same wide and varied technological applications for communication can be used on the intranet as on the internet (Curry and Stancich, 2000). An intranet can be defined as 'the use of internet technologies to link together the information resources of an organisation, from text to legacy databases to workflow and document management' (Desborough, 1996). Thus, it can be used as an excellent tool to improve project communication through information sharing between the staff (Curry and Stancich, 2000).

The extranet

The internet can be said to belong to all its users whereas an intranet exclusively belongs to the organisation that maintains and uses it. An extranet though, represents the bridge between the public internet and the private corporate intranet where the majority of business activity occurs (Angeles, 2001). An extranet can be defined as a 'slice of an intranet that provide a public window into company services or collected data' (Loshin, 1997). One can therefore argue that what is an intranet for one company is an extranet for another company, as illustrated in Figure 2.5.

Figure 2.5 The relationship between extranet, intranet and the internet

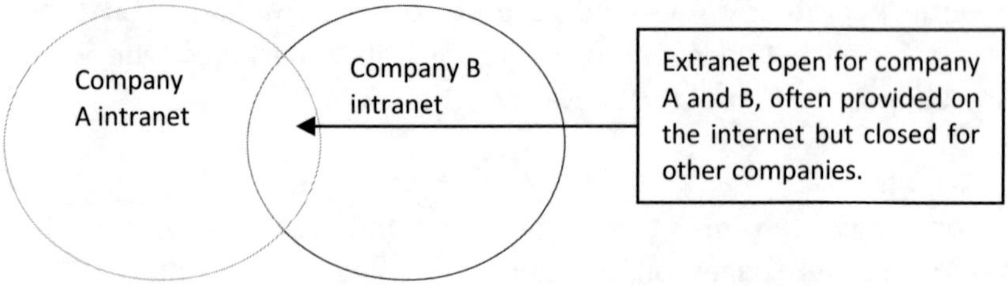

Source: Loshin (1997)

Data warehouse/business intelligence and analytical CRM

Analytical CRM deals with strategic, effective and efficient use of data in order to provide management with good decision-making possibilities. Because of information technology and e-business development, customer data accumulates. To understand this situation, analytical CRM requires support from robust, best practice enabled data processing and management technologies, a typical example of which is data warehousing. Data warehousing and business intelligence (BI) applications are essential elements of decision support, which has increasingly become a focus of the database industry. According to Blankenship *et al.* (1999) intelligence can be defined as 'the factual accumulation of the information that is organised and presented to help solve the problem or develop a plan or program'. However, Kahaner (1997) states that intelligence is another term for knowledge. Cook and Cook (2000) also distinguish between knowledge and intelligence, where knowledge is defined as analysed information whereas intelligence is defined as a gathering of knowledge that has been established, analysed and applied. Intelligence also concerns predicting future actions. Data warehousing can be defined as a collection of decision support technologies, aimed at enabling the knowledge worker (executive, manager and analyst) to make better and faster decisions (Chaudhuri and Dayal, 1997).

The connection between CRM and data warehousing is established by crucial requirements of easy, timely access to and effective use of valuable data and information for CRM decision making and process management, which entirely depends on the concern about a data warehouse. Todman (2001) stated that 'CRM cannot be practiced in business without a major source of information, which, of course, is the data warehouse'.

The data warehouse according to Glazer (1999) should contain information about the following:

- Transactions: purchase history with accompanying details e.g. (price paid, delivery data and item number).
- Customer contacts: there is an increasing number of customer contacts nowadays from multiple channels and contexts.
- Descriptive information: this is for segmentation and store data analysis purposes.

Thus, data warehousing and business intelligence applications are important for instant and real time access to information. According to Spil *et al.* (2002) research on the intranet and internet in combination with business intelligence is necessary to predict the future management communication. With the evolution of the internet, the universe of connected customers, suppliers and employees has expanded rapidly.

Supply chain management (SCM)

Supply chain management (SCM) has been evolving for a long time. Initially, emphasis was placed on the road to recovery of internal company processes and information flows. As IT improved and associated costs dropped radically, especially distributed computing via the internet, the focus broadened to include company processes that reached customers and suppliers. The focus will carry on emerging as the central field of competition in many industries. E-commerce technologies have the potential to revolutionise how firms co-ordinate and manage their supply chain activities.

Simchi-Levi *et al.* (2000) define SCM as:

> *… a set of approaches utilised to efficiently integrate suppliers, manufacturers, warehouses, and stores, so that merchandise is produced and distributed at the right quantities, to the right locations, and at the right time, in order to minimise system wide costs while satisfying service level requirements.*

As such, SCM encompasses the company's activities at all levels: strategic, tactical and operational. Yet another definition of SCM is given by Zheng *et al.*, (2000) as:

> *The delivery of enhanced customer and economic value through synchronized management of the flow of physical goods and associated information from sourcing through consumption.*

Thus, the supply chain takes an integrated, holistic approach to logistic management. It can be as a loop that starts, and ends with the customer. All materials, finished goods, services and information and transactions flow through the loop. According to Spekman *et al.* (1998) suppliers and customers cannot be treated in isolation since they are interrelated and therefore must be managed together to achieve success for both parties.

The key to acquisition success in this phenomenon has been widely attributed to effectively managing the firm's supply chain. Kalakota and Robinson (1999) noted how e-commerce can benefit SCM, by increasing the efficiency of logistics, lowering inventory and purchasing costs, reducing sales and marketing costs, and increasing sales. The importance of sharing information with members in the supply chain remains paramount and using e-commerce platforms to work closely with members enables more efficient business operations.

The value chain can be said to be a tool that can be used by an organisation to find ways to create more customer value. There are many activities performed in a company before selling a product. Design, marketing, delivery and support of the product are just a few steps to consider. According to Kotler (1997), the value chain identifies five primary activities and four support activities all of which are relevant in creating value, as illustrated in Table 2.3.

Table 2.3 The value chain

Secondary activities	Firms infrastructure				
	Human resource management				
	Technological development				
	Procurement				
Primary activities	Inbound logistics	Operations logistics	Outbound logistics	Marketing logistics	Services and sales

Source: adapted from Kotler (1997)

One of the primary activities is inbound logistics, where materials are brought into the organisation. Operation logistics is converting this material into final products. Outbound logistics is, as the name suggests, when the final products are delivered. The marketing of the product is the next step in the primary activities and the final one is service and sales of the product (Kotler, 1997).

The supportive activities are firm infrastructure, human resource management, technological development and procurement. Procurement is the purchasing of various inputs for each primary activity. The infrastructure support activity covers the costs of, for example, management, planning, finance, accounting and legal affairs. These are costs from all primary and support activities (Kotler, 1997). Investing in SCM involves a change in a firm's processes and position. Information systems form an infrastructure capable of supporting all this, yet they do not function without correct data entry and the willingness of people to work in an integrated way. The following section explains the role of e-commerce in SCM.

Electronic supply chain management

Information technology (IT) is essential to expand and maintain a successful SCM philosophy. Corporations implement information systems to monitor inventory levels and schedule production, to provide high levels of customer service, and to enhance their competitive position through partnerships. Moreover, the development of IT enables automation and execution in a supply chain. One of the most important contributions of IT to SCM is the emergence of e-commerce. Reynolds (2000) states that e-commerce in supply chain management facilitates globalisation and assists partners to contribute more efficiency and effectively. Kotzab *et al.* (2003) define electronic SCM as a management control, which concerns electronic supply chain integration on a practical, application and business management level.

With automation, the performance of tasks becomes immediate, and order times can be reduced significantly, especially if system-to-system communication is possible (Westland and Clark, 1999). De Souza *et al.* (2000) illustrated that close co-ordination between supply chain partners can reduce unwanted variations (e.g. order accumulations) in the supply chain. An organisation's supply chain is an 'extended enterprise with each individual firm serving as a business unit within the larger organisation' (Vokurka *et al.*, 2002). Close co-ordination can also be supported by IOSs.

There is an immense amount of literature on the integration and relationship of IOSs and supply chain management. SCM aims to integrate all key business activities through improved relationships at all levels of the supply chain, specifically internal operations, upstream supplier networks and downstream distribution channels (Al-Mashari and Zairi, 2000). The purpose of electronic SCM is to achieve a quick response to fluctuations in customer demand and at the same time reduce transaction costs for the entire supply chain, thereby creating maximal value for the end-user (Kotzab *et al.*,

2003). With technology-enabled IOSs and internet-based tools, the total flow of a channel from the first supplier of raw materials to the ultimate consumer is becoming more strongly related (Angeles, 2000). E-commerce technologies are eliminating the activities of middlemen and manual processing of invoices and other documents. E-commerce improves product flow co-ordination and allows companies to share product information, particularly inventory levels. Individual companies will no longer compete with each other, but companies will automate, integrate and collaborate so that supply chains will compete against supply chains (Vokurka *et al.*, 2002).

The majority of organisations are part of one or more supply chains. It has already been shown that the supply chain can be looked upon as a network of relationships among trading partners. Successful SCM requires a change from managing individual functions to integrating activities into key supply chain processes. Both upstream and downstream parts of the supply chain, according to Lambert *et al.* (1998), have interacted as disconnected entities that receive periodic flows of information over time. However, there still has to be a continued implementation and perhaps even an increase in electronic SCM initiatives in order to squeeze cost out of a supply chain, meaning managers must still be highly familiar and aware of new technology implementation and the opportunity for such implementation.

References

Ahmed, A., Zairi, M. and Alwabel, S. (2003) Global benchmarking for Internet and e-commerce applications, *Proceedings of the First International Conference on Performance Measures, Benchmarking and Best Practices in New Economy*, Business Excellence, 388-396, 10th-13th June, University of Minho, Braga, Portugal (ISBN 972-8692-08-0).

Aldrich, W. and Douglas, F. (1999) *Mastering the Digital Marketplace: Practical Strategies for Competitiveness in the New Economy*, John Wiley and Sons, New York; Chichester.

Al-Mashari, M., Al-Mudimigh, A. and Zairi, M. (2003) Enterprise resource planning: A taxonomy of critical factors, *European Journal of Operational Research; Amsterdam,* 146, 2, 352-364.

Al-Mashari, M. and Zairi, M. (2000) Supply-chain re-engineering using enterprise resource planning (ERP) systems: an analysis of a SAP R/3 implementation case, *International Journal of Physical Distribution and Logistics Management,* 30, ¾, 296–313.

Al-Mudimigh, A., Zairi, M. and Al-Mashari, M. (2001), ERP Software Implementation: An Integrative Framework, *European Journal of Information Systems; Basingstoke,* 10, 4, 216-226.

Alt, R. and Fleisch, E. (2001) Business Networking Systems: Characteristics and Lessons Learned, *International Journal of Electronic Commerce,* 5, 2, 7-28.

Alwabel, S. A., Ahmed, A. M. and Zairi, M. (2003) Drivers for change to reshape construction industry: Saudi's case, *Proceedings of the International Business Information Management Conference*, 16 -18 December 2003, Cairo, Egypt.

Alwabel, S. A. and Zairi, M. (2005b) The evolution of ERP and its relationship with e-business, Working Paper Series No. 05/19, *Bradford University School of Management*, May 2005, Bradford, 1-28.

Alwabel, S. A. and Zairi, M. (2005c) Factors influencing the implementation of e-commerce technologies by financial services in Saudi Arabia-an empirical study, Working Paper Series No. 05/17, *Bradford University School of Management,* May 2005, Bradford, 1-50.

Angeles, R. (2000) Revisiting the role of Internet-EDI in the current electronic commerce scene, *Logistics Information Management,* 13, 1, 45–57.

Angeles, R. (2001) Creating a digital marketspace presence: lessons in extranet implementation, *Internet Research; Bradford,* 11, 2, 167-184.

Archer, N. and Yuan, Y. (2000) Managing business-to-business relationships throughout the e-commerce procurement life cycle, *Internet Research: Electronic Networking Applications and Policy,* 10, 5, 385-395.

Argyris, C. (1971) Management information systems: The challenge to rationality and emotionality, *Management Science,* 17, 6, 275-292.

Arnold, J. R. T. (1998) *Introduction to Materials Management, (3rd)* Prentice-Hall International (UK), Upper Saddle River, N.J.; London.

Ballou, R. H. (1999) *Business Logistics Management: Planning, Organising, and Controlling the Supply Chain*, (4th) Prentice Hall, Upper Saddle River, NJ.

Bamfield, J. (1994) Learning by doing: electronic date interchange adoption by retailers, *Logistics Information Management,* 7, 6, 32-39.

Banaghan, M. and Bryant, G. (1998) Electronic commerce streamlines the supply chain, *Business Review Weekly*, 1, 7, 56-67.

Barrett, S. and Konsynski, B. R. (1982) Inter-organisation information sharing systems, *MIS Quarterly [special issue],* 12, 6, 93-105.

Bedworth, D. D. and Bailey, J. E. (1987) *Integrated Production Control Systems: Management, Analysis, Design*, (2nd) Wiley, New York; Chichester.

Blankenship, A. B., Breen, G. E. and Dutka, A. F. (1999) *State of the Art Marketing Research,* (2nd) NTC Business, Lincolnwood, Ill.

Cecil, J. L. and Hall, E. A. (1988) When IT really matters to business strategy, *The McKinsey Quarterly*, 1, 1, 2-26.

Chase, R. B. and Aquilano, N. J. (1995) *Production and Operations Management: Manufacturing and Services*, (7th) Irwin, Chicago; London.

Chaudhuri, S. and Dayal, U. (1997) An overview of data warehousing and OLAP technology, *ACM SIGMOD Record,* 26, 1, 65-74.

Chung, S. H. and Snyder, C. A. (2000) ERP adoption: a technological evolution approach, *International Journal of Agile Management Systems; Bradford,* 2, 1, 24-32.

Cook, M. and Cook, C. W. (2000) *Competitive Intelligence: Create an Intelligent Organisation and Compete to Win*, Kogan Page, London.

Curry, A. and Stancich, L. (2000) The intranet - an intrinsic component of strategic information management?, *International Journal of Information Management,* 20, 4, 249-268.

Daft, R. L. (1991) *Management,* (2nd) Dryden Press, Chicago; London.

Davenport, T. H. and Short, J. E. (1990) The new industrial engineering: information technology and business process redesign, *Sloan Management Review,* 31, 4, 11-27.

Davenport, T. H. and Stoddard, D. B. (1994) Re-engineering: business change of mythic proportions, *MIS Quarterly,* 18, 2, 121-127.

De Souza, R., Zice, S. and Chaoyang, L. (2000) Supply chain dynamics and optimization, *Integrated Manufacturing Systems,* 11, 5, 348-364.

Desborough, J. (1996) *Intranet web development*, New Riders Pub, Indianapolis, Ind.

Dornier, P. P. (1998) *Global Operations and Logistics: Text and Cases,* John Wiley and Sons, New York; Chichester.

Drury, D. H. and Farhoomand, A. (1996) Innovation adoption of EDI, *Information Resources Management Journal,* 9, 3, 5-13.

Egan, J. (1998) *Rethinking construction*, The report of the construction task force, department of the environment, Transport and the regions, HMSO, London.

Ernst, D. J. and Segall, P. (1995) Information resources and institutional effectiveness: The need for a holistic approach to planning and budgeting, *Cause/Effect Magazine,* 18, 1, 11-13.

Flores, F., Graves, M., Hartfield, B. and Winograd, T. (1988) Computer systems and the design of organisational interaction, *ACM Transactions on Office Information Systems,* 6, 2, 153-172.

Forrester Research (2000a), *E-marketplaces will lead US business e-commerce to $2.7 trillion in 2004*, available at http://www.forrester.com/ER/Press/Release/0.1769. 243.FF.html (Accessed August, 2003).

Forrester Research (2000b) *Worldwide E-commerce Growth*, available at http://www.forrester.com/ER/Press/ForrFind/0.1768.0.FF.html (Accessed May, 2003).

Fraser, J., Fraser, N. and McDonald, F. (2000) The strategic challenge of electronic commerce, *Supply Chain Management,* 5, 1, 7-14.

Gartner Group (2000) *Gartner Group Forecasts Regional B2B Outlook through 2004,* available at http://www.ncr.com/repository/research_reports/data_warehousing/gartner_dbcore.htm (Accessed July, 2003).

Gattiker, U. E., Perlusz, S. and Bohmann, K. (2000) Using the Internet for B2B activities: a review and future directions for research, *Internet Research,* 10, 2, 126-140.

Gelinas, U. J., Sutton, S. G. and Oram, A. E. (1999) *Accounting Information Systems,* (4th) South-Western College Pub, Cincinnati, Ohio; London.

Granlund, M. and Malmi, T. (2002) Moderate impact of ERPS on management accounting: a lag or permanent outcome?, *Management Accounting Research,* 13, 3, 299-322.

Greenberg, P. (2001) *CRM at the Speed of Light: Capturing and Keeping Customers in Internet Real Time*, Osborne/McGraw-Hill, Berkeley, CA: London.

Hamill, J. (1997) The Internet and international marketing, *International Marketing Review,* 14, 4/5, 300-323.

Hammer, M. (1990) Re-engineering work: don't automate, obliterate, *Harvard Business Review*, 68, 4, 104-112.

Hammer, M. and Champy, J. (1993) *Re-engineering the Corporation: A Manifesto for Business Revolution*, (1st) N. Brealey, London.

Hicks, D. A. (1997) The manager's guide to supply chain and logistics problem solving tools and techniques, part II: tools, companies, and industries, *IIE Solutions,* 29, 10, 24-29.

Higgins, P., Le Roy, P. and Tierney, L. (1996) *Manufacturing Planning and Control: Beyond MRP II,* Chapman and Hall, London.

Hiltz, S. R. and Turoff, M. (1993) *The Network Nation: Human Communication Via Computer,* (Rev.) MIT Press, Cambridge, Mass.; London.

Hope, J. and Hope, T. (1997) *Competing in the Third Wave: the Ten Key Issues that Managers Must Face in the Information Age*, Harvard Business School Press, Boston, Mass.

Ives, B. and Learmoth, G. P. (1984) The information system as a competitive weapon, *Communications of the ACM,* 27, 12, 1193-1201.

Jaiswal, M. P. (2002) Enhancing business value through ERP enabled e-business transformation, *Journal of E-Business,* 2, 2, 1-9.

Johnson, D. A., Allen, B. J. and Crum, M. R. (1992) The state of EDI usage in the motor carrier industry, *Journal of Business Logistics; Oak Brook,* 13, 2, 43-68.

Kahaner, L. (1997) Competitive Intelligence: *How to Gather, Analyze, and Use Information to Move your Business to the Top*, Touchstone, New York.

Kalakota, R. and Robinson, M. (1999) *E-Business: Roadmap for Success,* Addison-Wesley, Reading, Mass.; Harlow.

Kalakota, R. and Robinson, M. (2001) *E-business 2.0: Roadmap for Success,* Addison-Wesley, Boston, Mass.

Kalakota, R. and Whinston, A. B. (1997) *Electronic Commerce: A Manager's Guide,* Addison-Wesley, Reading, Mass.; Harlow, England.

Kaplan, S. and Sawhney, M. (2000) E-hubs: the new B2B marketplaces, *Harvard Business Review*, 78, 3, 97-103.

Keen, P. G. W. (1986) *Competing in Time: Using Telecommunications for Competitive Advantage*, Ballinger Pub. Co., Cambridge; Mass.

Kessler, J. (1991) MRP II: In the midst of a continuing evolution, *Industrial Engineering; Norcross,* 23, 3, 38-40.

Klaus, H., Rosemann, M. and Gable, G. G. (2000) What is ERP?, *Information Systems Frontiers,* 2, 2, 141-162.

Koh, S. C., Jones, M. H., Saad, S. M., Arunachalam, S. and Gunasekaran, A. (2000) Measuring uncertainties in MRP environments, *Logistics Information Management; Bradford,* 13, 3, 177-183.

Kotler, P. (1997) *Marketing Management: Analysis, Planning, Implementation, and Control*, (9th) Prentice Hall of India Private Limited, New Delhi.

Kotzab, H., Skjoldager, N. and Vinum, T. (2003) The development and empirical validation of an e-based supply chain strategy optimization model, *Industrial Management and Data Systems,* 103, 5, 347-360.

Lambert, D. M., Stock, J. R. and Ellram, L. M. (1998) *Fundamentals of Logistics Management,* Irwin/McGraw-Hill, Boston; London.

Laudon, K. C. and Laudon, J. P. (2000) *Management Information Systems: Organisation and Technology in the Networked Enterprise,* (6th) Prentice Hall: Prentice-Hall International, Upper Saddle River, N.J.; London.

Law, M., Lau, T. and Wong, Y. H. (2003) From customer relationship management to customer-managed relationship: unravelling the paradox with a co-creative perspective, *Marketing Intelligence and Planning,* 21, 1, 51-60.

Leavitt, H. J. and Whisler, T. L. (1958) Management in the 1980's, *Harvard Business Review,* 36, 6, 41-48.

Loshin, P. (1997) *Extranet Design and Implementation,* Sybex Network, San Francisco.

Macdonald, S., Lamberton, D. M. and Mandeville, T. (1983) *The Trouble With Technology: Explorations in the Process of Technological Change*, Pinter, London.

Maddox, K. and Blankenhorn, D. (1998) *Web Commerce: Building a Digital Business,* Wiley, New York; Chichester.

Malone, T. W., Yates, J. and Benjamin, R. I. (1987) Electronic markets and electronic hierarchies: effects of information technology on market structure and corporate strategies, *Communications of the ACM,* 30, 6, 484-497.

Markus, M. L. and Robey, D. (1988) Information technology and organisational change: causal structure in theory and research, *Management Science,* 34, 5, 583-598.

Markus, M. L. and Tanis, C. (2000) The Enterprise System Experience-from Adoption to Success, In R. W. Zmud, (eds.) *Framing the domains of IT management: projecting the future through the past*, Pinnaflex, Cincinnati.

Moorman, C. (1995) Organisational market information processing: cultural antecedents and new product outcomes, *Journal of Marketing Research,* 1, 32, 318-335.

Norris, G., Hurley, J. R., Hartly, K. M., Dunleavy, J. R. and Balls, J. D. (2000) *E-Business and ERP: Transforming the Enterprise,* John Wiley, New York; Chichester.

Organisation for Economic Co-operation and Development (OECD) (2000) *The economic and social Impact of electronic commerce*, Preliminary Findings and Research Agenda, USA.

O'Leary, D. E. (2000) *Enterprise Resource Planning Systems: Systems, Life Cycle, Electronic Commerce, and Risk*, Cambridge University Press, Cambridge.

Pawar, K. S. and Driva, H. (2000) Electronic trading in the supply chain: a holistic implementation framework, *Logistics Information Management,* 13, 1, 21-32.

Penrose, E. T. (1959) *The Theory of the Growth of the Firm,* Basil Blackwell, Oxford Eng.

Peppers, D. and Rogers, M. (1997) *Enterprise One to One: Tools for Competing in the Interactive Age*, Currency Doubleday, New York.

Plant, R. (2000) *E-Commerce: Formulation of Strategy,* Prentice Hall PTR, Upper Saddle River, N.J.

Porter, M. E. and Millar, V. E. (1985) How information gives you competitive advantage, *Harvard Business Review,* 63, 4, 149-160.

Raysman, R. (1981) Manager involvement needed in computer selection, *Harvard Business Review; Boston,* 59, 5, 54-58.

Reynolds, J. (2000) E-commerce: a critical review, *International Journal of Retail & Distribution Management Science,* 28, 10, 417-444.

Rockart, J. F. and Scott Morton, M. S. (1984) Implications of changes in information technology for corporate strategy, *Interfaces,* 14, 1, 84-95.

Romney, M. B. and Steinbart, P. J. (1999) *Accounting Information Systems,* (8th) Prentice Hall, Upper Saddle River, N.J.

Rooyen, J. H. (2002) Emerging role of corporate treasury management in cyber space, *South African Journal of Information Management,* 4, 4, 1-16.

Rosen, A. (2000) *The E-commerce Question and Answer Book: A Survival Guide for Business Managers*, Amacom, New York.

Rosetti, D. K. and DeZoort, F. A. (1989) Organisational adaptation to technology innovation, *Advanced Management Journal,* 54, 4, 29-33.

Rowley, J. E. (2002) *E-business: Principles and Practice,* Palgrave, Basingstoke.

Russell, R., S. and Taylor, B., W. (1998) *Operations Management: Focusing on Quality and Competitiveness,* (2nd) Prentice Hall: Prentice-Hall International, Upper Saddle River, N.J.; London.

Scarbrough, H. and Corbett, J. M. (1992) *Technology and Organisation: Power, Meaning and Design,* Routledge, London; New York.

Schneider, G. P. and Perry, J. T. (2000) *Electronic Commerce,* Course Technology, Cambridge, Mass.

Scott, W. R. (1992) *Organisations: Rational, Natural, and Open Systems,* (3rd) Prentice-Hall International, Englewood Cliffs, N.J.

Seybold, P. B. and Marshak, R. T. (1998) *Customers.com: How to Create a Profitable Business Strategy for the Internet and Beyond,* (1st) Sage, London.

Simchi-Levi, D., Simchi-Levi, E. and Kaminsky, P. (2000) *Designing and Managing the Supply Chain: Concepts, Strategies, and Cases Studies,* McGraw-Hill, Boston; London.

Spekman, R. E., Kamauff, J. W. and Myhr (1998) An empirical investigation into supply chain management: a perspective on partnership, *Supply Chain Management,* 3, 2, 53-67.

Spil, T. A., Stegwee, R. and Teitink, C. (2002) Business intelligence in healthcare organisations, *Proceedings of the 35th Hawaii International Conference on System Sciences*, Hawaii.

Stegwee, R. A. (1992) *Division for Conquest: Decision Support for Information Architecture Specification*, Wolters-Noordhof.

Steinfield, C., Kraut, R. and Plummer, A. (1995) The impact of interorganisational networks on buyer-seller relationships, *Journal of Computer Mediated Communication,* 1, 3, 1-16.

Sterne, J. (2000) *Customer Service on the Internet: Building Relationships, Increasing Loyalty, and Staying Competitive,* (2nd) John Wiley, New York; Chichester.

Sum, C. and Yang, K. (1993) A study on manufacturing resource planning (MRP II) practices in Singapore, *Omega; Oxford,* 21, 2, 187-198.

Swift, R. S. (2000) *Accelerating Customer Relationships: Using CRM and Relationship Technologies*, Prentice Hall PTR, Englewood Cliffs, N.J.; London.

Tapscott, D., Lowy, A. and Ticoll, D. (2000) *Digital Capital: Harnessing the Power of Business Webs,* Harvard Business School Press, Boston, Mass.

Timmers, P. (1999) *Electronic Commerce: Strategies and Models for Business-to-Business Trading*, Wiley, Chichester, West Sussex, England; New York.

Todman, C. (2001) *Designing a Data Warehouse Supporting Customer Relationship Management*, Prentice Hall PTR, Upper Saddle River, N.J.

Toomey, J. W. (1996) *MRP II: Planning for Manufacturing Excellence,* Chapman & Hall, New York; London.

Torkzadeh, G. and Sharma, N. (1991) MRP application in a small manufacturing company, *Industrial Engineering; Norcross,* 23, 6, 43-46.

Trice, H. M. and Beyer, J. M. (1993) *The Cultures of Work Organisations,* Prentice Hall: Prentice Hall International, Englewood Cliffs; London.

Turban, E., Lee, J., King, D., R and Chung, H. M. (2000) *Electronic Commerce: A Managerial Perspective,* Prentice Hall International, London.

Vokurka, R. J., Zank, G. M. and Lund, C. M. (2002) Improving competitiveness through supply chain management: a cumulative improvement approach, *Competitiveness Review,* 12, 1, 14-25.

Vollmann, T. E., Berry, W. L. and Whybark, D. C. (1992) *Manufacturing Planning and Control Systems,* (3rd) Irwin Professional Publishing, Chicago; London.

Walker, K. B. and Black, E. L. (2000) Re-engineering the undergraduate business core curriculum: aligning business schools with business for improved performance, *Business Process Management Journal,* 6, 3, 194-213.

Wallace, T. F. and Kremzar, M. H. (2001) *ERP: Making it Happen: The Implementers' Guide to Success with Enterprise Resource Planning,* Wiley, New York; Chichester.

Westland, J. C. and Clark, T. H. K. (1999) *Global Electronic Commerce: Theory and Case Studies,* MIT Press, Cambridge, Mass.; London.

Wilkes, R. B. (1991) Draining the swamp: defining strategic use of the information systems resource, *Information and Management,* 20, 1, 49-58.

Wilkinson, J. W. (2000) *Accounting Information Systems: Essential Concepts and Applications,* (4th) John Wiley, New York; Chichester.

Zheng, S., Yen, D. C. and Tarn, J. M. (2000) The new spectrum of the cross-enterprise solution: The integration of the supply chain and enterprise resource planning systems, *Journal of Computer Information Systems,* 41, 1, 84-93.

Chapter 3

Putting the *e* in business practice: The pervasiveness of internet applications

Analysis of current e-commerce practices

There are so many possible applications of e-business today and many more are predicted in the future. E-commerce, enabled by rapidly emerging new technologies, delivers global business interaction at the touch of a button. E-commerce extends a company out to broadening circles of impact. Advanced communications technologies are growing and evolving at a very rapid rate. Since the early 1990s when the internet was offered to business for commercial use, the way in which it has been used has evolved rapidly. Many businesses have developed websites with the purpose of promoting their companies automatically. According to Westland and Clark (1999) almost all of the Fortune 500 companies have commercial websites, yet only 10 percent of these use them for online selling.

Existing products and services that are promoted and sold via e-commerce, according to Frieden and Porter (1996), are home banking, electronic bill payment, computer software and computer hardware, video, cable television, photographs, books, gifts, flowers, newspapers and magazines, information databases, education and job training, travel services, health care services, customer service, online stock trading, and email; the most widely utilised forms of e-commerce. Moreover, recent studies done by Charles *et al.* (2002) have shown that only a small proportion of Canadian enterprises are embracing more advanced e-business applications such as selling (7 percent) and buying (22 percent) online. According to Charles *et al.* (2002) 'E-business allows organisations to streamline production, reduce operational costs, expand markets, enhance collaborative business partnerships and strengthen customer and supplier relationships'.

Companies continue using the internet as a medium to further language learning and discovery. It is not possible to provide a complete list of current e-commerce applications, but here are some of the activities of e-commerce available: electronic banking, online auctions, interactive marketing, direct marketing, online stock trading, electronic publishing, and travel package selling. In terms of physical movements a study by Forrester Research (2000a) shows that 20 percent of package traffic in the US is by electronic retailers. Moreover, according to the same Forrester Research, the potential of e-commerce caught public's attention as a result of ventures such as the electronic bookshop, Amazon.com, and the growing number of other internet-based retailers in the B2C e-commerce area.

However, B2B e-commerce is growing much more quickly than B2C forms of electronic trading. These two e-commerce applications are the major e-commerce usages nowadays, but there are other practices, which will be discussed later. To simplify matters, Bakos (1998) classifies all e-business activities into three different functions. The following section explains these functions.

Functions of e-commerce

Markets play an essential role in the economy, facilitating the exchange of information, goods, services and payments. In the process, they create economic value for buyers, sellers, market intermediaries and for society in general. Recently, information technology has played a major role in markets, both in traditional markets, and in the emergence of electronic marketplaces. The roles of intermediaries are generally based on the functions of a market, regardless of whether they are conventional or electronic market (Bakos, 1998). Bakos goes further and categorises market functions into three major services, namely matching buyers and suppliers, facilitating transactions, and providing institutional infrastructure.

- ***Matching buyers and suppliers***: involves determination of product offerings (by specifying facilitation or aggregation of different products), searching (of buyers for suppliers and suppliers for buyers) in terms of price and product information and matching suppliers' offers with buyers' preferences, and price discovery which may involve negotiation.
- ***Facilitating transaction***: is associated with logistics such as delivery of information, goods or services to buyers, settlement and trust. In an electronic market offer, the supplier and customer will agree to use an interoperable e-commerce infrastructure (i.e. EDI or the internet) so the value of a facilitator is reduced.
- ***Institutional infrastructure***: specifies the laws, rules and regulations that govern market transactions, such as issues related to commercial code, contract law and intellectual property protection (Bakos, 1998).

According to Giaglis *et al.* (1999), the first two services are provided by intermediaries, while the latter is carried out by government institutions. Thus, our focus is on the first two services. However, companies which adopt e-commerce do not need to be pure e-commerce and provide a digital channel for all their functions; most transactions are fulfilled through a combination of physical and digital channels (Turban *et al.*, 2000).

The functions differ amongst different e-commerce applications; however, most appear to offer at least matching buyers and suppliers' service, as this is fundamental to a marketplace (Bakos,

1998). Yet, through the latest developments in information technologies and e-commerce tools, electronic marketplaces are having a major impact on these roles (Giaglis *et al.*, 1999). The internet brings into existence a new way of pricing accuracy and flexibility (Laudon and Laudon, 2000). The primary advantage of an electronic market is efficient market search or electronic brokerage. Projected impacts of these lower search costs include disintermediation in the marketing channel, resulting in heightened price competition (Malone *et al.*, 1987; Bakos, 1998). E-commerce thus provides a significant reduction in the costs of production and distribution for these goods. This creates new opportunities for repackaging content through strategies such as bundling, site licensing, subscriptions, rentals, differential pricing and peruse fees. Sellers in internet marketplaces are typically responsible for delivery to their customers, and therefore delivery providers are emerging as major internet intermediaries (Bakos and Brynjolfsson, 2000).

Market-making applications

Market-making can be defined as the matching of demand and supply, and determining the prices in a market (Malone *et al.*, 1987). Market-making is said to be neutral if it is not buyer and seller controlled. It is either set up by a third party (e.g. a software provider) to match many buyers to many sellers (Berryman *et al.*, 1998) or several companies jointly forming a marketplace (Barrett and Konsynski, 1982). The electronic marketplace can be defined as an inter-organisational information system that allows the participating firms to interact to achieve one or more of the market-making activities which identify potential trading partners; facilitating the exchange of information, goods, services and payments and providing an infrastructure that enables the efficient functioning of the market (Bakos, 1998; Grieger, 2003). Thus, e-commerce effects are thought to be vital, for instance, for sites that function as third-party market-makers offering brokerage services. In order to improve the liquidity of the market such sites must be able to attract a critical mass of buyers and sellers. The more of each a site can attract, the better the possibility any member has of finding a desired match (Eid *et al.*, 2002).

E-commerce networks have provided opportunities to form electronic markets to match buyers and sellers (Bakos, 1998). Thus, it is necessary to provide secure means of exchanging information rapidly and successfully amongst the collaboration partners (O'Keefe *et al.*, 1998). However, so as to match buyers and sellers, B2B e-commerce should be applied. These B2B e-commerce networks employ a number of different market-making acuities to match buyers and sellers and to make possible price discovery.

Business models

A 'business model' has been used extensively in the e-commerce literature by various authors (Kalakota and Robinson, 1999; Timmers, 1999; Weill and Vitale, 2001; Turban *et al.*, 2002; Rappa, 2003; and Krishnamurthy, 2003). Turban *et al.* (2002) refer to business models as '...a method of doing business by which a company generates revenue to sustain itself. The model spells out how the company is positioned in the value chain'.

However, Timmers (1999) refers to business models as 'an architecture for the product, service and information flows, including a description of the various business actors, their roles, potential benefits and sources of revenues for the model', whereas Krishnamurthy (2003) states that: 'A business model is a path to a company's profitability, an integrated application of diverse concepts to ensure the business objectives are met. A business model consists of business objectives, a value delivery system, and a revenue model'. Others refer to business models as descriptions or specifications (Weill and Vitale, 2001).

> *In the most basic sense, a business model is a method of doing business by which a company can sustain itself that is, generate revenue. The business model spells out how a company makes money by specifying where it is positioned in the value chain* (Rappa, 2003).

The common feature evident in all the business model definitions mentioned above is the necessity that the business model represents the organisation in relation to the other entities that form part of the value network. Amit and Zott (2001) state that a business model '.....depicts the content, structure, and governance of transactions designed so as to create value through the exploitation of business opportunities'.

There have been several attempts to formally describe and classify a business model for the e-business era. Afuah and Tucci (2001) define the internet business model as '.....the system components, linkages, and associated dynamics that take advantage of the properties of the Internet to make money'. The e-business era radically and strategically changes traditional business models. Straight access to information and its rapid and cost-effective global reach enables fundamental changes in all economic sectors and changes in companies of all sizes and business actions. The widespread availability of information over the open network infrastructure widens organisations' boundaries towards being comprehensive organisations and strategic associations with modular or networked structures. Kalakota and Robinson (1999) stated that the ability to rationalise the structure, and influence and control the flow of information is radically more powerful and cost-effective than touching and manufacturing physical goods.

As mentioned earlier e-commerce networks employ a number of different market-making acuities to match buyers and sellers. These market-making mechanisms (Kaplan and Sawhney, 2000) can be divided into two mechanisms, an aggregation or a matching mechanism. Aggregates bring together buyers and suppliers in large numbers providing one stop shopping. Set prices are the norm in an aggregate marketplace, and the buyer and seller positions are fixed, whereas a matching mechanism bring together large numbers of buyers and suppliers to negotiate on dynamic and real-time deals. Matching marketplaces are often used more in spot markets because the prices are determined at the point of sale, and buyers and sellers are able to switch roles more readily (Kaplan and Sawhney, 2000). Various business models can be applied to implement each mechanism, yet according to the literature (Reck, 1997; Klein, 1997; Sculley and Woods, 1999; Kaplan and Sawhney, 2000; Skinner, 2000; Lucking-Reiley, 2000; Raisch and Gartner, 2001; and Grieger, 2003), the most regularly used business models in the electronic marketplace are electronic catalogues for aggregation, and electronic auction and exchange for matching.

Electronic catalogues

The catalogue model brings together large numbers of buyers and sellers. Virtual distributors aggregate; indexed product catalogues or content are available in a centralised location to suppliers and customers (Skinner, 2000). The catalogue model aggregates product catalogues of many competing suppliers to provide a one-stop procurement venue for buyers. It is usually applied to the sale of low-value items that are bought frequently but in small quantities at fixed prices (Sculley and Woods, 1999). Yet, catalogue hubs automate the procurement of non-commodity manufacturing inputs, creating value by reducing transaction costs (Kaplan and Sawhney, 2000). The electronic catalogue is an information system which puts emphasis on multimedia representations of the products, services and/or information of an organisation (Raisch and Gartner, 2001). In addition, an e-catalogue contains some functionality in selecting and ordering products, services and/or information. Although a catalogue mechanism enables suppliers to change product or service prices, buyers and suppliers cannot negotiate prices in a bid and ask system; as a result prices in e-catalogues are generally static (Kaplan and Sawhney, 2000).

Electronic auctions

Auctions are a new pricing model for many markets, in which multiple buyers and sellers bid competitively on a contract (Sculley and Woods, 1999). Electronic auctions (e-auctions) are a special case of mechanised negotiation, where the auction patterns vary with the deal objectives and rules (Reck, 1997). The role of the auctioneer in most e-auctions is replaced by an automated negotiation system (Klein, 1997). The auction method relies on dynamic pricing where buyers or sellers transparently bid on prices of clearly specified items (Reck, 1997). Both buyer- and seller-driven auction formats are expected to become increasingly popular for B2B marketplaces since they enhance efficiency while maximising the return for the buyer or the seller. Moreover, the auction format is well-suited to the interactive, real-time attributes of the internet (Sculley and Woods, 1999). Although e-auctions can provide ideal pricing information since prices of product/services are transparent to buyers and sellers, they are more time consuming as auctions are completed when the biding time is closed (Lucking-Reiley, 2000). However, to overcome this disadvantage electronic exchanges have appeared.

Electronic exchanges

The exchange mechanism enables buyers and suppliers to negotiate prices in a bid and ask system, similar to Stock Exchange Systems. This internet based electronic marketplace allows both upward and downward price changes. This model performs well for near-commodity items and can make substantial value in volatile markets, allowing organisations to manage excess supply and peak load demand (Grieger, 2003). Exchanges stabilise peaks and valleys in demand and supply by quickly exchanging the near-commodities

(Kaplan and Sawhney, 2000). However, a successful exchange format requires a critical mass to provide liquidity, allowing buyers' access to numerous suppliers (Raisch and Gartner, 2001; Grieger, 2003). To sum up, the unique feature of electronic exchanges is that they almost bring multiple buyers and sellers together in one central market space and enable those players to conduct transactions at a price which is determined in accordance with the rules of the exchange (Sculley and Woods, 1999).

Electronic shop

Electronic shop (e-shop) is a web advertisement of a company or a shop in order to promote the company and its products or services. Progressively more is added, including the possibility to order and pay on-line (Timmers, 1999).

Revenue models

Revenue models for generating profit in e-commerce vary from organisation to organisation. Some firms may believe more powerfully in the subscription model; other may desire the pay-per-use approach; whereas others rely on product sales margins as in more traditional transactions (Kerrigan *et al.*, 2001).

The revenue model dimension refers to 'the specific modes in which a business model enables revenue generation' (Amit and Zott, 2001). B2B e-marketplaces can capitalise on a selection of basic revenue generating modes. First, B2B pricing most often takes the form of transaction fees, which are charged to the supplier, to the customer, or to both. While there are countless variations on transaction fees, most of them are based on a percentage of the transaction price, typically ranging from 0.5 to 5 percent of the transaction volume (Kerrigan *et al.*, 2001). Instead of collecting fees by serving as a venue for transactions, B2B firms can charge membership or subscription fees, which avoid the difficulty of calculating myriad transaction fees (Kerrigan *et al.*, 2001). If the intermediary is just providing the software package for operating the marketplace a license fee is charged to the users (Windham and Samsel, 1999).

The second basic B2B revenue stream is generated through a combination of service contributions. Digital value-added services comprise information services such as customised data mining analyses, content services such as industry news, and transaction-related services such as insurance and payment. Physical value-added services (VAS) are offered to support warehousing, freight consolidation, and logistical requirements of the corporate members (Raisch and Gartner, 2001). As mentioned earlier most VAS offered by e-marketplace intermediaries are related to the facilitation of the transactions, since the institutional infrastructure function is naturally performed by government (Giaglis *et al.*, 1999).

From the above discussion it can be seen that business models are various. Thus, according to Symonds (1999), companies that apply e-commerce should offer more than one business model in order to allow buyers and sellers to choose the most suitable. Kalakota and Robinson (1999) maintain that 'e-business is about redefining old business models, with the aid of technology, to maximise customer value'. The numbers of business models vary from author to author. Each author and/or researcher seems to have their own list of necessary business models, as can be seen from Table 3.1, both because they appeared over a period of years and therefore reflect the ongoing development of research into business models, and also because they are particularly well suited to the financial services sector.

Table 3.1 Business models

Authors	Business models
Kalakota and Robinson (1999)	Category killer, channel reconfiguration, transaction intermediary, infomediary, self-service innovator, supply-chain innovator, channel mastery.
Timmers (1999)	E-shop, e-procurement, e-malls, e-auctions, virtual communities, collaboration platforms, third-party marketplaces, value-chain integrators, value-chain service providers, information brokerage, trust services.
Weill and Vitale (2001)	Content provider, direct to customer, full-service provider, intermediary, shared infrastructure, value net integrator, virtual community, whole-of enterprise/ govt.
Turban *et al* (2002)	Name your price, find the best price, affiliate marketing, group purchasing, electronic tendering system, customisation and personalisation, electronic marketplaces and exchanges, supply chain improvers, collaborative commerce.
Rappa (2003)	• *Broker models*: buy/sell fulfilment, market exchange, business trading community, buyer aggregator, distributor, virtual mall, metamediary, auction broker, reverse auction, classifieds, search agent, bounty broker. • *Advertising models*: generalised portal, personalised portal, specialised portal, attention/incentive marketing, free model, bargain discounter. • *Merchant models*: virtual merchant, catalogue merchant, bit vendor, click and mortar. • *Infomediary models*: recommended system, registration model. • *Manufacturer models*: brand integrated content. • *Community Models*: Voluntary contributor, knowledge networks, subscription model, utility model.
Krishnamurthy (2003)	• Bricks-and-clicks, pure-play • *B2C*: Direct sellers intermediaries, advertising-based models, community-based models, fee-based models. • *B2B*: EDI, extranets, e-marketplaces • *C2C:* Auctions, peer-to-peer • *C2B:* Idea collectors, reverse auctions, complaint centres, paid advertising models.

E-commerce practices

The recognised practices of e-commerce activities are based on the type of stakeholders involved in the transactions supported, automated, or integrated with information and communication technologies (Kalakota and Whinston, 1996). Consequently 11 categories of e-commerce are identified as shown in Table 3.2.

Table 3.2 E-commerce applications

E-commerce practices	Explanation
Business-to-business (B2B)	Refers to e-commerce transactions between or among multiple businesses (Aljifri *et al.*, 2003).
Business-to-consumer (B2C)	Refers to e-commerce that focuses on direct transactions between businesses and end consumers (Ah-Wong *et al.*, 2001). Examples in B2C electronic commerce appear in online retailing of tangible goods such as books or computer hardware as well as intangible goods such as software or financial services (May, 2000).
Consumer-to-business (C2B)	Refers to transactions where individuals sell products to business. It can also mean individuals seeking a seller online to conduct a transaction (Monica *et al.*, 2003), for example Priceline.com is a site where consumers can 'name your own price' for products.
Consumer-to-consumer (C2C)	Often referred to as virtual communities, C2C enables consumers to sell goods or services, to share member-generated information, and to interact with each other (Hagel and Armstrong, 1997).
People-to-people (P2P) or peer-to-peer	A form of specific C2C transaction where people can exchange CDs, software, information, and other goods directly, e.g. Napster.com was once a popular online music exchange between individuals (Alfred and Choi, 2002).
Intra-organisational e-commerce	Is well represented by corporate intranets. An intranet can be defined as an extension of client/server networks with asset of IT standards, infrastructure, tools and applications that rely on the internet as network and development

	platform (Desborough, 1996).
Business-to-employees	Is about creating a strong channel of communication throughout the organisation; communication that moves instantly and directly from point to point, whether from the collaborative e-supply chain optimisation (CEO) to the human resource (HR) manager, from manager to employee, or from peer to peer (Alfred and Choi, 2002).
Government-to-citizens (G2C)	Refers to the transactions in which government bodies transact directly with citizens in order to provide them with information or services across the entire spectrum of public services (health, transport, education, taxation, etc.) (Alfred and Choi, 2002).
Exchange-to-exchange (E2E)	Exchanges are in virtual marketplace or e-markets where buyers and sellers congregate (Phan, 2003) e.g. PlasticsNet.com where it connects buyers and sellers of plastics.
Collaborative commerce (c-commerce)	Combined with the power of internet communications, it moves businesses to a new business model that looks beyond the internal supply chain (Selen, 2001).
Mobile commerce (m-commerce)	Transactions carried out in a wireless environment, e.g. using a mobile phone (Fenech, 2002).

Source: adapted from Alwabel *et al.* (2004)

Financial reporting through the internet

The number of firms posting financial reporting through the internet has increased rapidly over the last five years. In 1998 the Association for Investment Management and Research (AIMR) undertook a research project to investigate the extent to which firms are adopting and utilising technology to provide financial reports to the investment community. Analysts were required to evaluate these technologies as a source of information. Further requirements were to rate the quality, timeliness and specificity of information provided by companies. The majority of analysts (66%)

reported that 'almost all' of the companies had a corporate website. A further 44% of the analysts reported these companies having an investor relations section. Annual reports (76%) were the most frequent type of information that companies provided. Some 65% responded that the availability of a company website made it easier to provide an accurate analysis of a company. A further 84% reported that 'almost all' of the companies studied by the analysts used email to communicate with the investment community. Analysts reported that of those companies that make excellent use of technology in providing strategic/financial information, 61% were large cap companies (AIMR, 1998).

Debreceny and Gray (1999) conducted a survey in 1998 of the 15 largest companies in the UK, Germany and France. This amounted to 45 companies in total. These companies were identified from the Dow Jones Global Index. In total 36 companies (80%) posted annual reports on the web.

Craven and Marston (1999) surveyed the largest 200 companies as listed by market capitalisation in the Financial Times (22 January 1998). Of the 206 firms selected, 153 (74%) had websites. Of the companies surveyed, 67 (32.5%) disclosed detailed annual reports. This study also investigated whether there was a positive and significant association between company variables, such as size and industry type, and internet disclosure. It was found that larger companies are more likely to disclose financial information on the internet. Results indicated no significant relationship between the extent of internet financial disclosure and industry type.

There are many advantages to providing financial information on the internet. Large companies can virtually eliminate the substantial cost of printing and posting annual reports to the thousands of investors who request them every year, because most investors have access to the internet. The information can be accessed by a much wider audience than more conventional means of communication permit. The regular maintenance of websites means that the financial information provided can be kept up-to-date whereas paper reports have a very short shelf-life (Craven and Marston, 1999).

The trend towards the provision of financial reporting through the internet is unalterable and the following disadvantages are, by and large, matters that large firms simply have to live with – they are not factors to be taken into account when deciding whether or not to provide such reporting: the issue for all large firms now is not if, but when and how, they will provide financial reporting.

The financial infrastructure for stock markets refers to the environment in which financial transactions are carried out; it includes the legal and regulatory framework, the financial institutions involved and the trading mechanisms (Tigre and Dedrick, 2004). An important component of the financial infrastructure is the trading, clearing and settlement system. An efficient and effective trading environment can enhance investor participation and reduce systemic risk, such as the inability to complete a trade. These benefits are translated into a higher liquidity and a reduced cost of capital for listed companies. Improvements in the infrastructure of local stock markets can stimulate local investors to hold domestic stocks, thereby enhancing the robustness of the market. Most trading is now automated and investors should soon be reaping benefits in terms of cheaper transaction costs and better service.

The term stock market refers to the buying and selling of shares, or stock, in all kinds of companies. However, according to Pike and Neale (1999) one of the major requirements of stock market efficiency is that all participants have generally equal access to price-sensitive information. In the past, the big investors with online databases were able to obtain information, and hence enjoy a competitive advantage, well before the small investors who may have had to rely on the daily paper to keep abreast of recent events and price movements. Yet, e-commerce offers enormous scope for narrowing the information gap between big and small investors as follows:

- *Company information,* electronic reporting of firm information will result in a significant opportunity to shareholders and enable greater accountability and corporate governance. The electronic information revolution should also give rise to a movement away from conventional accounting-based information to more user-friendly shareholder information which focuses on the key value drivers. For example, customer satisfaction and market diffusion might be regular information as part of a 'balanced scorecard' performance measurement system.
- *Market information*, there are thousands of web pages existing that are devoted to investment and personal finance information.

The impacts of e-commerce

In order to discuss the benefits, obstacles and other factors affecting the application of e-business to financial services, clarity is needed about the potential impacts of e-business. E-business has affected the way in which organisations complete and assign work to employees, communicate with suppliers and customers, and sell their products and services. Consequently, the financial services sector has seen a growing intensity of competition within the marketplace over the last decade. In the UK this competition developed with a concentration on the traditional marketing mix elements of product, price, promotion and place. It has been argued that this led to homogeneity rather than differentiation, with a common market concept perceived by the customer (Ahmed *et al.*, 2003).

Over the last 20 years, the financial services industry has witnessed dramatic changes, largely driven by globalisation, deregulation and consolidation trends. Technological advances accelerated the process, reinforcing some of these trends particularly globalisation and deregulation, as well as facilitating the development of electronic finance (Nieto, 2001). This has blurred the boundaries between different financial institutions, enabling new financial products and services to appear and making the existing ones available in different packages (Ahmed *et al.*, 2003). Saatcioglu *et al.* (2001) introduced a business model called the 'financial portal'. This model develops proprietary indices that focus on individual and small business customers' needs as well as matching the financial instruments to these indices. Therefore, it uses a device that establishes and rebalances portfolios as needed. For example, the model provides clients with customised investment services, while not requiring the knowledge and resources for investing in individual securities, which are more tailored to specific needs than mutual funds or index-tracking stocks, and are much more affordable, and perhaps more comfortable than hiring financial consultants for investment advice. Implementing this business model would not be feasible without the use of the internet (Saatcioglu *et al.*, 2001). Consequently the impacts of e-commerce can be summarised as follows:

- The adoption of e-business can bring new business models such as those relating to different types of intermediaries. For instance according to Wyckoff (1999) online auctions are a new intermediary that has expanded and become a key feature of the information economy. Auctions of products and services give a major positive movement in customer transactions over the internet and provide growth to new business models (Wyckoff, 1999).

- Increased speed and opportunities are made possible by e-commerce where new values, products and information can be sent out around the globe in a significantly short time frame (Downes and Mui, 2000).

- The adoption of e-business can change the function and mission employees perform in organisations, and in turn can create new positions. May (2000) recognises that with the introduction of e-commerce, naturally individuals may encounter role confusion, with company departments unsure who will be responsible for the performance and maintenance of e-business. However, in order to avoid this, top management should assign responsibility for each major process to members of the existing senior management team (Armistead, 1996).

Turban *et al.* (2000) state that e-business has the potential to change everything in a business, from marketing theories and practices, to product innovation and supply chain management. Many of the aspects of e-business discussed above impact either directly or indirectly on financial services systems, as shown in the discussion below.

Potential e-commerce benefits

The internet continues to grow as a medium for commerce, allowing a company to conduct business everywhere, all the time. The characteristics of the new economy have increased the level of competition in all industries and the internet presents an important opportunity for even small firms to launch new products or services because of the speed and low cost of doing business. In today's new business environment, power has shifted toward consumers who demand intelligent products that deliver new dimensions of value, time and content in addition to the current ones of price and quality (Aldrich and Douglas, 1999). By assembling a network of partners that specialise and excel in the links of the value chain, it is possible for organisations to achieve new levels of quality, flexibility and cost savings.

The benefits of applying e-commerce principles and processes to financial services are different for customers and for the provider organisation. For instance, from a customer's perspective, modern e-business may be symbolised by automatic teller machine (ATMs), the World Wide Web (WWW) and electronic banking, meaning that e-business is about self-service. For an organisation, the benefits of applying e-business principles and processes to financial service systems include achieving an increased market reach, developing enhanced relationships with customers and finding new ways to access the intellectual assets of the organisation. Many authors recognise that e-commerce can provide several potential and actual benefits to organisations. E-business research extends these advantages and for the purposes of this study these have been divided into ten main areas:

Better collaboration with customers

E-business can improve the relationship with customers not just in the short term, but for life as well. The potential benefits for corporations of undertaking business via e-commerce can be significant, by bringing together a large number of buyers and sellers and by automating transactions, and enhancing collaboration between buyers and sellers (Bakos, 1998). As a result, firms applying e-commerce can increase revenue (Kalakota and Whinston, 1997), sales and profits (Schneider and Perry, 2000) as well as reduced inventories (Banaghan and Bryant, 1998). Hagel and Armstrong, (1997) suggest that:

> *By adapting to the culture of the Internet, however, and providing customers with the ability to interact with one another in addition to the company, businesses can build new and deeper relationships with customers. We believe that commercial success in the on-line arena will belong to those businesses that organise electronic communities to meet multiple social and commercial needs. By creating strong on-line communities, businesses will be able to build customer*

loyalty to a degree that today's marketers can only dream of and, in turn, generate strong economic returns.

Efficiency gains and quality improvements

Internet-based markets can lead to efficiency gains for the involved players in terms of transaction cost reductions, better supply chain management (Kalakota and Whinston, 1997), widening of markets to global level and maybe narrowly targeting marketing efforts (Schneider and Perry, 2000). Efficiency gains can be realised through faster transactions and cash generation (Vadapalli and Ramamurthy, 1997; Hasan and Tibbits, 2000; Boyer, 2002), automated buying processes and improved sales tracking (Banaghan and Bryant, 1998). The use of databases and electronic communication between service providers and customers is creating new levels of customer service, in terms of service information being better distributed (Schneider and Perry, 2000), problems solved faster (Honeycutt *et al.*, 1998) and communication improved (Kalakota and Whinston, 1997). To meet rising stakeholder expectations, company administrators will be increasingly required to identify new and improved customer services that can be provided electronically. Progress in this area may lead to more efficient production (Faramarz and Jamshid, 2001) and improve customer service quality (Grembergen and Amelincks, 2002) which can exert a positive influence on customer satisfaction (Hasan and Tibbits, 2000).

Therefore, it should be noted that since banking customers, with the advent of internet technology, can have unlimited access to financial information and enjoy a wider range of choices in selecting competitive products and financial institutions than ever before, the subtle 'differentiating' quality levels of bank products and their timely introduction on the marketplace have become a key driving force in attracting new customers and enhancing customers' satisfaction (Ahmed *et al.*, 2003).

Expansion of markets

E-commerce provides the opportunity for business to offer products and services in new potentially global markets (Greaves *et al.*, 1999). Without e-commerce, buyers can have great difficulty finding suppliers with the right products and prices, and suppliers with equal difficulty finding motivated buyers (Schneider and Perry, 2000). In e-business, sellers can discover and address new customers at much lower costs compared to traditional marketing avenues (Charles *et al.*, 2002). Especially for smaller suppliers, e-commerce comprises an affordable alternative to extend their reach beyond traditional boundaries and to gain access to potential customers on a global level. The barriers of national boundaries are eliminated because e-business can be accessed from any place. According to Honeycutt *et al.* (1998) e-commerce eliminates some national and global barriers to entry for example, marketing costs, distribution and shelf-space acquisition. This enables companies to extend their market both nationally and internationally without additional capital outlay (Turban *et al.*, 2002; Faramarz and Jamshid, 2001).

Connection improvements

E-commerce provides companies with more diverse business activities and economies of scope (Kalakota and Whinston, 1997), shorter product development cycles (Banaghan and Bryant, 1998), increased flexibility and responsiveness (Schneider and Perry, 2000) and access to commercial research (Honeycutt *et al.*, 1998). On the demand side, electronic intermediaries potentially reduce buyers' search costs of finding suppliers and present better information about product characteristics, prices and availability (Kaplan and Garicano, 2000).

Customised product and service

When a company interacts electronically with customers, buying behaviour can be analysed so that the company can customise its product and service offerings to the individual customers in the new economy (Skjoett-Larsen, 2000). Customisation is the essence of the one-to-one marketing revolution. The ability to customise products, combined with the ability of sellers to access substantial information about prospective buyers, such as demographics, preferences and past shopping behaviour, is also an opportunity for improving a sellers' ability for price discrimination; this allows sellers to charge different prices to different buyers (Bakos, 1998). Factors such as quality, timing of deliveries and customisation are often more important in determining the overall value provided by a supplier (Molla and Licker, 2001).

Better management information

E-commerce allows management to deal better and faster with sales data reporting and analysis (Kalakota and Whinston, 1997). Progress in this area may lead to more well-organised production, inventory and distribution, marketing and sales, better financial planning, and more successful research and development and product development (Faramarz and Jamshid, 2001; Hasan and Tibbits, 2000).

Potentials for cost savings

One of the most important benefits of e-business is its ability to reduce cost and produce efficiency improvements. Companies can decrease the cost of creating, processing, distributing, storing and retrieving of paper-based information. Turban *et al.* (2002) suggest that an electronic procurement system can save administrative costs by as much as 85 percent. Turban *et al.* (2002) and Faramarz and Jamshid (2001) also demonstrated that an internet bank transaction could produce a saving of 90 percent compared to a traditional bank teller transaction. According to Anandarajan *et al.* (1998) implementation of an extranet will reduce cost. Cost saving comes, to a large extent, from the integration of SCM resulting in more consolidation and the use of smaller numbers of suppliers (Pawar and Driva, 2000). This means lower logistic costs, lower postal costs, lower storage costs and lower personnel costs (Kalakota and Robinson, 2001). A shared database between partners is also a cost reducer since it reduces relevant costs of market research (Anandarajan *et al.*, 1998). Through websites that facilitate efficient functioning at a higher level of quality, firms are able to provide customers with various self-service and delivery options (Molla and Licker, 2001). These offer considerable benefits to firms in increasing productivity and in saving costs (Dabholkar, 1996). For example, websites allow firms to decrease the number of phone calls, shorten transaction times, and reduce manpower, publishing and mailing costs (Dabholkar, 1996). According to Moon and Fre (2000), for banks, it costs just two cents for an internet transaction, compared with 36 cents for an ATM transaction and $1.15 for a teller-assisted transaction, as illustrated in Table 3.3. Charles *et al.* (2002) also point out that e-commerce enables suppliers to reach customers at very low unit costs.

Table 3.3 Service delivery channels and associated transaction costs

Delivery mechanism	Transaction costs US $
In-branch teller	1.15
ATM	0.36
Internet banking	0.02

Source: adapted from Moon and Fre (2000)

Time reduction

In addition to cost saving, e-commerce also impacts the order cycle time between the producing company and its customers. A reduction in purchasing time allows for smaller orders to be placed more often resulting in lower inventory costs (Anandarajan *et al.*, 1998). With e-commerce, savings can be made along the entire supply chain. Time saving can be made since paper handling is more time consuming than electronic transactions (Hasan and Tibbits, 2000). E-commerce has the potential to achieve a key objective of SCM, which is to cut 'cycle time'.

Empowered customers

The confidence of empowered consumers on the web is contributing to their increased control of e-commerce (Windham and Samsel, 1999). Customers' shopping options, and knowledge about those options, are no longer in the sole control of the seller, owing to the internet informational sources. Bergeron (2001) states that:

> *Thanks to the Web, customers now have access to information that effects informed decisions. Consumers are now using software to quickly identify the right [shopping] choices with the optional features and prices.*

Better market understanding

E-business transactions can be automated to extract information regarding their customers. This allows companies to interact more closely with their customers with regard to their buying behaviours and patterns. This produces better CRM and increased customer loyalty based on a one-to-one relationship (Faramarz and Jamshid, 2001).

Potential e-commerce obstacles

The introduction of new technology such as e-commerce gives, as described above, many benefits to firms. Costs can be decreased. More or less everything in the world has, however, both benefits and obstacles. Challenges with e-commerce are mainly concerned with security and legal issues, as emphasised by many authors (O'Keefe *et al.*, 1998; Ratnasingham, 1998; Doyle and Melanson, 2001; Lee and Turban, 2001; Eid *et al.*, 2002; Mukherjee and Nath, 2003). E-business research extends these disadvantages and for the purposes of this research these have been divided into six main areas:

Lack of financial resources and higher cost

One fundamental challenge for e-commerce is to increase market liquidity and to pass a certain number of parties in the network, specifically to reach the critical mass of users (Timmers, 1999), which might cause higher costs in staying on top of ICT. A collection of subscribers must be induced to join simultaneously or join in anticipation of others' participation to form an economically practicable set of subscribers. The minimum practicable set of subscribers is defined as the critical mass of users (Oren and Smith, 1981).

Electronic payment systems according to Walker and Johnson (2001) encompass those transactions involving consumers. These transactions involve the use of such payment mechanisms as credit cards, ATMs, debit cards, point-of-sale (POS) terminals, home banking, and telephone bill-paying services. Payments for these mechanisms are conducted online. However, the absence of a worldwide standard for the settlement of e-commerce transactions is causing difficulties. Requirements for online receipt processes vary depending on the monetary amount of the contract and how an individual contract fits within the overall receipt process. The complete sales/receipt process, according to Walker and Johnson (2001), includes the following mechanisms: order entry, pricing, discounts and taxes, invoicing and collections. Yet, the difficulty in this regard is not on making the site itself, rather it is how the electronic payment systems will work.

Lack of IT expertise and skills and knowledge

The top three barriers facing e-commerce listed by World Information Technology and Service Alliance's (WITSA) international survey of e-commerce (WITSA, 2000) were familiarity with e-commerce (26 percent), lack of understanding of e-commerce (21 percent), and unavailability of skilled workers (10 percent) the remaining barriers varied, as shown in Figure 3.1. As a result, the implementation of e-commerce leads to the requirement for specific skills (Schneider and Perry, 2000).

Figure 3.1 The most significant barriers facing e-commerce

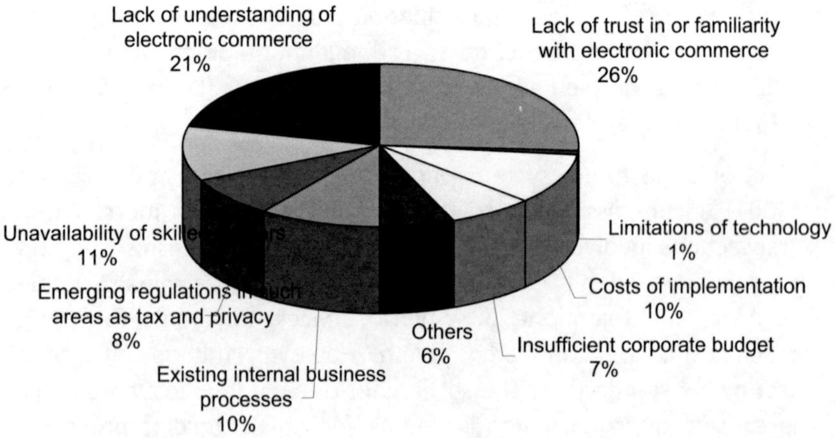

Source: adapted from WITSA (2007)

Securities issues

Besides IT expertise and skills and knowledge issues, there can be serious security concerns among e-commerce participants. As no internet security firewall is guaranteed to be perfect, both sellers and buyers may be concerned that competitors will be able to extract sensitive or proprietary information, or a virus might spread from one participant in an exchange with others (Doyle and Melanson, 2001). O'Keefe *et al.* (1998) argue that trust towards technology and trading partners is an important factor in improving the security. Ratnasingham (1998) looks further into how trust influences the process of managing the security of an organisation operating in an e-commerce environment. In electronic transactions, customers cannot view the queues in a bank branch or talk to the employees (Lee and Turban, 2001). Thus, they cannot assess the quality of the bank and its products and services before making any business deals (Mukherjee and Nath, 2003).

Culture and human behaviour

E-commerce has to overcome barriers of corporate culture and human behaviour, which are characterised as soft factors, but are very important. The long-lasting relationships between buyer and seller are crucial to human decision-makers in the targeted industries. Frequently, people prefer to interact personally with well-known, trustworthy business partners than with an anonymous website (Doyle and Melanson, 2001). Simultaneously, a customer who is resistant to change and satisfied with the current order habit may resist the internet as an innovation that threatens to alter the established habit (Deeter-Schmelz *et al.*, 2001). However, changing corporate culture has an important effect on resources. Thus, organisations should be aware of the need to exploit the intellectual assets of their workforces as effectively as possible. The emphasis on knowledge management and on new styles of organisation, such as remote working and distance communications, is an indication of the need to respond to the increase speed of business change (WITSA, 2000).

Lack of personal contact

According to Spekman *et al.* (1998) personal contact between trading partners in the supply chain is changing due to the introduction of e-commerce. As a result, the amount of face-to-face personal contact is reduced. La and Kandampully (2002) argue that the lack of direct personal contact with customers reduces the opportunity to look further into the customers' desires, and usually leaves firms with no clue as to why potential customers leave without making a purchase.

Vulnerable to money laundering

Money-laundering methods have become more creative due to the expansion of products and services that are new offered, more complicated financial relationships, advances in technology, and the increased speed of money flows worldwide. Electronic banking is vulnerable to money laundering because of its user anonymity, rapid transaction speed, and its wide geographic availability (Alwabel *et al.*, 2004). Therefore, it is vital for online banks to remain alert against cyber-laundering. It will be necessary to put tough stops and checks into place to increase the probability of reporting of suspicious transactions. Employees need to be trained in order that they are aware of what to look for. Businesses need to be positive in establishing these types of actions to stand any possibility of detecting cyber-laundering (Philippsohn, 2001). A summary of these e-commerce benefits and obstacles can be seen in Figure 3.2.

Figure 3.2 The possible benefits and obstacles of e-commerce

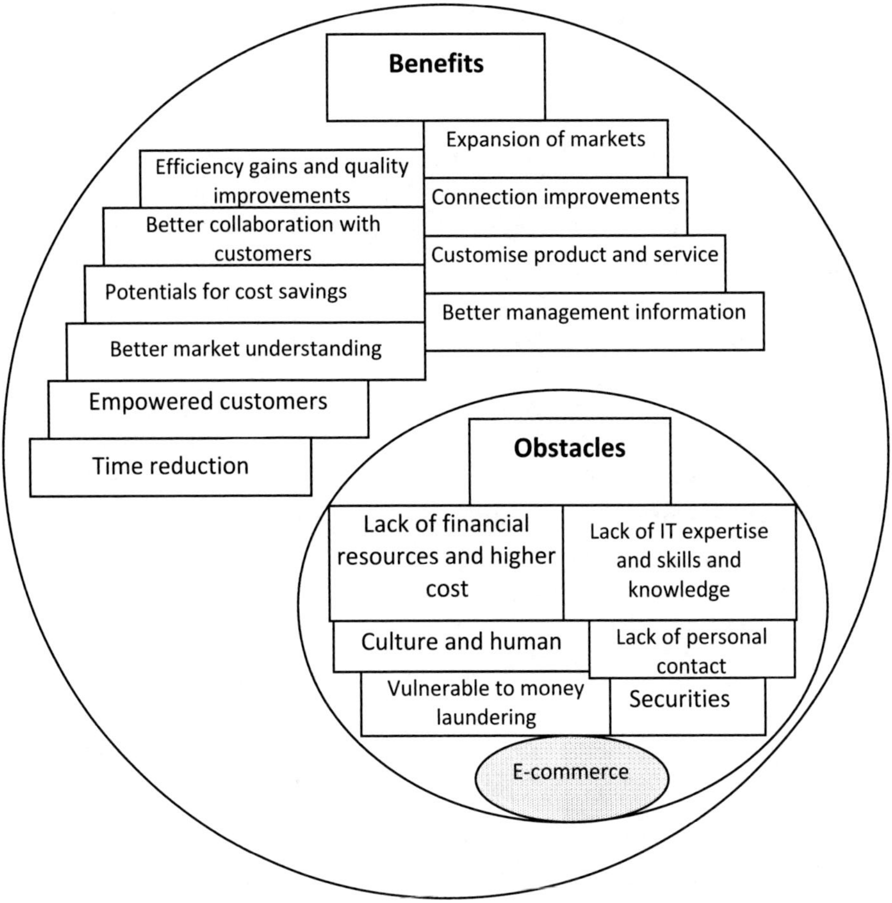

Source: adapted from Alwabel *et al.* (2004)

E-commerce future trends

E-commerce is no longer an alternative; it is crucial (Damanpour, 2001). Although there are still a number of barriers, as described above, that limit financial services and other organisations in the adoption of e-business, in time those limitations will diminish or be overcome. 'The key question is not whether to deploy Internet technology – companies have no choice if they want to stay competitive – but how to deploy it' (Porter, 2001). Porter believes that success in e-business can be achieved if it is used to complement the 'traditional ways of competing'. The challenge to organisations is how quickly they can leverage their traditional business strengths with e-business (Damanpour, 2001). A diversity of trends will drive the growth and development of e-commerce in the future. The more people learn about e-commerce the greater the e-commerce expansion will be (Turban *et al.*, 2000). However, to ensure the future of e-commerce, secure electronic payment systems and online banking facilities need to be developed (Andrieu, 2001). The key trends in the future of e-commerce, based on the literature can be summarised as follows:

- *Carrying on changes in technology:* continuous changes in technology are likely to facilitate significant cost reductions, improved capabilities of organisations and the increased availability of technological infrastructure (Turban *et al.*, 2000).
- *Integration:* more and more powerful and advanced computers will carry on integrating with smaller devices, letting faster and cheaper processes be developed (Turban *et al.*, 2000).
- *Improved digitisation:* all forms of information will turn out to be digital, specifically access to such information will be unrestricted, irrespective of geographic location (Lawrence *et al.*, 1998).
- *Security issues:* the future of e-commerce on the internet requires new authentication schemes to provide convenient and

safe billing systems. Since performance is a key issue, it would be beneficial to integrate authentication tightly into the firewall (Andrieu, 2001).

- *Electronic payment:* Andrieu (2001) states that secure online payment systems will be the single most important element of the e-commerce infrastructure. Hence, without electronic payments, e-commerce is unlikely to launch. A transformation is taking place as the world is changing from a paper-based money world to an electronic money world.

References

Afuah, A. and Tucci, C. L. (2001) *Internet Business Models and Strategies: Text and Cases,* Irwin/McGraw-Hill, Boston, Mass.; London.

Ahmed, A., Zairi, M. and Alwabel, S. (2003) Global benchmarking for Internet and e-commerce applications, *Proceedings of the First International Conference on Performance Measures, Benchmarking and Best Practices in New Economy,* Business Excellence, 388-396, 10th-13th June, University of Minho, Braga, Portugal (ISBN 972-8692-08-0).

Ah-Wong, J., Gandhi, P. and Patel, H. (2001) E-commerce progress: Enablers, inhibitors and the short-term future, *European Business Journal,* 13, 2, 98-107.

Aldrich, W. and Douglas, F. (1999) *Mastering the Digital Marketplace: Practical Strategies for Competitiveness in the New Economy,* John Wiley and Sons, New York; Chichester.

Alfred, L. and Choi, Y. K. (2002) A peer-to-peer distributed selection algorithm for the Internet, *Internet Research: Electronic Networking Applications and Policy,* 12, 1, 16-30.

Aljifri, H. A., Pons, A. and Collins, D. (2003) Global e-commerce: a framework for understanding and overcoming the trust barrier, *Information Management and Computer Security,* 11, 3, 130-138.

Alwabel, S. A., Ahmed, A. M., Gouda, S. and Zairi, M. (2004) What, Why and How: Critical review of e-commerce era, *Proceedings of the International Conference on Responsive Supply Chain and Organisational Competitiveness (RSC-2004),* 5-7 January, Coimbatore, India.

Amit, R. and Zott, C. (2001), Value creation in e-business, *Strategic Management Journal,* 22, 6-7, 493-520.

Anandarajan, M., Anandarajan, A. and Wen, H. J. (1998) Extranets: a tool for cost control in a value chain framework, *Industrial Marketing Management and Data System,* 98, 3, 120-128.

Andrieu, M. (2001) The future of e-money: main trends and driving forces, *The Journal of Future Studies, Strategic Thinking and Policy,* 3, 5, 429-451.

Armistead, C. (1996) Principles of business process management, *Managing Service Quality,* 6, 6, 48-52.

Association for Investment Management and Research (1999) *Auditing and reporting using technology and the Internet: Researching corporate strategic and financial information*, (AIMR).

Bakos, Y. (1998) The emerging role of electronic marketplace on the Internet, *Communications of the ACM,* 41, 8, 35-42.

Bakos, Y. and Brynjolfsson, E. (2000) Bundling and competition on the Internet, *Marketing Science,* 19, 1, 63-82.

Banaghan, M. and Bryant, G. (1998) Electronic commerce streamlines the supply chain, *Business Review Weekly*, 1, 7, 56-67.

Barrett, S. and Konsynski, B. R. (1982) Inter-organisation information sharing systems, *MIS Quarterly [special issue],* 12, 6, 93-105.

Bergeron, B., P. (2001) *The Eternal E-customer: How Emotionally Intelligent Interfaces Can Create Long-Lasting Customer Relationships*, McGraw-Hill, New York; London.

Berryman, K., Harrington, L., Layton-Rodin, D. and Rerolle, V. (1998) Electronic commerce: Three emerging strategies, *McKinsey Quart,* I, 1, 152-159.

Boyer, K. K., Hallowell, R. and Roth, A. V. (2002) E-services: Operating strategy - A case study and a method for analysing operational benefits, *Journal of Operations Management; Columbia,* 20, 2, 175-188.

Charles, S., Ives, M. and Leduc, A. (2002) *Embracing e-business: does size matter?* Research Report, Statistics, Canada.

Craven, B. M. and Marston, C. L. (1999) Financial reporting on the Internet by leading UK companies, *European Accounting Review*, 8, 2, 321-333.

Dabholkar, P. A. (1996) Consumer evaluations of new technology-based self-service options: an investigation of alternative models of service quality, *International Journal of Research in Marketing,* 1, 13, 29-51.

Damanpour, F. (2001) E-Business e-commerce evolution: perspective and strategy, *Managerial Finance,* 27, 7, 16-33.

Debreceny, R. and Gray, G. L. (1999) Financial reporting on the Internet and the external audit, *European Accounting Review,* 8, 2, 335-350.

Deeter-Schmelz, D. R., Bizzari, A., Graham, R. and Howdyshell, C. (2001) Business-to-Business on-line purchasing: suppliers' impact on buyers' adoption and usage Internet, *Journal of Supply Chain Management,* 37, 1, 4-10.

Desborough, J. (1996) *Intranet web development*, New Riders Pub, Indianapolis, Ind.

Downes, L. and Mui, C. (2000) *Unleashing the Killer App: Digital Strategies for Market Dominance, (Rev.)* Harvard Business School Press, Boston, Mass.

Doyle, T. and Melanson, J. (2001) B2B web exchanges: Easier hyped than done, *Journal of Business Strategy,* 22, 3, 10-13.

Eid, R., Trueman, M. and Ahmed, A. M. (2002) A cross-industry review of B2B critical success factors, *Internet Research: Electronic Networking Applications and Policy,* 12, 2, 110-123.

Faramarz, D. and Jamshid, A. D. (2001) E-business e-commerce evolution: perspective and strategy, *Managerial Finance,* 27, 7, 16-33.

Fenech, T. (2002) Exploratory study into wireless application protocol shopping, *International Journal of Retail and Distribution Management,* 30, 10, 482-497.

Forrester Research (2000a), *E-marketplaces will lead US business e-commerce to $2.7 trillion in 2004*, available at http://www.forrester.com/ER/Press/Release/0.1769. 243.FF.html (Accessed August, 2003).

Frieden, K. A. and Porter, M. E. (1996) *The taxation of cyberspace,* available at http://www.caltax.org (Accessed January, 2004).

Giaglis, G. M., Klein, S. and O'Keefe, R. M. (1999) Disintermediation, reintermediation, or cybermediation? The Future of Intermediaries in Electronic Marketplaces, *Proceedings of the 12th International Electronic Commerce Conference*, 389-407, Bled, Slovenia, 7-9 June.

Greaves, C., Kipling, P. and Wilson, T. (1999) Business use of the world wide web, with particular reference to UK companies, *International Journal of Information Management,* 19, 6, 449-470.

Grembergen, W. V. and Amelincks, I. (2002) Measuring and managing e-business projects through the balanced scorecard, *Proceedings of the 35th Hawaii Internal Conference on System Science, Big Island (Hawaii),* Organizational Systems and Technologies Track, 1-9, IEEE Computer Society Press.

Grieger, M. (2003) An empirical study of business processes across Internet-based electronic marketplaces: A supply chain management perspective, *Business Process Management Journal,* 10, 1, 80-100.

Hagel, J. and Armstrong, A. (1997) *Net Gain: Expanding Markets through Virtual Communities,* Harvard Business School Press, Boston, Mass.

Hasan, H. and Tibbits, H. R. (2000) Strategic management of electronic commerce: an adaptation of the balanced scorecard, *Internet Research; Bradford,* 10, 5, 439-450.

Honeycutt, J., E, Flaherty, T. and Benassi, K. (1998) Marketing industrial products on the Internet, *Industrial Marketing Management,* 27, 1, 63-72.

Kalakota, R. and Robinson, M. (1999) *E-Business: Roadmap for Success,* Addison-Wesley, Reading, Mass.; Harlow.

Kalakota, R. and Robinson, M. (2001) *E-business 2.0: Roadmap for Success,* Addison-Wesley, Boston, Mass.

Kalakota, R. and Whinston, A. B. (1996) *Frontiers of Electronic Commerce,* Addison-Wesley Pub. Co., Reading, Mass.; Wokingham.

Kalakota, R. and Whinston, A. B. (1997) *Electronic Commerce: A Manager's Guide,* Addison-Wesley, Reading, Mass.; Harlow, England.

Kaplan, S. and Sawhney, M. (2000) E-hubs: the new B2B marketplaces, *Harvard Business Review*, 78, 3, 97-103.

Kaplan, S. N. and Garicano, L. (2000) *The Effects of Business-to-Business E-commerce on Transaction Costs,* National Bureau of Economic Research, Cambridge; Mass.

Kerrigan, R., Roegner, E. V., Swinford, D. D. and Zawada, C. C. (2001) B2Basics, *The McKinsey Quarterly,* 1, 1, 44-53.

Klein, S. (1997) Introduction to electronic auctions, *International Journal of Electronic Markets,* 7, 4, 3-6.

Krishnamurthy, S. (2003) *E-commerce Management: Text and Cases,* Thomson/South-Western, Mason and Ohio.

La, K. V. and Kandampully, J. (2002) Electronic retailing and distribution of services: cyber intermediaries that serve customers and service providers, *Managing Service Quality,* 12, 2, 100-116.

Laudon, K. C. and Laudon, J. P. (2000) *Management Information Systems: Organisation and Technology in the Networked Enterprise,* (6th) Prentice Hall: Prentice-Hall International, Upper Saddle River, N.J.; London.

Lawrence, E., Newton, S., Corbitt, B., Lawrence, J., Dann, S. and Thanasankit, T. (1998) *Internet Commerce: Digital Models for Business,* (3rd) Wiley, Brisbane; Chichester.

Lee, M. K. O. and Turban, E. (2001) A trust model for consumer Internet shopping, *International Journal of Electronic Commerce,* 6, 4, 75-91.

Lucking-Reiley, D. (2000) Auctions on the Internet: What's being auctioned, and how? *The Journal of Industrial Economics,* 48, 3, 227-252.

Malone, T. W., Yates, J. and Benjamin, R. I. (1987) Electronic markets and electronic hierarchies: effects of information technology on market structure and corporate strategies, *Communications of the ACM,* 30, 6, 484-497.

May, P. (2000) *The business of E-commerce: From Corporate Strategy to Technology,* Cambridge University Press in association with Sigs Books, Cambridge; New York.

Molla, A. and Licker, P. S. (2001) E-commerce system success: An attempt to extend and respecify the Delone and Maclean model of IS success, *Journal of Electronic Commerce Research,* 2, 4, 131-141.

Monica, L., Theresa, L. and Wong, Y. H. (2003) From customer relationship management to customer-managed relationship: unraveling the paradox with a co-creative perspective, *Marketing Intelligence & Planning,* 21, 1, 51-60.

Moon, Y. and Fre, F. X. (2000) Exploding the self-service myth, *Harvard Business Review,* 78, 3, 26-27.

Mukherjee, A. and Nath, P. (2003) A model of trust in online relationship banking, *International Journal of Bank Marketing,* 21, 1, 5-15.

Nieto, J. (2001) Reflections on the regulatory approach to e-finance, electronic finance: a new perspective and challenges, *BIS Papers*, 1, 7, 90-97.

O'Keefe, R., O'Connor, G. and Kung, H. J. (1998) Early adopters of the Web as a retail medium: small company winners and losers, *European Journal of Marketing,* 32, 7/8, 629-643.

Oren, S. and Smith, S. (1981) Critical mass and tariff structure in electronic communications markets, *Bell-Journal-of-Economics,* 12, 2, 467-487.

Pawar, K. S. and Driva, H. (2000) Electronic trading in the supply chain: a holistic implementation framework, *Logistics Information Management,* 13, 1, 21-32.

Phan, D. D. (2003) E-business development for competitive advantages: a case study, *Information and Management,* 40, 6, 581-590.

Philippsohn, S. (2001) Money laundering on the Internet, *Computers and Security,* 20, 6, 485-490.

Pike, R. and Neale, B. (1999) Corporate finance and investment: decisions and strategies, (3rd) Prentice Hall Europe, London.

Porter, M. E. (2001) Strategy and the Internet, *Harvard Business Review,* 79, 3, 62-78.

Porter, M. E. and Millar, V. E. (1985) How information gives you competitive advantage, *Harvard Business Review,* 63, 4, 149-160.

Raisch, W. D. and Gartner (2001) *The e-marketplace: strategies for success in B2B ecommerce,* McGraw-Hill, New York; London.

Rappa, P. (2003) *Business models on the web,* available at http://digitalenterprise.org/models/models.html (Accessed December, 2003).

Ratnasingham, P. (1998) The importance of trust in electronic commerce, *Internet Research: Electronic Networking Applications and Policy,* 8, 4, 313-321.

Reck, M. (1997) Trading-process characteristics of electronic auctions, *International Journal of Electronic Markets,* 7, 4, 17-23.

Saatcioglu, K., Stallaert, J. and Whinston, A. (2001) Design of a financial portal, *Communications of the ACM,* 44, 6, 33-38.

Schneider, G. P. and Perry, J. T. (2000) *Electronic Commerce,* Course Technology, Cambridge, Mass.

Sculley, A. B. and Woods, W. W. A. (1999) *B2B Exchanges: The Killer Application in the Business-to-Business Internet Revolution*, ISI, Hong Kong.

Selen, W. (2001) Learning in the new business school setting: A collaborative model, *The Learning Organisation,* 8, 3, 106-113.

Skinner, S. (2000) *Business to Business E-commerce-Investment Perspective,* Durlacher research, London.

Skjoett-Larsen, T. (2000) European logistics beyond 2000, *International Journal of Physical Distribution and Logistics Management,* 30, 5, 377-387.

Spekman, R. E., Kamauff, J. W. and Myhr (1998) An empirical investigation into supply chain management: a perspective on partnership, *Supply Chain Management,* 3, 2, 53-67.

Symonds, M. (1999) The rise of the infomediary, *The Economist,* 351, 8125, 21-24.

Tigre, P. B. and Dedrick, J. (2004) E-commerce in Brazil: local adaptation of a global technology, *Electronic Markets; London,* 14, 1, 36-47.

Timmers, P. (1999) *Electronic Commerce: Strategies and Models for Business-to-Business Trading*, Wiley, Chichester, West Sussex, England; New York.

Turban, E., King, D., Jee, J., Warkentin, M. and Chung, H. M. (2002) *Electronic Commerce 2002: A Managerial Perspective,* Prentice Hall: Pearson Education, Upper Saddle River, N.J.

Turban, E., Lee, J., King, D., R and Chung, H. M. (2000) *Electronic Commerce: A Managerial Perspective,* Prentice Hall International, London.

Vadapalli, A. and Ramamurthy, K. (1997) Business use of the Internet: an analytical framework and exploratory case study, *International Journal of Electronic Commerce,* 2, 2, 57-69.

Walker, K. B. and Johnson, E. N. (2001) Planning a revenue stream system in an e-business environment, *Industrial Management and Data Systems; Wembley,* 101, 8/9, 406-413.

Weill, P. and Vitale, M. R. (2001) *Place to Space: Migrating to E-business Models,* Harvard Business School Press, Boston, Mass.; Great Britain.

Westland, J. C. and Clark, T. H. K. (1999) *Global Electronic Commerce: Theory and Case Studies,* MIT Press, Cambridge, Mass.; London.

Windham, L. and Samsel, J. (1999) *Dead Ahead: the Web Dilemma and the New Rules of Business,* Allworth Press, New York.

WITSA: The World Information Technology and Services Alliance, (2000) *International Survey of Electronic Commerce*, 20 Red Lion Street London, WC1R 4QN, United Kingdom.

Wyckoff, A. (1999) *The Economic and Social Impact of Electronic Commerce: Preliminary Findings and Research Agenda*, Organisation for Economic Co-operation and Development, Paris.

Chapter 4

Building Q in *e*: The foundation of e-commerce

Introduction

Faced with intensive global competition, more demanding customers, rapidly shrinking product life cycles and shorter response times, the financial services industry in Saudi Arabia is now pursuing competitiveness by aiming for higher levels of product and service value and thus, higher customer satisfaction. All these challenges may be achieved by the implementation of e-commerce. Nevertheless, e-commerce activities normally do not just crop-up within a firm; their development goes through a certain life cycle. However, e-commerce investment in organisations could be full of disappointment. It is not that e-commerce systems have not been acquired, but that, in many organisations, they have consistently failed to be utilised to their full potential (Dos Santos and Peffers, 1998).

Moreover, effective e-commerce is an ongoing concern for academia and organisations. Nowadays the most important challenge facing the organisation's manager is implementation of changes aimed at the improvement in organisational performance. The problem is associated with the difficulty of attaining appropriate and reliable approaches that can be used systematically. In addition, achievement of accurate results for e-commerce measurement and evaluation is crucial; since improving performance requires information about how good performance currently is and getting feedback on the success of efforts to improve the organisation's performance.

Without doubt, evaluation of e-commerce is useful and has more credibility if a good approach to measurement is applied, providing evidence of whether the system is improving over time or tends to respond less well to the information needs. Organisation theories suggest that organisations are dynamic and e-commerce systems need to be under continuous review to ensure that they remain in harmony with their environments. Therefore, evaluation plays a particularly important role in the evolution of organisation and e-commerce systems.

Problems with implementing e-commerce without quality factors

The implementation of e-commerce systems change the way organisations do business and how people complete their work (Alwabel *et al.*, 2004). Consequently, the implementation of e-commerce ultimately results in changes to processes (business-orientated activities), which in turn inflicts changes on work practices (people-orientated activities).

E-commerce implementation should involve the analysis of current business processes and the chance of re-engineering, rather than designing an application to make the best of bad processes (Edwards and Peppard, 1994).

Moreover, the implementation of e-commerce is not a technical task. The implementation of e-commerce is a business-based endeavour, as organisations try to match the technological imperatives of e-commerce with the business needs of the company. Corbitt *et al.* (1997) states that technical challenges are not the main reasons why e-commerce fails. Organisations fail to reconcile the technological imperatives of e-commerce with the business needs of the enterprise itself. Although statistics are quoted showing many companies are adopting e-commerce technology (Forrester Research, 2000a), it may be contested that these are simply 'jumping on the bandwagon', rather than making sound business decisions (Dos Santos and Peffers, 1998). Primary implementation motivators are often cited as a desire to integrate all parts of a business, achieve business change, replace outdated, unsupported software, consider tax implications and, overall, to improve company stability and increase competitive advantage and profit (Davenport, 1998).

Furthermore, in spite of spending immense resources on technology implementation, the rejection of technology occurs commonly, since organisations cannot overcome the struggle. Socio-economic and political impediments for the success of implementing and diffusing processes are lack of higher education institutions, poor facilities, difficulties in retaining qualified, technical people, differences in culture and work habits, insufficient management support and user attitudes (Pradhan, 1994). The following problems, which hinder the implementation of e-commerce, have been obtained from the existing literature:

- Poor link between e-business strategy and business processes (Edwards and Peppard, 1994);
- Lack of managerial and technological skills (Schneider and Perry, 2000);
- Lack of systems integration (Kalakota and Robinson, 2001);
- The inability to leverage existing e-commerce infrastructures (Zorfass and Michel, 1994 and Eid *et al.*, 2002);
- Another problem is that the issue of e-commerce seems to be more of a management problem, rather than a technical one (Corbitt *et al.*, 1997).
- A lot of e-commerce adopters appear to have had an excessive focus on the technology in the mistaken belief that, 'if we build it, they [the benefits] will come' (Fingar and Aronica, 2001).

Some factors that need to be considered when implementing e-commerce, according to Duffy (2000), are:

- Technological know-how
- Human capital
- Business processes.

Consequently, when developing the specification for e-commerce applications or tools, it is significant that current business processes are reviewed and areas for improvement, discovered from implementing e-commerce, are highlighted for planning. The new processes obtainable through e-commerce implementation are also necessary for e-commerce project success. Wheelen and Hunger (2000) define implementation as the process, directed by a manager, to install planned change in an organisation. They further add that implementing change can become more successful depending on the different tactics used by managers. A plan can be defined as, 'any detailed method, formulated beforehand, for doing or making something' (Guralnik, 1986). More specifically, an activity plan (for doing something) usually begins with a system at some initial state, specifies some desired final or goal state and identifies constraints on the allowable sequence of actions that will take the system from the initial to final state.

Critical review of e-commerce implementation models and processes

There have been numerous cases of information system failures reported in the information systems (IS) literature (Hirschheim and Lyytinen, 1987). Therefore, a significant number of IS research papers in the 1990s (Bowtell *et al.*, 1999) were published, attempting to discover the reasons for e-commerce project failures and how to ensure project success (Vadapalli and Ramamurthy, 1997; Teo *et al.*, 1997; O'Keefe *et al.*, 1998; Teo and Tan, 2000;

Molla and Licker, 2001; Eid *et al.*, 2002; Grandon and Pearson, 2003; Scupola, 2003; Lertwongsatien and Wongpinunwatana, 2003; Gibbs and Kraemer, 2004; Tigre and Dedrick, 2004). DeLone and Mclean (1992) argue in theirs, that there is no consensus in the IT/IS literature on the measure of information success. Hence, it is equally hard to define IS success and they developed six different factors in an 'IS Success Model'.

The six success categories identified are system quality, information quality, use, user satisfaction, individual impact and organisational impact. DeLone and McLean's model (Figure 4.1) is selected, because it is one of the most popular models related to implementation success. Their study included an analysis of the literature with reference to practitioners' and academics' views on information system success and how it was achieved.

Figure 4.1 Information systems success model

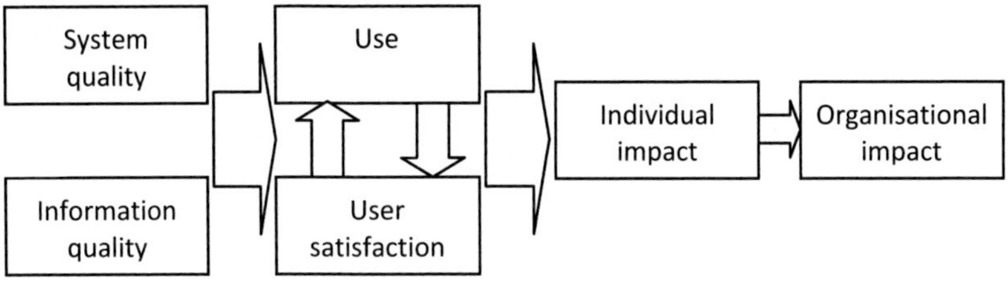

Source: adapted from DeLone and McLean (1992)

The model above, according to Seddon and Kiew (1996), provides a more supportive evaluation structure, since it offers a method for classifying the multitude of IS success measures proposed by the literature into six categories and suggests a model of interdependencies between them. Moreover, Ballantine *et al.* (1996) point out that this model has been accepted as one of the most comprehensive and well-known models to have been widely used as a basis of empirical research.

The relationships between system quality and information quality is that they have an individual and joint effect on both use and user satisfaction. The quantity of use can influence the degree of user satisfaction and vice versa. Use and user satisfaction offers the background to the individual impact and this individual impact was found to eventually have some organisational impact (DeLone and McLean, 1992).

This model has been found to be very relevant to IS researchers (Bowtell *et al.*, 1999) and with a selected mix of e-commerce success factors (see Table 4.1 below).

Consequently, Molla and Licker (2001) extended the DeLone and MacLean model and came up with the following categories: customer e-commerce satisfaction, e-commerce system quality, content quality, use, trust and support.

On the other hand, a fundamental approach to studying the adoption of new technologies is one that examines the diffusion of innovations (Rogers, 1995). Table 4.1 provides an overview of 16 major studies investigating explanatory variables for IS, EDI, e-commerce and internet banking adoption and satisfaction.

The eleven studies comprising of either e-commerce or internet banking adoption are summarised here. Vadapalli and Ramamurthy (1997), studied large US-based, communications companies and found some support for their proposition that organisational boundaries, transaction costs, economics and organisational cognition were determinants of company adoption of the internet. They also proposed that the inherent self-fulfilling characteristics of the internet affects levels of use: The greater the benefits, the greater the level of use of the internet.

Table 4.1 Summary of literature review identifying key factors influencing e-commerce adoption

Technology type	Company type	Factors	Reference
IS		• System quality • Information quality • Use, user satisfaction • Individual impact • Organisational impact	DeLone and Mclean (1992)
EDI		• Relative advantage, • Costs • Technical compatibility	Premkumar *et al.* (1994)
EDI		• Business process re-engineering • Standardisation and infrastructure • Automation and flexible computing • Integration and interoperability	Zorfass and Michel (1994)
EDI	Retailers	• Innovation to disseminate EDI know-how • Cost and performance improvements to the technology • Management learning	Bamfield (1994)
EDI	SMEs	• Perceived EDI benefits • Organisational readiness for EDI • External pressure to adopt EDI	Iacovou *et al.* (1995)
E-commerce	Large US-based, communications	• Organisational boundaries transaction costs • Economics • Organisational cognition	Vadapalli and Ramamurthy (1997)
E-commerce	Large business	• Compatibility • Governmental support • Relative advantages	Teo *et al.*, (1997)

Internet	Small businesses	• Low risk • Security	O'Keefe *et al.*, (1998)
Internet banking	Banking	• Relative advantage Compatibility • Trialability • Self-efficacy • Governmental support	Teo and Tan (2000)
E-commerce		• Customer e-commerce satisfaction • E-commerce system quality • E-commerce content quality • Use, Trust and Support	Molla and Licker (2001)
Internet B2B	B2B	• Top management support and commitment • Setting strategic goals • Integrating the internet with marketing strategy • Collaboration • Deciding on who are the potential audiences, website designing • Understanding foreign marketing environment • Resources required for working globally • Multilanguage website • Culture considerations • International delivery availability • Technological infrastructure • Internal culture • Sales force role • Training programme • Trust, security • Successful relationship • Internet affordable access • Customer acceptance	Eid *et al.*, (2002)
E-commerce	SMEs	• Organisational support • Managerial productivity • Strategic decision aid	Grandon and Pearson

		• Organisational readiness • External pressure • Perceived ease of use and • Perceived usefulness	(2003)
E-commerce	Small businesses	• Government intervention Public administration • External pressure from competitors, suppliers and buyers	Scupola (2003)
E-commerce	SMEs	• Business size • Top management support for e-commerce • Existence of IT department Compatibility • Relative advantages Competitiveness	Lertwong-satien and Wongpinun watana (2003)
E-commerce	Global survey	• Strong leadership • IT capabilities • Adequate legal and regulatory environment • Competitive pressure • Enterprise integration	Tigre and Dedrick (2004)
E-commerce	Global survey	• Technology resources • Perceived benefits • Lack of organisational capabilities • Financial resources • Firm size, external pressure • Government promotion • Legislation barriers	Gibbs and Kraemer (2004)

Similarly, Teo *et al.* (1997) examined factors affecting internet adoption amongst large businesses, based in Singapore, using a contingency model. They found that factors like compatibility and governmental support were significant comparative to relative advantages. Teo and Tan (2000) further studied 188 Singapore business companies and the characteristics of adopters and non-adopters of the internet and found that the benefits to adopter companies were lower operational costs, new business opportunities and improved customer services. In addition, they found that factors such as relative advantage, compatibility, trialability, self-efficacy and governmental support had an impact on the adoption of internet banking.

O'Keefe *et al.* (1998) observed small business adopters of the internet, seeking to identify factors which affect successful performance of websites. They concluded that perceptions related to the cost of doing business online (e.g. low cost and low risk) and consumer concerns (i.e. security, credit risks) were significant. However, product type and business size were not seen as differentiating characteristics of companies likely to perform well on the internet, but the extent of interactiveness of their web offer appeared to affect the overall success.

Moreover, in connecting with customers in B2B, several factors have been identified as contributing to successful implementation (Eid *et al.*, 2002).

- *Combine the e-business application with the marketing strategy*: get support from the top management, integrate the internet with the marketing strategy and identify who is the potential audience at the internet transaction.
- *Website design factor*: websites should be well designed, accessible, accurate, integrated, customer driven and fast. Personalise the e-experience for the customers and customise *their* website.
- *Global related factors*: understand foreign marketing environments, get the resources required for working globally, launch multi-language websites, take customers' culture into consideration and make international delivery available.
- *Internal factors*: make sure the technology infrastructure can support the e-business functioning, create customer-driven culture and provide training programs for employees to provide high-quality e-service.

- *External related factors*: build a sense of trust and security with the customers, making special efforts to motivate customers to make the move to an online environment.

On the other hand, Grandon and Pearson (2003) combine two independent research streams to examine the determinant factors of strategic value and adoption of e-commerce as perceived by top managers in SMEs in the Midwest region of the US. Their study revealed a significant relationship between the perceived strategic value of e-commerce variables, such as organisational support, managerial productivity and factors such as organisational readiness, ease of use and compatibility, which influence e-commerce adoption in SMEs.

Moreover, Scupola (2003) studied the environmental drivers of internet commerce adoption and implementation in seven small businesses located in Southern Italy. The study shows that the environmental context has a key role in the adoption and implementation of e-commerce in SMEs. Scupola (2003) found that environmental factors of special importance are government intervention, public administration and external pressure from competitors, suppliers and buyers.

In another study investigating e-commerce development in Thailand, Lertwongsatien and Wongpinunwatana (2003) surveyed the factors influencing e-commerce adoption decisions in Thai SMEs. The study focused on organisational factors, such as business size, top management support for e-commerce and existence of an IT department; technology factors, such as compatibility and relative advantages and external factors that affect competitiveness.

Lertwongsatien and Wongpinunwatana (2003) found that the amount of strategic emphasis firms give to IT (i.e. IT-related knowledge, resources, and capabilities) has an impact on e-commerce adoption intention. Firms that strongly advocate the use of IT by formally establishing an IT department are more likely to adopt e-commerce earlier than firms with less IT support. Firms that have IT assets (i.e. IT knowledge, IT capabilities) readily in place should be in a better position to implement e-commerce than firms that need to start building technology knowledge and infrastructure required for e-commerce adoption. However, business size was not seen as a differentiating characteristic of companies likely to adopt e-commerce.

Moreover, Tigre and Dedrick (2204) investigated e-commerce in a ten country survey of 2,100 organisations, including 200 in Brazil. They found that strong leadership, IT capabilities, adequate legal and regulatory environments, competitive pressure and enterprise integration are all critical in implementing e-commerce. They also found that there are different e-commerce drivers across sectors. (E.g. financial companies are most often driven by the desire to expand markets for existing products or services (91.2%), followed by the need to improve coordination with clients and dealers (67.8%).

In another study investigating the scope of e-commerce, Gibbs and Kraemer (2004) surveyed the factors influencing e-commerce adoption decisions in different industries in 10 different countries. They found that the most important factors were technology resources, perceived benefits, financial resources, legislation barriers, external pressure and the least important factor was government promotion. However, Tigre and Dedrick (2004) do not support Gibbs and Kraemer's (2204) conclusion and contend that government plays a more effective role as a user and promoter of e-commerce practices than regulators.

Thus, IS success factors will vary depending on the different stakeholders (Bowtell *et al.*, 1999) and the different viewpoints one can have when regarding IS (Alter, 1996) and thus, it has been hard to define a set of success factors that fit specific and individual IS implementation projects, because each project can have unique characteristics. Bowtell *et al.* (1999) disagrees with DeLone and McLean's (1992) IS success findings. Bowtell *et al.* (1999) concluded that they had no problem identifying a number of specific factors for IS success, rather than the six, broad, fixed factors that DeLone and McLean (1992) formed.

The literature reviews undertaken revealed a lack of research concerning some critical factors of e-commerce implementation in the financial services industry (e.g. investment appraisal evaluation, value chain process, quality orientation and corporate governance), and this could be due to the fact that e-commerce is a new phenomenon and no such comprehensive research has been done in order for these factors to be covered.

Putting Q in *e* through critical factors

There are three main categories of critical Q-factors that impinge directly on the successful implementation of e-commerce projects. These include dominant strategic factors, organisational factors, environmental factors and communication factors.

Dominant strategic factors

Top management support and commitment

Any project without top management support and commitment cannot be successful. Managers should give the necessary priority to e-commerce implementation so that people in the organisation can be committed to the project and also valuable resources can be allocated to the implementation effort. For that purpose, managers should create more effective awareness for the e-commerce system by communicating its benefits to its stakeholders (Turban *et al.*, 2000). According to Zairi (2000):

> *The key drivers for adding optimum value to society and the communities in which specific business organisations operate*

is through having strong commitment to corporate and social governance, having an open dialogue with external stakeholders and having the determination to achieve environmental sustainability.

Moreover, the issue of e-commerce implementation is about business process rather than technology (Corbitt *et al.*, 1997). Many researchers have found that through lack of top management support, technology cannot be successfully implemented (Schneider and Perry, 2000; Al-Mashari, 2002; Al-Mashari *et al.*, 2003; Eid *et al.*, 2002; Grandon and Pearson, 2003; Lertwongsatien and Wongpinunwatana, 2003).

Thus, top management support has been identified as a key critical factor to e-commerce effectiveness in SMEs (Lertwongsatien and Wongpinunwatana, 2003). Turban *et al.* (2000) emphasised that a critical success factor for e-commerce initiatives is top management support. Therefore, by high competence of the organisational leadership role, top management are able to ensure sufficient allocation of resources and perform as a change agent to create a more conducive environment for e-commerce implementation (Teo and Tan, 2000; Tigre and Dedrick, 2004). Furthermore, top management have the authority to influence other members of the business and through influence and their support, implement e-commerce (Teo *et al.*, 1997).

E-commerce strategic goals

The word strategic in this context concerns the adjustment of a plan to the anticipated reactions of those who will be affected by the plans, such as competitors, customers and the actual organisation. Often plans can differ in structure, but a strategy commonly contains a mission, vision, values, strategic directions, objectives, key strategies, performance outcomes, operational plans and accountabilities (Drucker, 1990). Obviously, in strategic factors, it will be relevant to investigate the strategic use of information systems to gain or improve competitive advantage for the organisation (Porter and Millar, 1985). E-commerce has been reported to improve an organisations' competitiveness in a given market, while also improving organisational flexibility (Aldrich and Douglas, 1999).

Moreover, D'Antoni (2000) examined the results of a survey by the Yankee Group's e-sourcing strategic unit among 100 IT and business managers regarding their e-commerce activities. From the entire survey, 53% of managers indicated that their company did not have an evidently defined e-commerce strategy. Nevertheless, the survey concluded that e-commerce projects usually move faster when accompanied by an official plan of action, whether it is detailed or broadly sketched. These conclusions all give a clear indication that a clearly defined e-commerce strategy is needed.

Thus, with clear e-commerce strategic goals that provide all potential users with a strategic decision aid, the various possibilities for reducing rejection rates are increased (Grandon and Pearson, 2003). This in turn will lead employees to embrace e-commerce.

Investment appraisal evaluation

Organisations have limited resources and these resources are expected to be invested in anticipation of the highest future gains. The initial interest for e-commerce has more recently been overtaken by a sense of practicality. Senior management started seeking real evidence of the contribution e-commerce makes to the success of the business and the value organisations are getting from their extensive e-commerce investments.

Successful e-commerce results do not occur by default; they are highly uncertain and in order to achieve organisational success, e-commerce has to be managed effectively and be considered broadly. The additional difficulties in identifying and measuring potential benefits and costs, deriving from current organisational practices, forced many organisations to establish management control systems. Among these systems are the thorough 'appraisals' of potential e-commerce investments and the 'evaluation' of their distributable outcomes (Hasan and Tibbits, 2000).

A very significant study by Willcocks (1996), investigating IT ex-post evaluation, found that 80% of firms reported having some post evaluation process. However, only 12% constantly fed this information back into the firm and only 32% measured the impact of IT on business performance.

Despite the existence of various approaches and techniques for IT investment evaluation, most companies still use simple accounting methods. These are the methods that come from the notion of discounted cash flows (DCF), which is derived from estimating and comparing the outflows 'costs' and inflows 'benefits' of a proposed investment and using a given discount factor to calculate the present value of future monetary estimations (Erben, 2002). Some of these methods are return on investment (ROI), net present value (NPV), and internal rate of return (IRR). The main advantage of these methods is that they have been widely used and tested in a variety of investment appraisal evaluation settings (Erben, 2002).

However, they are not without limitations. The main shortcoming is that they focus entirely on the estimation of cash flows and, as a result, tend to be based on data that satisfy accounting principles and that can be officially permitted via appearance in financial statements, and this in turn can lead to unclear results (Farbey *et al.*, 1993). In addition, Martinsons *et al.* (1999) argue that 'evaluation methods that rely on financial measures are not as well-suited for newer generations of IT applications' (in this context of e-commerce) where there is a necessity to include less tangible factors, such as customer satisfaction, organisational improvement, know-how, gaining competitive advantages and so on. Generally, DCF is not appropriate for evaluating investments that are expected to generate benefits that are primarily intangible or indirect (Brown, 1994).

It is therefore important to understand the process by which e-commerce investment decisions are made and justified, its organisational context, the methods and tools that support it and the means by which this process can be made more effective and efficient. Hence, the management of e-commerce investments becomes a vital process for both creating and appropriating the business value of e-commerce, as well as for the overall organisational success.

Moreover, organisations need to adopt investment appraisal evaluations that include the full value derived from their e-commerce investments

Employee's skills and core competence

Implementing new technology may require changes in employees' work attitudes, skills, core competencies, performance levels and learning what e-commerce can offer the firm. In one survey, Teo and Tan (2000) found that one of the main reasons for not adopting the internet is the lack of internal expertise. Irani *et al.* (1999) argue that at each instance an innovative IT project is implemented by the organisation, employees need to go through a learning curve while adapting to the new system and procedure.

Moreover, many companies are tempted to delay adoption of an innovation or a new technology until they have satisfactory internal expertise (Thong, 1999). As a result, the implementation of e-commerce leads to the requirement of specific skills and techniques (Schneider and Perry, 2000). Based on this, it is expected that if a firm possesses the core capabilities needed for a technological project, then they will be more ready, willing and have an easier time implementing such a project – for example, e-commerce systems.

Empowerment and involvement

One of the least effectively applied factors in business and organisation is that of employee empowerment and involvement. Employee involvement can be defined as '...a participative process to use the entire capacity of workers, designed to encourage employee commitment to organisational success' (Cotton, 1993). On the other hand, employee empowerment can be defined as a leadership process of building, developing and increasing power of the company to perform through cooperation, sharing and working together in teams (Ozaralli, 2003). From these two definitions, it is generally believed that involvement is an indication towards empowerment.

Consequently, an essential component of technological development is that it must be sustained by increased investment in the 'softer' side of the firm. Zuboff (1988) provides a powerful description of this by distinguishing between the automating and informating capacity of IT. The more traditional approach, automating, mainly describes how the use of IT can save mental or physical labour in the management of data. On the contrary, an informating approach focuses on learning as a continuous process, seeking to transform the organisation and add value through learning. Informating breaks down barriers within the organisation and shares knowledge freely. In providing workers with more responsibility, greater independence to make decisions, and more training to develop skills that can be used to exploit the full potential of new technologies, an informating approach is better than automating. Consequently, e-commerce technologies force management into a new role, that of managing intellectual capital, not equipment. Once a technology is in place, management's job is to care for the intellectual capabilities of employees so as to create a competitive advantage. Poon and Swatman (1998) found that direct management involvement is the norm for e-commerce successful adoption.

Customer-centric approach

The implementation of e-commerce can change the systems of service to be demand-driven and not supply-driven (Turban *et al.*, 2000). Thus, e-business encourages a more customer-centric, demand-driven approach to service delivery. For that purpose, organisations need to move from a product-centric to a customer-centric model, which serves customers with tailor-made products and services over the entire lifecycle, based on the interaction with these customers (Seybold and Marshak, 1998). Thus, engaging with e-commerce along with CRM technologies assists organisations to retrieve detailed customer information and to create opportunities for dynamic, real-time reaction (Tapscott *et al.*, 2000). Consequently, integrating customer acquisition, satisfaction and retention with a strategy to move from a product-centric to a customer-centric approach is critical in order for e-commerce to be implemented successfully (Kalakota and Robinson, 2001; Molla and Licker, 2001; Eid *et al.*, 2002; Clarke and Doherty, 2004).

Affordability of resources

While benefits of participation in e-commerce can be significant, firms constantly consider and assess the costs of such participative initiatives. Costs refer to the perceived potential costs of participating in e-commerce. Costs of participation might be related to the costs of acquiring the necessary technology for participation, including technological infrastructure upgrades, e-commerce integration with existing systems, investments in bandwidth and applications (website, intranet, extranet, etc), as well as the training costs.

Landsbergen and Wolken (2001) state that firms usually lack the resources for sharing information electronically and, thus, it is difficult to encourage their participation in a system where the benefits are indefinable and costs are unclear or uncertain. It is recognised that, for e-commerce to be successful, the initial capital outlay will exceed benefits, in the short-term at least (Poon and Swatman, 1998).

Since information sharing with other firms diverts resources from the firm's other priorities (Dawes 1996), it is difficult for firms to use their limited resources to make information available for the benefit of another firm when they already have serious and much more pressing information systems needs (Landsbergen and Wolken 2001). In the absence of profitability or return on investment, the cost of implementation might be the most important variable (Gibbs and Kraemer, 2004). Therefore, only firms that have slack resources can afford costly innovations, can absorb failure and can explore new ideas in advance of the actual need (Premkumar *et al.*, 1994). commerce implementation success.

Q-organisational factors

In addition to the aforementioned factors, there are various Q-organisational factors which are those variables affecting the organisational structure that the organisation could adjust or change to suit its changing environment (Vadapalli and Ramamurthy, 1997; Teo *et al.*, 1997). Six organisational factors can be identified: value chain process, enterprise IT experience, quality orientation, organisational culture, organisational structure and e-commerce implementation strategy.

Value chain process

In the field of information management, there are several information transfer models that have been identified. One information transfer model has been described as a value chain process – the creation, production, dissemination, organisation, diffusion, utilisation and preservation of information (Achleitner *et al.*, 1998).

Kotler (1997) explores how changes to the traditional value chain are affecting organisations and their ability to manage and add value to information. In the traditional physical value chain, information is treated as a supporting element of the value-adding process, not as a source of value itself.

However, the internet and related technologies have enabled firms to change the way they interact and coordinate value chain activities with customers and suppliers with the objective of improving operational and financial performance. These changes are referred to as net-enabled business transformation (NBT) (Straub and Watson, 2001).

These involve substitution of everyday business activities involving paper/phone/fax-based communication with electronic transaction and information exchange and significant redesigning of processes, incentives and IT to enable tighter coordination with customers and suppliers. Such changes may enable firms to enhance customer satisfaction, understand customer preferences, reduce inventory, increase inventory turnover, decrease stock-out situations and improve response time and time-to-market, which may eventually lead to financial benefits. By being aware of the value chain, businesses can collect data and add value to it, for example, by developing enhanced customer relationships and by providing a suite of tailored services to their customers and clients (Steinfield *et al.*, 1995). Chen *et al.* (2003) and Norris *et al.* (2000) point out that a value chain process is essential for e-commerce to be successful.

Enterprise IT experience

Although IT was unheard of 30 years ago in most business circles, nowadays business cannot live without it. Yet, in the past, the person who was in charge of the computer was just that, the person who ran the computer (Ernst and Segall, 1995). However, a lot has changed in technology and continues to do so at break neck speed.

Changes are occurring at unprecedented levels and require people who are familiar with and have experience with information technology to take care of such things on an ongoing and up-to-date basis (Kinder, 2000). In his research about the emerging e-commerce business models, Kinder (2002) concluded accordingly, that companies who have had little experience of IT are struggling when it comes to implementing e-commerce. Ageshin (2001) point out that an organisation's IT experience is needed for e-commerce to be implemented successfully.

Quality orientation

Quality orientation can be defined as the extent to which a company lays emphasis on quality, creates a commitment to quality among its employees and practices total quality management (TQM) (Bounds *et al.*, 1994). According to Kanji and Asher (1996), TQM is a continuous process of improvement for individuals, groups of people, and whole firms; it encompasses a set of four principles (delight the customer, management by fact, people-based management and continuous improvement) and eight core concepts (customer satisfaction, internal customers are real, all work is process, measurement, teamwork, people make quality, continuous improvement cycle and prevention).

TQM provides people with opportunities to learn and develop themselves through joint problem-solving efforts. Meeting clear and often challenging customer requirements and working to improve work processes continuously provides challenges that should both test and stretch members' skills. Insistent emphasis on teamwork and cross-functional relationships provides many opportunities for social interaction and social reinforcement (Hackman and Wageman, 1995).

Zairi *et al.* (1994) states that the rapid evolution of technology and higher customer expectations have been two of the most important reasons for hospitality companies to restate from top to bottom the quality management issue. In discussions of business behaviour, very often it is possible to hear that TQM is a journey and not a destination. They further suggest that TQM leads to improvement of bottom-line results such as profits.

According to Poulymenakou and Tsironis (2003), in the context of e-commerce processes, the primary objective of an e-commerce system is to help integrate an organisation's business operations and processes effectively and efficiently. Not all organisations have been successful in their e-business implementations and to that end research has assisted in identifying many factors that might be critical to a successful implementation. Such factors, such as establishing a total quality management (TQM) culture have all shown to play significant roles in e-commerce implementation.

Therefore, a strong quality orientation in the firm should generally urge the members of a product development team to strive for higher quality outcomes (Bounds *et al.*, 1994). On the other hand, without a commitment to quality on the part of various functional areas in the company, a team may not be able to develop a quality product. Since teams are dependent on these functional resources and facilities to complete their tasks, a lack of quality culture among these functional areas may hinder a teams' ability to translate their ideas for improving quality into high-quality products.

Organisational culture

Many authors point out that cultural factors have a significant effect on e-commerce success (Eid *et al.*, 2002). The effects of the organisation's culture on the implementation are based upon Pliskin *et al.* (1993) research into the resistance towards implementation of an information system. These authors identify the effects of the users' culture, the organisational structure, the political power and the environment of the organisation as primary influences on the successful implementation of an information system. In the context of e-commerce processes, cultural factors influence the introduction of new processes and the modification and evolution of existing approaches to e-commerce development (Eid *et al.*, 2002).

As business owners throughout the world are introducing new technologies into their organisations, the many factors affecting diffusion should be given careful consideration in order to minimise difficulties and failures associated with diffusion (Rogers, 1995). Therefore, organisations with a culture that encourage its members to try new things to meet environmental demands are much more likely to adopt technical innovations. Grandon and Pearson (2003) point out that adoption of technology often fail because a particular innovation may not fit well with an organisation's perceived problem, or the expected consequences are perceived by the organisation's members as more negative than positive.

Organisational structure

Many researchers, including Rosetti and DeZoort (1989), have described the traditional model of a hierarchical structured organisation as not competitive in a fast changing marketplace. In the context of e-commerce, Grandon and Pearson (2003) explain that traditional organisational structures and approaches cannot provide the competitive basis that are required in the business environment, because they break down the product development process across the specialist functional departments, which results in poor communication.

According to Egan (1998), new technical aids, working materials and work processes are only valuable and beneficial if the workers are put in a position where they can meet with the associated requirements and exploit the associated potential. As a result, in order for a company to achieve its aims there is an acknowledgment that it must improve, in particular, management and supervisory skills at all levels and provide more and better training (Alwabel *et al.*, 2003). In addition, there have been strong indications that the benefits from IT implementation are actually derived from the change in the organisation and that the IT system is just an enabler for these changes (Davenport and Stoddard, 1994).

On the other hand, organisational structures and processes can hinder the successful application of good and acceptable design principles, resulting in poor design features (Poltrock and Grudin, 1994). Lynex and Layzell (1997) found that in some organisations, the structure encouraged people not to co-operate or share strategic information and instead promoted competition amongst the business units and this inhibited software reuse.

E-commerce implementation strategy

E-commerce may have suffered recently from a decline of industry interest towards it, but 'it is not a fad, a trend or fashion that we will soon discard' (Kendall and Kendall, 2001). There is a growing consensus in the literature about the need to observe and explain the paradoxes and other phenomena related to e-commerce when engaging in management and information systems (IS) research in a networked economy (Kendall and Kendall, 2001).

The financial services professionals' need for successful e-commerce development and implementation, within both industry and academia, has led, in recent years, to a surge in e-commerce research and development in the financial services industry. The successful implementation of new and innovative e-commerce in financial services requires the development of strategic implementation plans prior to e-commerce project commencement.

Implementation can be defined as 'the process by which strategies and policies are put into action through the development of programs, budgets and procedure' (Wheelen and Hunger, 2000). Strategy implementation can be defined, according to Parsa (1999), as 'the process of accomplishing strategic objectives'. Thus, before an organisation dives into the world of internet business, a clearly planned e-commerce implementation strategy should be studied. Moreover, strategy should precede e-commerce investments.

One of the focuses of research in the implementation process has been the role played by middle managers in such a process. Floyd and Wooldridge (1990) found a positive relationship between overall middle management involvement in strategy and organisational performance. While D'Antoni (2000) found that middle managers actively influenced the formulated strategy in the e-commerce implementation process.

There are two main types of e-commerce implementation strategy that are used in practice. These are top-down analytic planning process (Kalakota and Robinson, 2001), and bottom-up 'just do it' tactical approach (Herman, 2000). Top-down planning takes a broad view of the environment. It identifies options and then defines the organisation's mission and direction. While it ensures a detailed analysis of the implementation, its biggest problem is the separation of strategy analysis and implementation. This can lead to good strategic plans that are never applied, or strategic plans that are not used to set clear objectives and targets, but are used as a reason to start a certain execution. In addition, it can lead to plans that do not get the right feedback when the planning and execution are separated. Thus, little is learned from the mistakes made during the planning process.

On the other hand, a bottom-up 'just do it' tactical approach takes a more focused view of the environment and performs the essential activities required to produce short-term results. These approaches mostly occur as a large amount of small-scale projects. While this approach can lead to fast decision making and quick results, it has the disadvantage that its conclusions are hardly integrated with the rest of the company's processes, since they are mainly 'stand alone' results.

Due to these advantages and disadvantages, Kalakota and Robinson (2001) prefer to use the 'continuous planning with feedback' approach, as shown in Figure 4.2.

Figure 4.2 Continuous planning with feedback

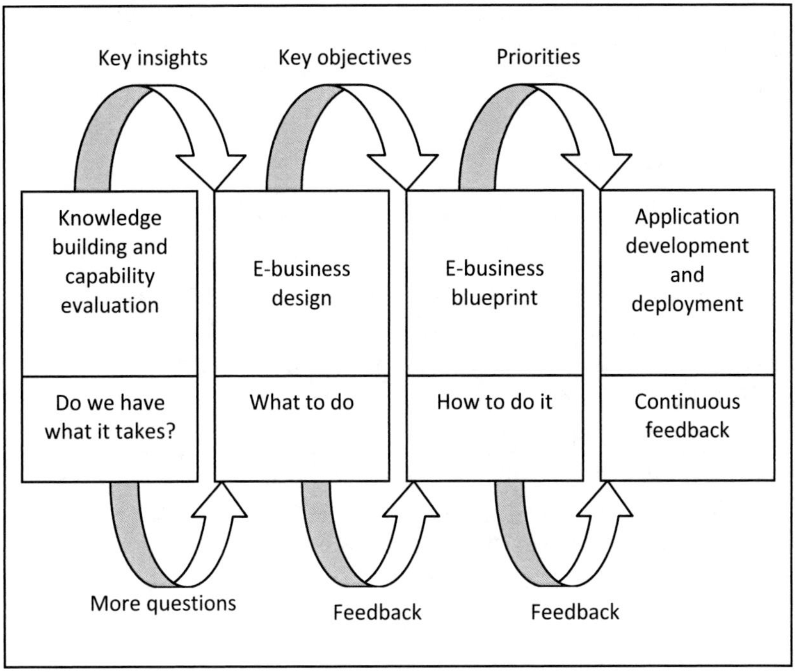

Source: adapted from Kalakota and Robinson (2001)

Brache and Webb (2000) point out that building e-commerce implementation strategy needs to be strongly based on a specific need in the marketplace with very clear steps to make a profit or extend service offerings by meeting that need.

Environmental factors

Environmental factors are those changes in the business environment that create threats in addition to opportunities for an organisation and are usually beyond the control of management. Environmental factors cover the scope in which a firm conducts its business, its industry, competitors, access to resources supplied by others and dealings with government (Tornatzky and Fleischer 1990).

Competitive intensity

Competitive intensity refers to the degree that the company is affected by competitors within the market (Zhu, 2004). Porter (1980) proposed a 'Five-Factor Model of Profitability', which indicated that firms have to deal with five competitive forces – the threat of potential entrants, bargaining power of customers, threat of substitute products, bargaining power of suppliers and competition among existing firms. The strength of the competitive force of potential entrants is largely a function of the height of barriers to entry, which stem from brand loyalty, absolute cost advantages, economies of scale, switching cost and government regulation (Hill and Jones, 2001).

According to Porter (1985), under the following situations, the competitiveness increases:

- when customers have power to demand lower prices or better services from the firm;
- when suppliers are able to force up the price that a firm must pay for its inputs or reduce the quality of the inputs they supply;
- when close substitutes exist for the firm's products or services.

Due to the nature of e-commerce, being very close to IT and the internet as a technology, it can be argued that competitive intensity increases the need for e-commerce implementation by firms. In the case of e-commerce, Thong (1999), Lertwongsatien and Wongpinunwatana (2003) and Scupola (2003) argue that competition leads to environmental uncertainty and increases both the need and the rate of adoption for those technologies. E-commerce is among the most powerful tools available today for enhancing operational effectiveness, as well as strategic positioning (Porter, 2001). Therefore, firms facing a greater degree of competition tend to attribute more value to e-commerce innovations.

External support

Although external support plays an important role in the adoption of new technologies, it was not included in many empirical studies (Larsen and McGuire, 1998). External support can be defined as the availability of support for implementing and using the innovation, where firms are more willing to risk trying new technologies if they feel there is an adequate vendor or third-party support for the technology (Premkumar and Roberts, 1999). Rogers (1995) emphasised the significant role played by technology vendors, consultants and change agents in persuading potential adopters about new innovations.

In addition, government units are among the most powerful institutional forces affecting innovation. The rapid spread of information technology and electronic commerce was due largely to the knowledge building development, and standard setting roles played by institutions of higher education in developed countries (Teo *et al.*, 1997) and these were assisted by governmental subsidies in the development stages of the internet. The impact of government policies and initiatives has been shown to have direct stimulation to the supply of information which produces faster technology diffusion (Teo *et al.*, 1997).

Moreover, consultants and technology vendors can add significant value to business planning to SMEs (McDonagh and Prothero, 2000). Soh *et al.* (1992) found a positive correlation between using external consultants and IS success in small business, although they tended not to meet the planned deadlines and budgets. Therefore, firms facing a greater degree of external support tend to attribute more value to IS innovations.

Supplier/customer pressure

Although supplier and customer pressure play a significant role in the adoption of new technologies, they were not included in many empirical studies (Larsen and McGuire, 1998). According to Poon (2000), there is pressure from suppliers and customers and this could be divided into pressure from consumers and pressure from other businesses. Such collaboration could result in having different e-commerce activities, such as sending purchase-orders, monitoring delivery status, price and inventory enquiries and stock monitoring. Iacovou *et al.* (1995) point out that there is a lack of mass consumers/suppliers over the internet, which discourages many businesses from adopting e-commerce.

However, Poon and Swatman (1998) state that if a small business retained a high percentage of customers and competitors online, this would increase the chances of adopting e-commerce.

Moreover, companies may be forced to adopt an innovative technology, simply because of their powerful partners' demands, as opposed to their internal needs (Poon, 2000). Yet, Provan (1980) suggested that the pressure exercised by trading partners is a function of two factors: the potential power of the imposing partner and its chosen weight strategy.

According to Iacovou *et al.* (1995), a powerful partner may use three different strategies to induce a weaker partner to adopt an innovative technology: recommendations, promises and threats.

Therefore, Iacovou *et al.* (1995) proposed that an imposition from trading partners is expected to be one of the most critical factors for innovative technology adoption.

In the context of e-commerce processes, supplier/customer pressure factors influence the introduction of new processes and the adaptation and evolution of existing approaches to e-commerce development (Grandon and Pearson, 2003; Scupola, 2003).

Regulatory issues

In recent years, the pressures of global competition have prompted governments of developed and developing countries to explore the means to use emerging networking technologies to achieve economic and social benefits. Evidence from country policy reports in the past decade has shown that countries around the world have embraced the new opportunities offered by the internet and e-commerce (Forrester Research, 2000a).

However, the development of innovative e-commerce raises numerous legal and regulatory issues that must be addressed. These include finding acceptable methods for authentication and protection of information, accommodating the special needs of law enforcement and creating the requisite means of settling disputes.

Unfortunately, prior e-commerce research does not offer much help in addressing their concerns regarding regulatory issues. This is, because most e-commerce research in Marketing Science and information systems (IS) disciplines (e.g. Vadapalli and Ramamurthy, 1997; Teo *et al.*, 1997; O'Keefe *et al.*, 1998; Teo and Tan, 2000; Molla and Licker, 2001; Eid *et al.*, 2002; Grandon and Pearson, 2003; Scupola, 2003; Lertwongsatien and Wongpinunwatana, 2003) focus on examining variables that affect the entire e-commerce diffusion process. As a result, little is known about salient factors in the various states of e-commerce diffusion.

However, Europe, Asia and North America have many projects and programmes to promote e-commerce, especially initiatives to demonstrate technological and business feasibility, to improve and harmonise the regulatory environment and to improve infrastructure and information for e-commerce. For example, the G7 (Group of Seven: Canada, France, Germany, Italy, Japan, United Kingdom, and United States) have a global pilot project entitled, 'A Global Marketplace for SMEs', with initiatives to establish a global information network, assess the legal, technical and institutional requirements for SMEs to engage in e-commerce and establish international e-commerce test beds (G7, 1998).

Consequently, Gibbs and Kraemer (2004) point out that regulatory issues have been recognised as a critical environmental factor affecting innovation diffusion. Governments could facilitate e-commerce usage by utilising supportive business and tax laws and regulating the internet to make it a trustworthy business platform, for example, dealing with fraud and credit card misuse (UNCTAD, 2002). Given that financial transactions often involve very sensitive information, an adequate regulatory and institutional framework is considered more critical for the financial services industry than for others (Distr, 2003).

Moreover, Tigre and Dedrick (2004) and Gibbs and Kraemer (2004) agree that regulatory issues have been documented as a critical environmental factor affecting e-commerce implementation success.

Corporate governance

The concept of governance appears to have been significantly developed in corporate law. Corporate governance issues cover the entire functioning and distribution of powers within large corporations (Hopt and Wymeersch, 1997). According to the OECD (1999):

> *Corporate governance is the system by which business corporations are directed and controlled. The corporate governance structure specifies the distribution of rights and responsibilities among different participants in the organisation, such as the board, managers, shareholders and other stakeholders, and spells out the rules and procedures for making decisions on corporate affairs. By doing this, it also provides the structure through which the company objectives are set and the means of attaining those objectives and monitoring performance.*

In addition, the OECD (1997) indicated that, close to the use of the term governance in corporate law is the concept of internet governance, for instance regarding the issue of domain names and complex power relations in a decentralised network structure, where some essential technical and economic elements still need a certain amount of central control and relevant contractual obligations, international law and conventions must be respected.

Weill and Ross (2004) define IT governance as 'specifying the decision rights and accountability framework to encourage desirable behaviour in the use of IT'. IT governance requires a lot of time, work and attention so there has to be something that encourages it. Weil and Ross (2004) point out some reasons why a firm should attempt to implement effective IT governance. First, high-quality IT governance recompenses. Research that they undertook showed that organisations that were successful in their IT governance had more than 20% higher return on assets (ROA) than similar organisations with the same strategy but with ineffective IT governance. IT governance was not the only factor that affected the outcome, but good government often comes with good management. Another reason is that IT is costly and it is therefore vital to focus on strategic priorities. In many firms the IT investments exceed 50% of the total capital invested. The third reason for effective IT governance is to avoid hidden IT spending.

In the context of e-commerce processes, corporate governance factors influence the introduction of new processes and the adoption and evolution of existing approaches to e-commerce development (Murphy and Bruce, 2003).

Communication factors

The importance of communication for holding a relationship together has been stressed in the literature as, 'the glue that holds together a channel of distribution' (Mohr and Nevin, 1990). The new approach emphasises two-track communication by better listening to customers and interactivity and the idea that communication before, during and after transactions can build or destroy important relationships (Duncan and Moriarty, 1997).

To achieve an effective communication strategy, the basic problems to be resolved, according to Hill *et al.* (1977), concern the questions of the target, media, message and timing.

Target

For e-commerce to be successful, the target audience should be identified. To identify the target audience or the customers the company intends to reach, first, define the problem, research the problem, analyse short and long-range goals, establish objectives and execute a marketing plan. This identification is important, since it will affect the other parts in designing the communication, for example, it will determine the nature of the information required, as well as the most desirable form of communication (Hill *et al.*, 1977).

However, identifying the target audience is a complicated and sizeable process, because the different types of users need to be identified. It is essential that an organisation considers what type of users are most important to it and then focuses on the segments most likely to use them, since limited IT budgets generally mean you cannot reach everyone. Identifying the user audience, where they are located geographically and what their needs are before making huge IT investments in web-based e-business services is imperative to the success of all serious e-businesses (Hawk, 2002). To avoid an e-business disaster, a company must concentrate on identifying the target audience who will bring the most value and IT managers must decide what information is required and how this can best be distributed (Chen *et al.*, 2003).

Media

The key difference between traditional marketing media and e-commerce is the degree of interactivity it allows (Deighton, 1997). Interactivity, according to Alba *et al.* (1997), can be defined as a communication situation with give and take between at least two parties where they respond to each other and the exchanges are based on previous communications.

Gordon (1998) hypothesises that, 'the competitive position of a company and its relative profitability is [most] likely tied directly to the cumulative volume of data it maintains on its customers, relative to its competitors.' In order to achieve this competitive advantage, the use of interactive technology that enables feedback from its customers is crucial.

Thus, the use of interactive media draws attention to the theoretical differences between traditional conceptualisations on advertising and its applications to today's marketplace. Traditional methods to advertising practice have implicitly assumed that advertising is something the marketer does to the customer. On the contrary, interactive advertising makes it clear that what advertising does to the customer is only one limited dimension of advertising, highlighting the need to understand what customers do to advertising (Alba *et al.*, 1997) and how interactive media affect this two-way interaction. The reasons customers seek, self-select, use and respond to information are critical for understanding interactive marketing communication.

Furthermore, communication among multiple customers over interactive media (e.g. portals, chat-rooms) has the potential to alter the way in which customers respond to the marketers' communications. Customers play a major active task in not only looking for information relevant to their needs, but also in communicating these needs to the company by entering an ongoing dialogue with the company (Deighton, 1997).

Message

Communication is an exchange of messages (Hill *et al.*, 1977). The message sent by suppliers may have to be modified specifically to meet the needs of the individual customer, taking into account their role in the buying process. To decide upon a message, it could be appropriate to consider the different buying criteria used by the customers in areas, such as price, quality, ease of communication, reputation and additional services (Duncan and Moriarty, 1998).

Both Hawk (2002) and Chen *et al.* (2003) agreed that a convenient message is essential for organisations when communicating with its customers. E-commerce is not a technology play; it is a relationship (Eid *et al.*, 2002).

Timing

What should be taken into consideration is when the customer wants to communicate, according to Sterne (2000). Customer service is about '…being there when the customer wants something, needs something, or just wants to gripe about something'.

Thus, the timing of deliveries, according to Molla and Licker (2001), is crucial in determining the overall value provided by a supplier. Since the administrative processes in e-commerce can be minimised, organisations can be tied closer to each other. This enables firms to implement new business strategies, such as Just-in-Time (JIT) delivery systems, which enable the stock flow to be optimised, resulting in decreased stocks for both the suppliers and buyers (Dornier, 1998).

Chen *et al.* (2003) stated that convenient timing is vital for an organisation when communicating with its customer.

Technological factors

Technological factors represent the existing, planned and possible technologies that can form part of e-commerce success. Technological factors include enterprise integration, compatibility, relative advantage and security of e-commerce.

Enterprise integration

The effective use of information requires integrating the technology within an organisation (Kalakota and Whinston, 1997). Zhu (2004) states that the potential for value creation inhibits an organisations' ability to effectively convert internet technologies into technological capabilities. At the front end, customer-facing website services assist organisations in providing real-time information to consumers, updating product and pricing offers and facilitating self-service using online account management and research tools, thus improving customer services and expanding revenue sources. At the back end, the open-standard data exchange of the internet potentially reduces inappropriateness of the legacy information systems and achieves data integration among various databases in an attempt to provide integrated accounts for customers (Zhu, 2004).

Therefore, front-end e-commerce systems must be aligned with the back-end ERP (enterprise resource planning) systems to provide total integration for e-commerce and the customer (Kalakota and Whinston, 1997).

Compatibility

Compatibility is the degree to which an innovation is perceived as being harmonious with formerly introduced ideas, existing socio-cultural values and beliefs and any needs of potential adopters (Rogers, 1995; Teo *et al.*, 1997; Thong, 1999). Teo and Tan (2000) found that internet banking is more likely to be adopted when it is compatible with individuals' job responsibility and value system. It will be likely to be adopted, not only if it is compatible with deeply held cultural values, but also if it is compatible with previous ideas.

Since resistance to change is an element faced by many firms, most firms would implement e-commerce when there is a match between e-commerce and the firms' culture, values, working processes and IT infrastructure. Thus, organisations naturally attempt to choose forms of e-commerce that conform to certain internal values and experiences. In this way, the organisation will need to make minimal adjustments and changes, which implies less resistance to the adoption. In addition, compatibility ensures greater security and less risk to the potential adopter and makes the innovation idea more meaningful to the organisation (Teo *et al.*, 1997).

Relative advantage

Relative advantage is the degree to which a new idea or practice is superior to the idea or practice it is intended to replace (Rogers, 1995). The positive perceptions of the benefits of e-commerce should provide encouragement for the business to adopt e-commerce. The degree of relative advantage is often expressed in economic profitability, cost reduction and savings in time and effort (Pawar and Driva, 2000). The commonly commended benefits of using e-commerce for businesses include, the creation of a worldwide customer base, rapid information access, global scale information distribution, lower costs, extended global market reach and improved customer service (Teo *et al.*, 1997; Vadapalli and Ramamurthy, 1997; Teo and Tan, 2000; Poon and Swatman, 1998 Thong, 1999;).

Moreover, Teo *et al.* (1997), Teo and Tan (2000), and Lertwongsatien and Wongpinunwatana (2003) found relative advantage to be an important factor in determining adoption of e-commerce. In general, the perceived relative advantage of an innovation is positively related to its rate of adoption (Rogers 1995).

Security

Security and the ability of the organisation to ensure confidentiality, integrity and availability of information assets is the major barrier to the wider adoption of e-commerce (Doyle and Melanson 2001). Any system that runs over the internet is vulnerable to encroachment from unauthorised personnel, which can result in the loss of intellectual property to those who can breach system controls and access commercially valuable information. Thus, security of transactions and information is an integral part of the successful conduct of e-commerce; thus for e-commerce to be effectively conducted, it must be ensured that the transaction environment is secure (Ratnasingham, 1998; Doyle and Melanson, 2001; Lee and Turban, 2001; Mukherjee and Nath, 2003; Ahmed *et al.*, 2003).

Nevertheless, maintaining mechanisms, such as digital signatures, encryption and firewalls provide sufficient security for e-commerce and this is an area that is constantly evolving. Businesses can take several steps to improve the security of online transactions, for example, by using a global public key infrastructure, which is a spectrum of products that protects the integrity and confidentiality of online transactions (Andrieu, 2001).

Measuring the value of quality in e-commerce

As mentioned earlier, the main concern for many firms is the requirement to prove that e-commerce puts in some value to business processes. Traditional accounting and measurement systems were drawn on to reveal the increased efficiency that followed from e-commerce applications. However, there were some important problems with these traditional systems. Most significantly, they related to tangible inputs and outputs and were not well organised to measure e-commerce performance as a tangible and intangible benefit.

Moreover, there is consensus of the limitations of traditional performance measurements (Bakos and Kemerer, 1992; Farbey *et al.*, 1993; Kaplan and Norton, 1996; Hasan and Tibbits, 2000; Andriessen, 2004). Traditional accounting and measurement systems are not efficient any more for evaluating e-commerce and, therefore, companies need to look for other methods to perform evaluation for their e-commerce systems.

The nature of investment evaluation

According to the Oxford English Dictionary, the word 'evaluation' comes from the old French evaluer, which was first noted in 1779 as meaning the action of evaluating. The Oxford Dictionary later defines this, as 'the activity of finding out or forming an idea of the amount or value of something or somebody'.

Evaluation, according to the European Commission (2001), can be defined as:

> *... a periodic assessment of the relevance, efficiency, effectiveness, economic and financial viability and sustainability of the project/programme in the context of its stated objectives. The purpose of evaluation is to review the achievements of a project/programme against planned expectations and to use experience from the*

project/programme to improve its design and/or the design of future projects and programmes.

In fact, evaluation began to make tracks from the computer information storage and retrieval systems to focus on other operational information system environments (King and Rodriguez, 1978). King and Rodriguez (1978) further point out that the nature of system evaluation, as well as methods of evaluation, has changed dramatically. Yet, due to the expansive function of IT, some problems occur when evaluating it. Thus, the following section discusses these problems

The problem of IT investment evaluation

Information technology has been recognised as a major enabler of business change (Davenport and Stoddard, 1994), since it allows firms to adopt operating exercises that would not have been likely without the opportunities accessible by new technologies (Hammer and Champy, 1993). Nevertheless, firms may face different problems when measuring new IT applications that will support business processes. IT can affect business processes in different ways and the ultimate impact on business performance relies on a variety of factors. These factors relate to what is being measured, since IT has an impact at several levels in an organisation, but only indirectly contributes to profitability (Farbey *et al.*, 1993). At all levels of analysis, external factors and measurement problems can lead to conflicting or unclear results.

Moreover, another problem, according to Willcocks (1992), has been the identification of suitable techniques that give reliable results. Meanwhile, the results of past empirical studies on the impact of IT investment on a firm's performance are not uniform – some report little or negative impacts of IT investments, while others have found significant positive impacts of IT on a firm's performance. Thus, Willcocks (1992) suggests the utilisation of multiple measures.

In addition, any evaluation involves the measurement of specific aspects and the judgment of these measurements against specific criteria. These could be according to DeLone and McLean (1992) technical measures (e.g. response time), financial measures (e.g. costs, benefits), measures of system or information quality and, ultimately, consumer satisfaction.

Bititci *et al.* (1997) elucidate the difference between performance management and measurement: Performance management is observed as 'a closed loop control system that deploys policy and strategy and obtains feedback from various levels in order to manage the performance of the system'. A performance measurement system 'is the information system which is at the heart of the performance management process and is of critical importance to the effective and efficient functioning of the performance management system'.

Thus, performance measurement 'involves the selection, definition and application of performance indicators, which quantifies the efficiency and effectiveness of service delivery methods' (Fine and Snyder, 1999). Consequently, performance measurement involves many challenges, such as finding suitable performance indicators, collecting performance measures from lower organisational levels to measure total organisational performance, the reliability of standards of measurement and measuring outcomes that are defined accordingly, by Hatry and Wholey (1999), as 'the events, occurrences, or changes in conditions, behaviour, or attitudes that indicate progress toward achievement of the mission and objectives of the program'.

Measurement is a critical part of evaluation and as Andriessen (2004) states, 'what gets measured gets managed'. Effective evaluation is important for appropriate operation and use of IT, especially in the current environment of changing financial services.

However, the broad range of roles and environments in which technology is used, challenges traditional evaluation approaches. Measurement difficulties have been experienced in traditional evaluation approaches (Bakos and Kemerer, 1992; Farbey *et al.*, 1993; Kaplan and Norton, 1996; Hasan and Tibbits, 2000). As a result, firms need to undertake investment appraisal evaluations that include the full value derived from their e-commerce investments. The following section discusses the need of an effective e-commerce performance measurement.

Need of an e-commerce performance measurement

Current researches indicate that issues relating to e-commerce evaluation and management are becoming more important to managers (Hasan and Tibbits, 2000). The measurement of the various variables and criteria (e.g. costs, productivity, user satisfaction) associated with IS are a critical component of evaluation and the necessary link between evaluation and the tools and methods of evaluation (e.g. Grembergen and Amelincks, 2002; Milis and Mercken, 2004).

The difficult economic environment and its increasingly competitive nature have amplified the need to monitor and measure e-commerce operational performance. However, empirical studies on the impact of IT investment on organisational performance have failed to produce reliable results (Willcocks, 1992). The problem of identifying the business value of IT investments is complicated by the fact that IT has an impact at several levels in an organisation, but only indirectly contributes to profitability (Farbey *et al.*, 1993). Hasan and Tibbits (2000) argue that 'there appears to be a paradox between the positive correlation of IT investment with revenue and its lack of correlation with profitability or productivity, at least on traditional measures'.

Martinsons *et al.* (1999) believe that 'traditional financial accounting measures (like the ROI and payback period) offer a narrow and incomplete picture of business performance and that a reliance on such data hinders the creation of future business value'. This has required a shift from highlighting financial figures to a broader perspective since business competition is now on the basis of product quality, delivery, after sales services and customer satisfaction (Zairi, 1994). Moreover, firms now find that they have to share information internally more effectively and efficiently in order to retain their competitive advantage. It is, as Zairi (1996) states, that business performance measurement should look beyond traditional financial metrics and adapt essential commerce drivers that determine and influence a firm's future business.

Several firms have started searching for new approaches to measure the payback from their e-commerce systems (Hasan and Tibbits, 2000). According to Zairi (1992), the main reasons for failure of traditional performance measurement systems are:

- Failure to define performance functioning.
- Failure to relate performance to the process.
- Failure to distinguish between control and improvement measures.
- Fear of exposing poor performance.

These reasons have produced new research on methods to measure organisational performance effectively, with weight on a balance between financial (quantitative) and non-financial (qualitative) measures (Farbey *et al.*, 1993).

Concerning alternative methods, several researchers have proposed models that link IT investment to organisational performance through some intermediate processes. These process-oriented models trace the path or chain of activities that IT investment takes on the way to reaching firm-level performance. Bakos and Kemerer

(1992) state that it is more relevant to look at intermediate outputs derived from time, quality, cost and flexibility, which are more directly linked to e-commerce than revenue or other financial measures of performance. Mooney *et al.* (1995) argue that firms derive business value from IT through its impacts on intermediate business processes. The intermediate processes include the operational processes that comprise a company's value chain and the management processes of information processing, control and coordination.

Another approach to the problem is called 'information economics' (IE) (Parker *et al.*, 1988). This method enables more intangible benefits, like better customer service or a higher degree of competitiveness, to be explained. It also separates the benefits and risks into two domains (a business domain and a technological domain) and evaluates these domains jointly.

Recently, a balanced scorecard (BSC) approach has been proposed for the evaluation, specifically, of e-commerce systems (Hasan and Tibbits, 2000). The BSC was proposed by Kaplan and Norton (1992) for the evaluation of business performance, but it can also be applied for the evaluation of IT projects.

The balanced scorecard (BSC) as a performance measurement method

The balanced scorecard (BSC) is an evaluation tool being increasingly used by corporations to measure performance. The firm's strategy is evaluated by using financial, customer perspective and operational measures. The BSC was first introduced by Kaplan and Norton (1992) to enable managers to look at their business performance from four important perspectives. The BSC approach can be useful in evaluating e-commerce, since, in addition to financial measures, it takes into account a wider range of e-commerce effects (Hasan and Tibbits, 2000).

Although the BSC measures organisational performance with emphasis on financial objectives, it also includes the performance drivers of these financial objectives and measures organisational performance across four balanced perspectives; (1) financial, (2) customer, (3) internal business processes and (4) learning and growth. This scorecard ensures that corporate vision and strategy is linked to the business unit and operational level measures. For instance, a firm looks to enhance the efficiency of its data centre operation, thereby reducing costs and increasing corporate profitability. While the objective in this case is focused on operational issues, the four BSC indicators and the links between them still apply. Moreover, the return on investment in personnel training can be traced to other indicators such as enhanced customer satisfaction, improved mainframe disk utilisation and lower unit costs (Kaplan and Norton, 1992).

The e-commerce balanced scorecard (BSC)

In recent times, several researchers (e.g. Willcocks, 1996; Van Grembergen and Van Bruggen, 1997; Martinsons *et al.*, 1999; Hasan and Tibbits, 2000, Grembergen and Saull, 2001; Grembergen and Amelincks, 2002; Grembergen *et al.*, 2003, Milis and Mercken 2004) have suggested that the balanced scorecard might also help to evaluate the performance of an information system (IS) or e-commerce system and to evaluate their investments in a holistic manner. Table 4.2 summarises several studies, indicating their context and illustrates the perspectives they have used to evaluate the performance of either information technology or e-commerce. The table also details some strategic goals and methods of measuring performance for the business value perspective of e-commerce BSC. Thus, as Hammer (1990) argues, IT has the necessary capability to transform outdated business processes. Hence, it is believed that the value of e-commerce investments should then become apparent with improvements in business processes. Accordingly, activity performance measures should also be considered as dependent variables in evaluating the business value of e-commerce.

The four perspectives of performance measurement

The balanced scorecard, according to Kaplan and Norton (1992), consists of four perspectives. These are the financial perspective, the customer perspective, the internal business process perspective, and the learning and growth perspective. These four perspectives present the framework for the scorecard, and measure the performance of a company during the past, present and the future.

To achieve 'balance' within the scorecard, the four perspectives need to be equally dependent in order for the effects of different actions not to offset each other. The purpose of the concept is to put the company's vision and strategy into action, as well as to outline business strategy in four different respects. The four perspectives are described by Kaplan and Norton (1996) in the following terms:

Customer perspective

In customer perspective, the company establishes its customers and market segments in which they want to compete. Then they must arrive at satisfactory objectives and core measures, and determine which critical success factors influence company competitiveness. The customer perspective focuses on measures that reflect how the company is creating customer value through its strategy and actions (Kaplan and Norton, 1996). From the customer perspective, the value of e-commerce is based largely on the extent to which it helps customers to trade more efficiently and effectively. Areas such as customer satisfaction, customer profitability, market share and the number of new customers need to be analysed.

Internal process perspective

The internal process perspective represents one of the strongest distinctions between the balanced scorecard and traditional accounting measurement systems. The balanced scorecard usually reveals entirely new business processes. Objectives and measures for the internal process are derived from explicit strategies so as to meet shareholder and target customer expectations. A common limitation of traditional accounting measurement systems is that they attempt to improve performance of individual departments rather than integrated business processes. A second limitation is that traditional accounting measurement systems tend to focus only on products and services for today's customers, whereas the balanced scorecard model put the focus on wholly new products and services for future customers, with the intention of achieving long-term financial success (Kaplan and Norton, 1996). Thus, in the context of e-commerce implementation this perspective is concerned mainly with the integration of e-commerce into the organisation and the role it plays in process coordination and integration between the organisation and its counterparts. It is expected that the evaluation of the newly coordinated and integrated processes should provide useful data about the impact e-commerce has had on the productivity and efficiency of these processes. Areas such as on-time delivery, the number of new products launched and product defects need to be measured.

Financial perspective

The financial measures define the long-run objectives of the business component (Kaplan and Norton, 1996). These objectives are established in the strategy and linked to sequences of action that should be taken within the four different perspectives in order to achieve the desired long-term outcome. The different measures selected in the BSC should be links in a chain of cause-and-effect relationships that establish the means to ensure that the financial benefits are realised. Ultimately, all objectives and measures in the other scorecard perspectives should be linked to achieving one or more of the objectives in the financial perspective (Kaplan and Norton, 1996). By undertaking that, the company recognises that the long-run goal for the business is to generate financial returns to all stakeholders, and that all strategies should enable the business unit to achieve its financial objectives. Thus, financial measures reflect the fiscal consequences of e-commerce actions already taken. They are valuable in summarising the easily measured aspects of a company's e-commerce financial performance and they indicate whether a company's e-commerce strategy, implementation and execution are contributing to the bottom line.

Learning and growth perspective

The learning and growth perspective identifies the internal structure that the organisation must build to create long-term growth and improvement. Internal business processes and customer perspectives identify factors critical for current and future e-commerce success, and this is unlikely to be achieved if employees, systems and technologies are not developed. Companies should attempt to identify and measure their core competencies, the critical technologies needed to ensure continued market leadership (Kaplan and Norton, 1992).

Figure 4.2 E-commerce strategies and measuring performance

References / Strategies	Methods of measuring performance	Will-cocks (1996)	Van Grem-bergen & Van Bruggen (1997)	Martins-ons *et al.* (1999)	Hasan & Tibbits (2000)	Grem-bergen & Saull (2001)	Grem-bergen and Amelincks, (2002)	Grem-bergen *et al.* (2003)	Milis & Mercken (2004)
			IT	MIS	EC	IT	EC	IT	ICT
Customer									
Customer satisfaction	Satisfactory level and frequency of e-commerce training	*	*	*	*	*	*	*	
Customer retention	Retention rates of customers who use the internet compared with those who do not						*		
Effective internet marketing	The percentage of users who visit the company site						*		
Time to market	New products/services introduced versus competition								*
Application delivery performance	Delivered quality	*			*	*		*	
Acquiring new customers	Sales generated directly and indirectly by the website						*		
Partnership with users	Satisfactory level and frequency of e-commerce support		*	*				*	

Preferred suppliers of application	New leads generated by the website		*	*				*	*
Satisfy end-user requirements	Effective e-commerce utilisation		*	*					
Internal process									
Service excellence	Enhanced processing of progress							*	*
Employee efficiency	Improved employee efficiency	*			*	*			
Quality improvement	Enhanced decision making		*	*	*				
Flexibility	Enhanced systems development process excellence				*			*	
Better management information	Enhanced communication		*	*	*	*			*
Control IS cost	Controlled cost		*	*				*	
Continue to focus on improving overall performance management	Enhanced co-ordination			*		*			*
Security and safety	Absence of major e-commerce issues in internal/external audit report				*	*	*		
System development	On–time delivery of products and services		*		*		*		
Fulfilment process	Faster reporting		*		*	*	*	*	
Cost management	Organised cost management	*						*	

Organisational impact	Enhanced processing of progress								
Financial									
Profitability	Time saving due to efficient documentation management	*		*	*				*
E-commerce strategic plan achievements	Completion of steps of the e-commerce project plan					*	*	*	
Compliance with budget	Actual versus budgeted expenses (ongoing development and maintenance)						*		
Strategic contribution	Completion of initiative					*	*		
Synergy achievement	Achievement of group synergies					*			
Management of e-commerce investment	Actual versus budget expenses					*		*	
Business value of system projects	Cost reduction of CRM Lower unit costs		*	*	*	*	*	*	*
Sell appropriate products and services to third parties	Increase market share		*	*					
Learning and growth									
Staff management effectiveness	Average workload per developer	*				*	*	*	

Personnel development	Percent of work done by contractors	*							
Support investment in innovative learning approaches	Training and education of IT staff	*	*	*			*	*	
Implementation of new technology	Percent of IT budget allocated to research new and updated technologies	*		*		*		*	*
Enhance the diversity and flexibility of our workforce	Workforce profile reports		*					*	
Develop skills and effective knowledge management relevant to future needs	Training and development reports							*	

References

Achleitner, H. K., Vowell, F. and Wyatt, R. B. (1998) Global conversations: New horizons for information professionals and students, *First Monday,* 3, 1, 1-10.

Ageshin, E. A. (2001) E-procurement at work: A case study, *Production and Inventory Management Journal; Alexandria,* 42, 1, 48-53.

Ahmed, A., Zairi, M. and Alwabel, S. (2003) Global benchmarking for Internet and e-commerce applications, *Proceedings of the First International Conference on Performance Measures, Benchmarking and Best Practices in New Economy,* Business Excellence, 388-396, 10th-13th June, Univ. of Minho, Braga, Portugal.

Alba, J., Lynch, J., Weitz, B., Janiszewski, C., Lutz, R. and Wood, S. (1997) Interactive home shopping: consumer, retailers and manufacturer incentives to participate in electronic marketplaces, *Journal of Marketing,* 61, 3, 38-53.

Aldrich, W. and Douglas, F. (1999) *Mastering the Digital Marketplace: Practical Strategies for Competitiveness in the New Economy*, John Wiley and Sons, NY.

Al-Mashari, M. (2002) Electronic commerce: A comparative study of organisational experiences, *Benchmarking: An International Journal,* 9, 2, 182-189.

Al-Mashari, M., Al-Mudimigh, A. and Zairi, M. (2003) Enterprise resource planning: A taxonomy of critical factors, *European Journal of Operational Research; Amsterdam,* 146, 2, 352-364.

Alter, S. (1996) *Information Systems: A Management Perspective, (2nd)* Benjamin/Cummings Pub. Co, Menlo Park, Calif.; Wokingham.

Alwabel, S. A., Ahmed, A. M., Gouda, S. and Zairi, M. (2004) What, Why and How: Critical review of e-commerce era, *Proceedings of the International Conference on Responsive Supply Chain and Organisational Competitiveness (RSC-2004)*, 5-7 January, Coimbatore, India.

Alwabel, S. A., Ahmed, A. M. and Zairi, M. (2003) Drivers for change to reshape construction industry: Saudi's case, *Proceedings of the International Business Information Management Conference*, 16 -18 December 2003, Cairo, Egypt.

Andriessen, D. (2004) IC valuation and measurement: classifying the state of the art, *Journal of Intellectual Capital,* 5, 2, 230-242.

Andrieu, M. (2001) The future of e-money: main trends and driving forces, *The Journal of Future Studies, Strategic Thinking and Policy,* 3, 5, 429-451.

Bakos, J. Y. and Kemerer, C. F. (1992) Recent applications of economic theory in information technology research, *Decision Support Systems; Amsterdam,* 8, 5, 365-386.

Ballantine, J., Bonner, M., Levy, M. and Martin, A. (1996) The 3-D model of information systems success: the search for the dependent variable continues, *Information Resources Management Journal,* 9, 4, 5-14.

Bamfield, J. (1994) Learning by doing: electronic data interchange adoption by retailers, *Logistics Information Management,* 7, 6, 32-39.

Bititci, U. S., Carrie, A. S. and McDevitt, L. (1997) Integrated performance measurement systems: a development guide, *International Journal of Operations and Production,* 17, 5, 522-534.

Bounds, L. G., Yorks, M. A. and Ranney, G. (1994) *Beyond Total Quality Management: Toward the Emerging Paradigm,* McGraw-Hill, New York.

Bowtell, M., Patnayakuni, R., Seddon, P. B. and Staples, S. (1999) Dimensions of Information System Success, *Communications of the Association for Information Systems,* 2, 20, 1-39.

Brache, A. and Webb, J. (2000) The eight deadly assumptions of e-business, *The Journal of Business Strategy,* 21, 3, 13-17.

Brown, A. (1994) Appraising Intangible Benefits from Information Technology Investment, *Proceedings of the First European Conference on Information Technology Investment Evaluation*, Henley on Thames, UK, 13-14, September.

Chen, L. D., Haney, S., Pandzik, A., Spigarelli, J. and Jesseman, C. (2003) Small business internet commerce: A case study, *Information Resources Management Journal; Hershey,* 16, 3, 17-41.

Clarke, S. and Doherty, N. (2004) The importance of a strong business-IT relationship for the realisation of benefits in e-business projects: the experiences of Egg, *Qualitative Market Research; Bradford,* 7, 1, 58-66.

Corbitt, B., Behrendorf, G. and Brown-Parker, J. (1997) Small and medium-sized enterprises and electronic commerce, *The Australian Institute of Management,* 14, 1, 204-222.

Cotton, J. L. (1993) *Employee Involvement: Methods for Improving Performance and Work Attitudes*, Sage Publications, Newbury Park; London.

D'Antoni, H. (2000) E-business requires a coherent plan, *Information Week,* 1, 792, 252-256.

Davenport, T. H. (1998) Putting the enterprise into the enterprise system, *Harvard Business Review; Boston,* 76, 4, 121-131.

Davenport, T. H. and Stoddard, D. B. (1994) Re-engineering: business change of mythic proportions, *MIS Quarterly,* 18, 2, 121-127.

Dawes, S. S. (1996) Interagency information sharing: Expected benefits, manageable risks, *Journal of Policy Analysis and Management,* 15, 3, 377-394.

Deighton, J. (1997) Commentary on exploring the implications of the Internet for consumer marketing, *Journal of Academy of Marketing Science,* 25, 4, 347-353.

DeLone, W. H. and McLean, E. R. (1992) Information systems success: the quest for the dependent variable, *Information Systems Research,* 3, 1, March, 60-95.

Distr (2003) Development of e-commerce sectors in the Arab region, *Proceedings of the Western Asia Preparatory Conference for the World Summit on the Information Society (WSIS)*, 4-6 February 2003, Beirut.

Dornier, P. P. (1998) *Global Operations and Logistics: Text and Cases,* John Wiley and Sons, New York; Chichester.

Dos Santos, B. L. and Peffers, K. (1998) Competitor and vendor influence on the adoption of innovative applications in electronic commerce, *Information and Management,* 34, 3, 175-184.

Doyle, T. and Melanson, J. (2001) B2B web exchanges: Easier hyped than done, *Journal of Business Strategy,* 22, 3, 10-13.

Drucker, P. F. (1990) *Managing the Non-Profit Organisation: Practices and Principles*, Butterworth-Heinemann, London.

Duffy, J. (2000) Point of no return, *CMA Management; Hamilton,* 74, 2, 32-37.

Duncan, T. and Moriarty, S. E. (1998) A communication-based marketing model for managing relationships, *Journal of Marketing Intelligence and Planning,* 62, 2, 1-13.

Edwards, C. and Peppard, J. (1994) Forging a link between business strategy and business reengineering, *European Management Journal;* 12, 4, 407-415.

Egan, J. (1998) *Rethinking construction*, The report of the construction task force, department of the environment, Transport and the regions, HMSO, London.

Eid, R., Trueman, M. and Ahmed, A. M. (2002) A cross-industry review of B2B critical success factors, *Internet Research: Electronic Networking Applications and Policy,* 12, 2, 110-123.

Erben, R. F. (2002) E-controlling: ten challenges for controlling and management accounting, *The Journal of Corporate Accounting and Finance; Hoboken,* 13, 5, 55-62.

Ernst, D. J. and Segall, P. (1995) Information resources and institutional effectiveness: The need for a holistic approach to planning and budgeting, *Cause/Effect Magazine,* 18, 1, 11-13.

European Commission, (2001) *Evaluation in the European Commission: A Guide to the Evaluation Procedures and Structures Currently Operational in the Commission's External Co-operation Programmes*, Brussels.

Farbey, B., Land, F. and Targett, D. (1993) *How to Assess Your IT Investment: A Study of Methods and Practice,* Boston: Butterworth-Heinemann, Oxford.

Fine, T. and Snyder, L. (1999) What is the difference between performance measurement and benchmarking?, *PM. Public Management; Washington,* 81, 1, 24-25.

Fingar, P. and Aronica, R. C. (2001) *The Death of 'e' and the Birth of the Real New Economy: Business Models, Technologies and Strategies for the 21st Century,* Meghan-Kiffer, Tampa, FL.

Floyd, S. W. and Wooldridge, B. (1990) The strategy process, middle management involvement, and organisational performance, *Strategic Management Journal,* 11, 3, 231-241.

Forrester Research (2000a), *E-marketplaces will lead US business e-commerce to $2.7 trillion in 2004*, available at http://www.forrester.com

G7 (1998) *G7 pilot project, a global marketplace for SMEs*, available at http://www.ispo.cec.be/ecommerce/g7init.html (Accessed August, 2003).

Gibbs, J. L. and Kraemer, K. L. (2004) A cross-country investigation of the determinants of scope of e-commerce use and colon; an institutional approach, *Electronic Markets,* 14, 2, 124-137.

Gordon, I. (1998) *Relationship Marketing: New Strategies, Techniques and Technologies to Win the Customers you Want and Keep Them Forever,* John Wiley and Sons, Toronto; Chichester.

Grandon, E. and Pearson, J. M. (2003) Strategic value and adoption of electronic commerce: An empirical study of Chilean small and medium businesses, *Journal of Global Information Technology Management; Marietta,* 6, 3, 22-43.

Grembergen, W. V. and Amelincks, I. (2002) Measuring and managing e-business projects through the balanced scorecard, *Proceedings of the 35th Hawaii Internal Conference on System Science, Big Island (Hawaii),* Organizational Systems and Technologies Track, 1-9, IEEE Computer Society Press.

Grembergen, W. V. and Saull, R. (2001) Aligning business and information technology through the balanced scorecard at a major Canadian financial group: its status measured with an IT BSC maturity model, *Proceedings of the 34th Hawaii International Conference on System Sciences,* International Conference on System Sciences (HICSS-34)-Vol. 8, Jan 03 - 06, Maui, Hawaii.

Grembergen, W. V., Saull, R. and Haes, S. D. (2003) Linking the IT balanced scorecard to the business objectives at a major Canadian financial group, *Journal of Information Technology Cases and Applications,* 5, 1, 23-45.

Guralnik, D. B. (1986) *Webster's New World Dictionary of the American Language,* (2nd) Simon and Schuster, New York.

Hackman, J. R. and Wageman, R. (1995) Total quality management: Empirical, conceptual, and practical issues, *Administrative Science Quarterly,* 40, 1, 309-342.

Hagel, J. and Armstrong, A. (1997) *Net Gain: Expanding Markets through Virtual*

Hammer, M. (1990) Re-engineering work: don't automate, obliterate, *Harvard Business Review*, 68, 4, 104-112.

Hammer, M. and Champy, J. (1993) *Re-engineering the Corporation: A Manifesto for Business Revolution*, (1st) N. Brealey, London.

Hasan, H. and Tibbits, H. R. (2000) Strategic management of electronic commerce: an adaptation of the balanced scorecard, *Internet Research; Bradford,* 10, 5, 439-450.

Hatry, H. P. and Wholey, J. S. (1999) *Performance Measurement: Getting Results,* Urban Institute Press, Washington, D.C.

Hawk, S. (2002) The development of Russian e-commerce: The case of Ozon, *Management Decision; London,* 40, 7/8, 702-709.

Herman, J. (2000) What is an e-strategy? *Business Communications Review,* 30, 4, 24-26.

Hill, C. W. L. and Jones, G. R. (2001) *Strategic Management Theory: An Integrated Approach,* (5th) Houghton Mifflin, Boston, Mass.

Hill, R. W. and Hillier, T. J. (1977) *Organisational Buying Behaviour: the Key to More Effective Selling to Industrial Markets*, Macmillan, London.

Hirschheim, R. and Lyytinen, K. (1987) Information systems failures - a survey and classification of the empirical literature, *Oxford Surveys in Information Technology,* 4, 1, 257-309.

Hopt, K. J. and Wymeersch, E. (eds.) (1997) *Comparative Corporate Governance: Essays and Materials,* Walter de Gruyter, Berlin.

Iacovou, C., Benbasat, I. and Dexter, A. (1995) EDI and small organisations: Adoption and impact of technology, *MIS Quarterly,* 19, 4, 465-485.

Irani, Z., Love, P. E. D. and Li, H. (1999) IT/IS investment barriers to the decision-making process, *Proceedings of the Business Information Technology: The Global Imperative Conference*, Cape Town, 30th June – 2nd July, South Africa, CD Proceedings.

Kalakota, R. and Robinson, M. (2001) *E-business 2.0: Roadmap for Success,* Addison-Wesley, Boston, Mass.

Kalakota, R. and Whinston, A. B. (1997) *Electronic Commerce: A Manager's Guide,* Addison-Wesley, Reading, Mass.; Harlow, England.

Kanji, G. K. and Asher, M. (1996) *100 Methods for Total Quality Management,* Sage, London.

Kaplan, R. S. and Norton, D. P. (1992) The balanced scorecard – measures that drive performance, *Harvard Business Review,* 70, 1, 71-79.

Kaplan, R. and Norton, D. (1996) Using the balanced scorecard as a strategic management system, *Harvard Business Review,* 74, 1, 75-85.

Kendall, K. and Kendall, J. (2001) A Paradoxically peaceful coexistence between commerce and e-commerce, *The Journal of Information Technology Theory and Applications,* 3, 4, 1-6.

Kinder, T. (2000) The use of the Internet in recruitment-case studies from West Lothian, Scotland, *Technovation,* 20, 9, 461-475.

King, W. R. and Rodriguez, J. I. (1978) Evaluation management information systems, *MIS Quarterly,* 2, 3, 43-51.

Kotler, P. (1997) *Marketing Management: Analysis, Planning, Implementation, and Control,* (9th) Prentice Hall of India Private Limited, New Delhi.

Landsbergen, D. and Wolken, G. (2001) Realizing the promise: government information systems and the fourth generation of information technology, *Public Administration Review, Washington,* 61, 2, 206-218.

Larsen, T. J. and McGuire, E. (1998) *Information Systems Innovation and Diffusion: Issues and Directions,* Idea Group Pub., Hershey, PA; London.

Lee, M. K. O. and Turban, E. (2001) A trust model for consumer Internet shopping, *International Journal of Electronic Commerce,* 6, 4, 75-91.

Lertwongsatien, C. and Wongpinunwatana, N. (2003) E-commerce adoption in Thailand: An empirical study of Small and Medium Enterprises (SMEs), *Journal of Global Information Technology Management; Marietta,* 6, 3, 67-83.

Lynex, A. and Layzell, P. J. (1997) Understanding resistance to software reuse, *Proceedings of the 8th International Workshop on Software Technology and*

Engineering Practice (STEP97), IEEE computer society, 339-349, Los Alamitos, California.

Martinsons, M., Davison, R. and Tse, D. (1999) The balanced scorecard: A foundation for the strategic management of information systems, *Decision Support Systems; Amsterdam,* 25, 1, 71-88.

McDonagh, P. and Prothero, A. (2000) Euro clicking and the Irish SME: Prepared for e-commerce and the single currency, *Irish Marketing Review,* 13, 1, 21-33.

Milis, K. and Mercken, R. (2004) The use of the balanced scorecard for the evaluation of Information and Communication Technology projects, *International Journal of Project Management,* 22, 2, 87-97.

Mohr, J. and Nevin, J. R. (1990) Communication strategies in marketing channels: a theoretical perspective, *Journal of Marketing,* 54, 1, 36-51.

Molla, A. and Licker, P. S. (2001) E-commerce system success: An attempt to extend and respecify the Delone and Maclean model of IS success, *Journal of Electronic Commerce Research,* 2, 4, 131-141.

Mooney, J. G., Gurbaxani, V. and Kraemer, K. L. (1995) A process oriented framework for assessing the business value of information technology, *Proceedings of the Sixteenth International Conference on Information Systems,* 17-27, Amsterdam, The Netherlands, Dec. 10-13.

Mukherjee, A. and Nath, P. (2003) A model of trust in online relationship banking, *International Journal of Bank Marketing,* 21, 1, 5-15.

Norris, G., Hurley, J. R., Hartly, K. M., Dunleavy, J. R. and Balls, J. D. (2000) *E-Business and ERP: Transforming the Enterprise,* John Wiley, New York.

O'Keefe, R., O'Connor, G. and Kung, H. J. (1998) Early adopters of the Web as a retail medium: small company winners and losers, *European Journal of Marketing,* 32, 7/8, 629-643.

Organisation for Economic Co-operation and Development (OECD) (1997) *Internet Domain Names: Allocation Policies*, Paris.

Organisation for Economic Co-operation Development (OECD) (1999) *Principles of Corporate Governance*, Paris.

Ozaralli, N. (2003) Effects of transformational leadership on empowerment and team effectiveness, *Leadership and Organisation Development Journal,* 24, 6, 335-344.

Parker, M. M., Benson, R. J. and Trainor, H. E. (1988) *Information Economics: Linking Business Performance to Information Technology,* Prentice-Hall International, Englewood Cliffs, N.J.

Parsa, H. G. (1999) Interaction of strategy implementation and power perceptions in franchise systems: an empirical investigation, *Journal of Business Research,* 45, 2, 173-185.

Pliskin, N., Romm, T., Lee, A. and Weber, Y. (1993) Presumed versus actual organisational culture: managerial implications for implementation of information systems, *The Computer Journal,* 36, 2, 143-152.

Poltrock, S. E. and Grudin, J. (1994) Organisational obstacles to interface design and development: two participant-observer studies, *ACM Transaction on Computer-Human Interaction,* 1, 1, 52-80.

Poon, S. (2000) Business environment and Internet commerce benefits – a small business perspective, *European Journal of Information Systems,* 9, 2, 72-81.

Poon, S. and Swatman, P. (1998) A Combined-Method study of small business Internet commerce, *International Journal of Electronic Commerce,* 2, 3, 31-46.

Porter, M.E. (1980) Industry structure and competitive strategy: Keys to profitability, *Financial Analysis Journal,* 36, 4, 30-41.

Porter, M. E. (2001) Strategy & the Internet, *Harvard Business Review,* 79, 3, 62-78.

Porter, M. E. and Millar, V. E. (1985) How information gives you competitive advantage, *Harvard Business Review,* 63, 4, 149-160.

Poulymenakou, A. and Tsironis, L. (2003) Quality and electronic commerce: a partnership for growth, *The TQM Magazine,* 15, 3, 137-151.

Pradhan, B. D. (1994) Telecom Technology Transfer - Experience in India, *IFIP Transactions a Computer Science and Technology,* 94, 3, 456-462.

Premkumar, G., Ramamurthy, K. and Nilakanta, S. (1994) Implementation of electronic data interchange: An innovation diffusion perspective, *Journal of Management Information Systems; JMIS; Armonk,* 11, 2, 157-186.

Premkumar, G. and Roberts, M. (1999) Adoption of new information technologies in rural small businesses, *The International Journal of Management Science,* 27, 4, 467-484.

Ratnasingham, P. (1998) The importance of trust in electronic commerce, *Internet Research: Electronic Networking Applications and Policy,* 8, 4, 313-321.

Rogers, E. M. (1995) *Diffusion of Innovations,* (4th) Free Press, New York; London.

Rosetti, D. K. and DeZoort, F. A. (1989) Organisational adaptation to technology innovation, *Advanced Management Journal,* 54, 4, 29-33.

Schneider, G. P. and Perry, J. T. (2000) *Electronic Commerce,* Course Technology, Cambridge, Mass.

Scupola, A. (2003) The adoption of Internet commerce by SMEs in the south of Italy: An environmental, technological and organisational perspective, *Journal of Global Information Technology Management; Marietta,* 6, 1, 52-71.

Seddon, P. B. and Kiew, M. (1996) A partial test and development of DeLone and Mclean's model of IS success, *Australia Journal of Information Systems,* 4, 1, 90-109.

Seybold, P. B. and Marshak, R. T. (1998) *Customers.com: How to Create a Profitable Business Strategy for the Internet and Beyond,* (1st) Sage, London.

Soh, P., Yap, S. and Raman, S. (1992) Impact of consultants on computerisation success in small business, *Information and Management,* 22, 1, 309-313.

Steinfield, C., Kraut, R. and Plummer, A. (1995) The impact of interorganisational networks on buyer-seller relationships, *Journal of Computer Mediated Communication,* 1, 3, 1-16.

Straub, D. W. and Watson, R. T. (2001) Research commentary: Transformational issues in researching IS and net-enabled organisations, *Information Systems Research,* 12, 4, 337-345.

Tapscott, D., Lowy, A. and Ticoll, D. (2000) *Digital Capital: Harnessing the Power of Business Webs,* Harvard Business School Press, Boston, Mass.

Teo, T. S. H., Ang, J. S. K. and Pavri, F. N. (1997) The State of Strategic IS Planning Practices in Singapore, *Information and Management,* 33, 1, 13-23.

Teo, T. S. H. and Tan, M. (2000) Factors influencing the adoption of internet banking, *Journal of the Association for Information Systems,* 1, 5, 1-42.

Thong, J. Y. L. (1999) An integrated model of information systems adoption in small business, *Journal of Management Information Systems,* 15, 4, 187-214.

Tigre, P. B. and Dedrick, J. (2004) E-commerce in Brazil: local adaptation of a global technology, *Electronic Markets; London,* 14, 1, 36-47.

Tornatzky, L. G., Fleischer, M. and Chakrabarti, A. K. (1990) *The Processes of Technological Innovation,* Lexington Books, Lexington, Mass.

Turban, E., Lee, J., King, D., R and Chung, H. M. (2000) *Electronic Commerce: A Managerial Perspective,* Prentice Hall International, London.

UNCTAD (2002) E-commerce and development report, *Proceedings of the United Nations Conference on Trade and Development*, United Nations, New York.

Vadapalli, A. and Ramamurthy, K. (1997) Business use of the Internet: an analytical framework and exploratory case study, *International Journal of Electronic Commerce,* 2, 2, 57-69.

Van Grembergen, W. and Van Bruggen, R. (1997) Measuring and improving corporate information technology through the balanced scorecard technique, *Proceedings of the Fourth European Conference on the Evaluation of Information technology*, Antwerp, Belgium: UFSIA (University of Antwerp).

Weill, P. and Ross, J. W. (2004) *IT Governance: How Top Performers Manage IT Decision Rights for Superior Results,* Harvard Business School: McGraw-Hill, Boston, Mass.; London.

Wheelen, T. L. and Hunger, J. D. (2000) *Strategic Management and Business Policy: Entering 21st Century Global Society*, (7th) Prentice Hall, London.

Willcocks, L. (1992) Evaluating information technology investments: research findings and reappraisal, *Journal of Information Systems,* 2, 4, 243-268.

Zairi, M. (1994) *Measuring Performance for Business Results*, Chapman and Hall, London.

Zairi, M. (1996) *Benchmarking for Best Practice: Continuous Learning Through Sustainable Innovation*, Butterworth-Heinemann, Oxford.

Zairi, M. (2000) Social responsibility and impact on society, *The TQM Magazine; Bedford,* 12, 3, 172-178.

Zairi, M., Letza, S. R. and Oakland, J. S. (1994) Does TQM impact on bottom-line results, *TQM Magazine,* 6, 1, 38-43.

Zhu, K. (2004) Information transparency of business-to-business electronic markets: A game-theoretic analysis, *Management Science; Linthicum,* 50, 5, 670-685.

Zorfass, P. and Michel, C. (1994) Electronic data interchange, *The Secured Lender; New York,* 50, 5, 36-43.

Zuboff, S. (1988) *In the Age of the Smart Machine: the Future of Work and Power*, Basic Books, New York.

Chapter 5

Building Q in *e*: The foundation of e-government

Introduction

The internet has brought about profound changes in society, enabling users to access almost any information they desire. One effect is that internet users are becoming better informed than those who do not use the internet. At the same time, merchants have taken advantage of the internet to sell their wares to internet-connected buyers with the proliferation of e-commerce. This combination of receiving knowledge online together with the experience of receiving goods online is leading to user expectations of receiving government services online. This is a good result, because on the supply side, governments want to take advantage of the economies to be gained by supplying services online. To the user or consumer, receiving services on line means convenience and timeliness. Governments supplying their services online receive savings in the cost of staffing requirements and information distribution.

These benefits will multiply as more and more citizens use online government services. For example, once a government online service is established, the government's savings will increase as more people use the online service, instead of using the traditional more labour-intensive form of the service. However, Burn and Robins (2003) state that e-government is not just about putting existing forms and services online. It provides the opportunity for the government to rethink how it provides its services and how it links them in a way that is tailored to users' needs. It is also recognised that e-government is not simply about implementing a new IT system. It is about changing business models and processes to do things differently and better. Information technology offers the solutions, but e-government is about changing the way the agency operates. It recognises that there are situation-specific factors for each e-government project which will determine success and failure and, hence, strategies for success of the adoption (Heeks, 2002).

Many now describe e-government as a continuum that begins when organisations and public agencies publish static information to the internet. As public organisations become more advanced, they are able to provide more dynamic, transactional services. Ideally, the continuum runs from static content through dynamic and transactional services, ending ultimately at organisational transformation. Many feel that the potential of e-government to transform organisations will lead to increased transparency, greater citizen participation in government.

Public organisations are beginning e-government by publishing static information to the internet and establishing an online presence in the hope that they too will experience increases in efficiency, effectiveness, and organisational performance. As public agencies begin implementing e-government initiatives, agencies believe that performance will improve and agencies will be better equipped to interact with citizens and provide services over the internet. E-government initiatives now enable citizens to access government documents, order publications, reserve lodging, order vital records, and renew licenses and permits from any location, with an internet connection. In addition, there are already signs that e-government is transforming organisations by breaking down organisational boundaries, providing greater access to information, and enhancing communications.

However, public organisations need to proceed with optimism, as well as with caution. E-government initiatives, like many technical innovations, have the potential to unintentionally distance citizens from government, leading to disenfranchisement. Public organisations also need to ensure that all citizens have access to the basic skills and infrastructure needed to participate in an increasingly technological society. As the digital divide takes a different shape in different locations, public policies will need to address issues of universal access and the educational needs of their citizens.

There is already evidence to indicate that by automating service provision, e-government is increasing efficiency, effectiveness, and citizen satisfaction. However, more baseline data needs to be collected to determine the longitudinal effects of e-government on public agencies. Additionally, there is an ongoing academic debate regarding the structural effects of information technology on public and private organisations. For instance, researchers have debated for nearly forty years about whether technological innovations cause centralisation or decentralisation in organisations.

Electronic government results from a variety of reasons of which the most important ones are that the public demands higher quality service and government willingness to improve performance. Public administration plays a central role in modern economic and social relations, bureaucratic complexity tends to increase in an entropic style and 'Red Tape', and citizen and business productive time is precious and cost reduction minimal (possibly only communication costs).

According to Heeks (2001b), there is a strong argument for not making cost/benefit analysis the central plank of decision making. Indeed in developing countries, where ICT costs can be two or three times higher while clerical costs are up to ten times lower, even these basic projects would probably be struck out. Like it or not, one must take a leap of faith, an acceptance that e-government is the future of government and that we have to press ahead. Furthermore, he adds to the previous argument by saying:

> *I typically liken e-government to a runaway horse. Developing country governments' can either jump on and try to steer it as best they can, or they can stand aside and watch other nations ride off into the future without them* (p. 99).

E-government definition

Governments are embarking on providing e-access to their citizens for the public service delivery; it is on the agenda of many governments to benefit from the emerging shift from the conventional methods of paper work to the digital age. This agenda is triggered by the efficiencies and effectiveness attributed to the e-government perspectives. Such attributes have dual purpose, cost- and time efficiencies from the suppliers' perspectives and the satisfaction from the recipients of the quality services. So enhancing citizens' satisfaction through quality service delivery in terms of time space is the paramount concern in this direction. Citizens as users of the e-access interact with various services without hierarchical obstacles and the absence of bureaucratic barriers. So being able to access all different kinds of services without time and space constraints can achieve such objectives in terms of customer (citizen) requirements (Munson *et al.,* 2001).

The e-service contributes to the overall systems success in terms of customer satisfaction and it enables services providers to achieve long-term goals of user retention and expansion into other areas (Das, Soh, & Lee, 1999). For such defined goals, governments need to devise and implement a strategy of e-service adoption (Saanen *et al.,* 1999). This suggests that the e-service is a critical resource to achieving multifaceted goals. Despites its importance, e-service definition varies. Boyer *et al.* (2002) believe that 'e-service [is] ... the initial landing on [a] homepage until the requested service has been completed or the final product has been delivered and is fit for use'. Although they add to our understanding of e-service, these definitions are grounded in private sector service delivery.

E-service comprehension in terms of the public sector begs an understanding of e-government. E-government itself is surrounded by several definitions (JOAIA, 2002). Research reveals that e-government has been defined in various ways (Wassenaar, 2000; Howard, 2001; Tambouris *et al.,* 2001). For instance, Lieber (2000) defines it as 'implementing cost-effective models for citizens, industry, federal employees, and other stakeholders to conduct business transactions online'. The focus of this definition lies in strategy, process, organisation and technology. Another definition is proposed by Gartner (2000): 'the transformation of public sector internal and external relationships through net-enabled operations, IT and communications, in order to improve government services delivery, constituency participation, and internal government operations.' Similarly, Zweers and Planque (2001) suggest that e-government is to be viewed as the objective to supply or to make available information, services or products, through electronic medias, through public agencies, at any time, place and for any citizen, in order to add value to all. The flux of the definitions of e-government continues. For example, the Information Society of the European Commission (ISEC, 2001) defines e-government as:

> *The use of information and communication technology in public administrations combined with organisational change and new skills in order to improve public services and democratic processes and strengthen support to public policies.*

Apart from the functional dimension of e-government, it is suggested to be considered as 'the application of the internet and related technologies to provide more convenient and effective government services to individual citizens and businesses' (Mitretek Systems, 2002). Some parsimonious yet comprehensive definitions are associated with Norris, Fletcher and Holden (2001) who describe e-government as 'the delivery of services and information, electronically, to business and residents, twenty-four hours a day, seven days a week'. In this endeavour, West (2001b) goes a step further to simplify it as 'the delivery of information and services online through the internet'. This is followed by Tapscott's explicit inclusion of e-services in e-government and e-citizens by suggesting that 'connected in net, the government can surpass barriers of time and distance, and offer to the public services of better quality, the costs lowest' (Tapscott, 1997). E-government is sometimes referred to as a revolution in public management and according to Dow *et al.* (2002) it will transform not only the way in which most public services are delivered, but also the fundamental relationship between government and citizen.

According to Gouscos, Mentzas and Georgiadis (2001) electronic government should be considered an ***integral system*** of political objectives, organisational procedures, information content and ICT technologies; and operating within public administration so as to contribute to fulfilment of its mission. In addition, they refer to electronic government as not a mere technological infrastructure or strategy but rather a new integrated style of public administration organisation and operation which addresses all citizens and businesses that public administration has a mission to serve. Electronic government is electronic services are offered by government (G), including public or regional/local administration agencies to businesses (B) and citizens (C), in the form of G2G, G2B, G2C schemes (Gouscos, Mentzas and Georgiadis, 2001) and the electronic services should be characterised by:

- offering any service to any citizen or business, in any place at any time (24x7 availability), through any communication channel, in any native language and independently of IT skills;
- single point of service for all cases, single sign-on for all services, single session for any service, transparent complexity, virtual integration (true one-stop approach);
- no paper documents, no paper money, no physical transport, no physical waiting;

- maximum reliability of results, maximum quality of service, minimum time of completion, minimum difficulty of access, minimum cost of use.

In common understanding, e-government focuses upon relatively simple transactions between identifiable customers (citizens, enterprises), on one side, and a multitude of government organisations in charge of registering objects, issuing passports, collecting taxes or paying benefits, on the other (Lenk & Traunmuller, 2002).

E-government benefits

Implementing e-government will gain a government many benefits and opportunities. No government wants to be left behind in the movement to improve government through electronic delivery of information and services to citizens. In general, some of these benefits include reducing the time and cost (supplier and demand) of providing services to the general public; empowering employees, reducing bureaucracy and increasing the efficiency and effectiveness of civil agencies. However, while implementing the vision of e-government, the government should pay attention to the complex realities. E-government initiatives are complex mixtures of technological, managerial and policy related challenges. The risk of not understanding and addressing these complexities is costly failure (Pardo, 2000).

E-government adoption provides the following benefits (Reynolds and Regio, 2001; Heeks, 2001b, 99):

- Delivers electronic and integrated public services from a single point of access (one stop portal).
- Available 24 hours a day, 7 days a week.
- Speed up decision making and service delivery.
- Bridge the digital divide.

- Save costs and capture revenue.
- Provide the government with efficient and effective decision making.
- Improve the quality of service delivery to citizens and businesses and other arms of government.
- Re-build government-customer relationships.
- The education does not end when a person finishes school, it can be realised through widespread e-learning. An ensuing society of knowledge workers will continue to access sophisticated and personalised education tools online.
- Governments can help businesses to move online and assist them to use online tools and foster economic development.
- Enable innovative approaches to governance.
- Disseminate information about government procedures and rules.

Furthermore, the Comptroller and Auditor General (2002: 110) indicates three benefits:

- The public can access information and advice online.
- The public can interact online with departments to apply for and receive a wide range of services.
- Significant improvements in the departments' operational efficiency are possible.

According to Dawes (1996: 97) implementing e-government can lead to timely and accurate information for better decision making and problem solving, reduced costs and increased productivity, centralised source and support for current information, expanded professional networks, improved public image, and greater integration and coordination of government services; these are found to be among some of the benefits of interagency information sharing.

Finally, according to Sharifi and Zarei (2004), implementing e-government will help developing countries to reduce their existing gaps with developed countries and vice versa.

E-government stages

Figure 5.1 E-government stages model

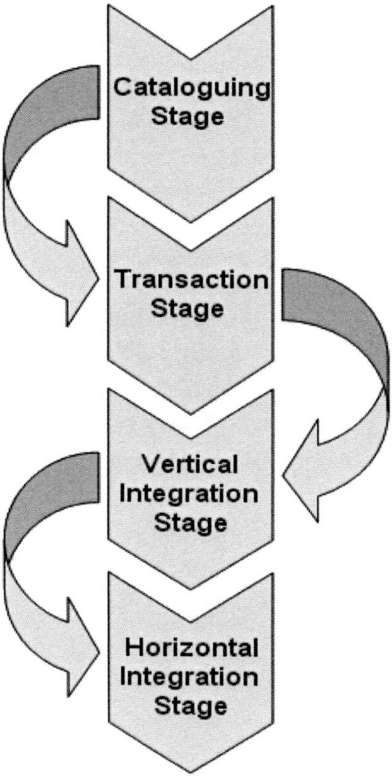

Source: Layne & Lee (2001)

Figure 5.1 provides a summary of the stages of e-government development according to Layne and Lee (2001). E-government can be adapted into four stages of development: In the first or early (cataloguing) stage, government establishes an online presence. It also should include in this stage downloadable forms that citizens and businesses have come to expect. The cataloguing stage has empirically been documented by a number of studies (Gant & Gant, 2002; Warkentin, Gefen, Pavlou & Rose, 2002). In this stage, single or a few independent government websites are emerged. The websites provide a user with static information e.g. addresses, phone numbers, office hours, calendars, etc. The functionality of the cataloguing stage provides minimal but efficient information to users, and the cataloguing should be organised at first on the basis of departments and then by service, actions, or events. The benefits of cataloguing involve increased convenience to citizens and businesses, reduced workload of government and established departmental presence of government functions as well as learning tools for citizens for processes and procedures.

After that comes the transaction stage: Enhanced and expanded web presence where services are made available for online use and databases are readied for the support of such transactions (Gant & Gant, 2002; Huang & Chao, 2001). Users can access dynamic and specialised information. An official national government website or homepage may serve as an entry point linking users to other branches. Furthermore, government publications, legislation, newsletters and other useful documents can be downloaded or ordered online. It could include formal interactions between citizens and service providers which take place on a more sophisticated level. Users can search specialised databases, or download forms and make applications online.

It includes allowing for dealing with the government directly through online interfaces with live databases. It provides the start of e-government as an entity, changing the way people interact with their government. The functionality of the transaction stage encompasses the government moving from providing only facts to becoming an active respondent, i.e. two-way communication, forms are filled out and the government responds with confirmation and receipts, citizens move from passive to active roles and can participate in online forums. The one-stop portal provides all service needs rather than citizens traversing numerous sites to find the correct information. The benefits of the transaction stage involve empowering citizens through availability, paperwork, travel, improved efficiency and increased savings.

In the vertical integration stage systems in all branches of government (legislative and executive) serving similar functions are linked together. This stage involves the ability to conduct complete and secure transactions online, such as obtaining visas, passports, birth and death records, licenses, permits or specialised government services. It includes the government being connected for different functions and services of government which will have permanent changes in government processes and concepts of government.

Vertical integration allows counterpart systems to communicate with each other, a central database or a connected web of databases and seamlessly integrates the government for cross-referencing and checking. The benefits of vertical integration involve: allowing citizens to access the service from a portal, emerging into a government-to-government interaction for consistency and accuracy of data; availability of knowledge to all levels of government; and continued improved efficiencies.

Finally, in the horizontal integration phase, systems of all levels and branches and across functions are linked in a one-stop-shop. All transactional services offered by government will be available online. By clicking on the government's official site, users will have the ability to instantly access any service made available. A single national government website will allow the user to customise a secure one-stop-shop portal that will enable direct access to services based on a user's specific need.

Horizontal integration allows databases across functional areas to communicate and share information, information obtained by one agency will propagate throughout all government functions. The benefits of horizontal integration include citizens having online access to ubiquitous government services, with various levels of government and the functional walls inside government being transparent to them. This recognises the full potential of information technology from a citizen's perspective; citizens can conduct business across a wide variety of requirements and eliminates redundancies and inconsistencies in government information bases for citizens.

The Layne and Lee model bears a certain resemblance to the original IT-growth model presented by Gibson and Nolan, and also to its revised and more frequently cited version by Nolan (Gibson & Nolan, 1974; Nolan, 1979). While the first Layne and Lee stage does not yet require any business process change or change management, more fundamental, complex and substantial changes become the norm in subsequent stages.

Following this, the e-government can be displayed in the following points: (1) e-communication between government departments; (2) e-procurement; (3) e-payment for social welfare recipients and the respective government departments; (4) e-commerce; (5) databases; (6) e-documents; (7) e-taxation; (8) digital confirmation of personal identity cards. (GOPSC, 2000a)

E-government challenges

However, all that sounds promising is not free from challenges. In order to implement an e-government programme, governments need to develop specific and reasonably attainable goals and understand what resources are available to achieve those goals. Only then will they be able to formulate a plan that can be implemented in full, rather than being cut short before any gains are realised due to lack of resources. Once governments commit to strategies transforming their processes, significant challenges will arise during their implementation. The most pertinent challenges that are expected to be encountered during the implementation of an e-government have been indicated in previous studies:

- Many countries do not have the information technology (IT) infrastructure necessary to immediately deploy e-government services; developing IT infrastructure is an important component in e-government implementation.
- E-literacy refers to those who are unable to make use of ICT because they are computer illiterate.
- Protecting the privacy of citizens' personal information stored on these databases after they collect vast quantities of their data.
- Developing an information management framework is necessary to make sense of available data. Without it, government could not derive useful analysis quickly enough to react to social and economic developments.
- Lack of communication infrastructure that affects government integration and citizen access to e-government services.
- Security is costly, but must be addressed in the design phase, as security breaches can shatter public trust in e-government.
- The application of ICT to government may encounter legal or policy barriers. While implementing e-government the responsible people must consider the impact of law and the public.
- E-government services are only useful if people are familiar with them; education will be needed.
- E-government involves changes; according to Mabin, Forgeson and Green (2001) change may fail due to what is often termed 'resistance to change'.

IT enabling factors

The emergence of information technology has contributed to the diffusion of internet, e-commerce and e-government. But the definitions of information technology, due to its evolving nature, have been used differently in different contexts. The importance and significance has emerged in almost all aspects of life. A number of IT projects have increased in the last few years, and the growing body of knowledge is descriptive, theoretical, and practical. Increasingly, previous studies have indicated large scale IT project failure (Booty, 1998).

Evolution is apparently dependent on the contextual factors for adoption. The most fundamental factors are: information technology (IT) infrastructure; prevalent IT standards; national information infrastructure (NII); collaboration and integration capabilities among agencies and institutions; and last, but not the least, security. Each one of the important IT factors is illustrated in the model depicted in Figure 5.2.

Figure 5.2 IT Enabler factors for e-government adoption

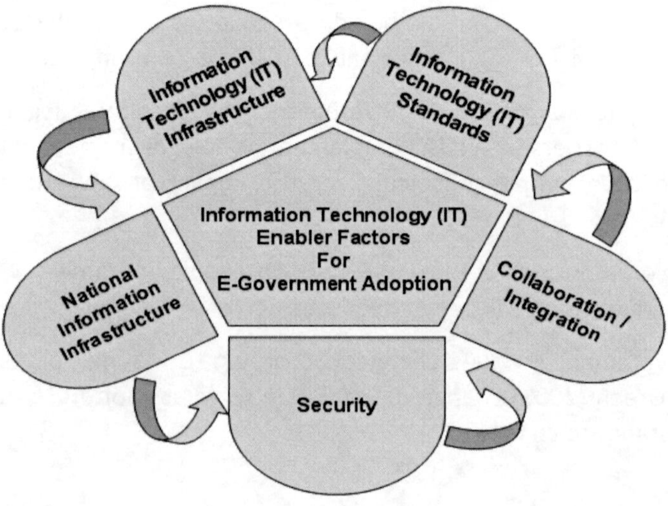

Hard Q-factors in e-government implementation

Strategy in e-government adoption

Any project that involves change should develop a specific plan of action and include a strategy to motivate the organisation toward achievement of the goals (Burn and Robins, 2003). Several technical/economic conditions are relevant for the design and formulation of a national e-government strategy. A good strategy needs to first assess the current condition as the first step to developing a path to the desired results. The national information and communication technology infrastructure is the first critical element for assessment. In particular, the UN/ASPA (2002) report has pointed out the importance of network availability.

The availability of a high-speed network for both government and private use is an important indicator of the maturity of an infrastructure. Second, computer availability and use determines whether the information and communication infrastructure is utilised. Citizens and businesses need to have computers and internet service providers for them to get access to government information and services online. This is usually measured by the number of computers per capita. Wide disparity is seen among countries around the world. Third, the distribution of use and accessibility among various groups also shapes national e-government strategies. Digital divide is usually the term used to capture this issue. Different groups have unique needs and uses for e-government.

Electronic government should be planned and deployed taking into consideration strategic objectives like the following (Gouscos, Mentzas and Georgiadis, 2001):

- Cater first and foremost for citizen and business needs, and support 'e-citizens' and 'e-businesses'.

- Facilitate access, cater for quality of results and minimize problems, errors and dissatisfaction.
- Exploit information content, add value to offered services, promote shift of culture towards quality and effectiveness and create prestige for public service.

A strategic plan needs to identify and anticipate those uncertainties such as technology. A leading technology today may be obsolete tomorrow. As a result, the cost projection for information technology may be incorrect. Moreover, a strategic plan needs to allocate necessary resources to critical programmes. One main challenge of e-government initiatives is finding the resources. A plan without committed resources is very likely to fail. One important resource that most countries are short of is skilled IT personnel. A strategic plan needs to address the recruiting and training of IT staff or critical programmes. Security control of government information resources is at the centre of any successful national e-government strategic plan. Ensuring the security of information is the necessary groundwork for disseminating government information and providing government services online.

A national e-government strategy needs to address both privacy and security to win the trust and willingness of citizens and businesses to submit personal information and conduct transactions online. If privacy is not adequately protected to facilitate private and business transactions with government online, a national e-government strategy needs to include efforts to pass relevant laws and regulations. A national e-government strategy should also address gaps in the area of security. Some countries have launched the Public Key Infrastructure Initiative and other security measures to address this issue.

For example, Singapore's success on providing public services online can be attributed to the strategies that it has adopted (Ke and Wei, 2004). Furthermore, many governments developed an online strategy such as Western Australian Government (2001). The major aim of this strategy is to develop a 'technology-enriched community'. In this social milieu: the technology is used to its full advantage to enrich the lives of its citizens, the 'digital divide' is replaced with 'digital inclusion'. For instance, children are skilled to take charge of the future and reap its benefits and it is made easier for the citizen to interact with the social, economic and political environment. Furthermore, the technology flows to all members of the community and is available for all to utilise if they so desire. Communities embrace technology to improve their ability to interact and to communicate. This suggests that the elements of a system are essential to take into consideration for e-government.

Taking the Singaporean case as a hallmark, there are five e-government strategic thrusts: reinventing the government, delivering integrated electronic services, being proactive and responsive, using ICT to build new capabilities and capacities, and innovating with ICT. The plan also provided government agencies with specific guiding principles to follow in e-government development (Ke & Wei, 2004).

Vision in e-government adoption

The purpose of government is to further the shared goals of a society. Therefore, begin the planning process by establishing a broad vision of e-government. The broad vision should flow from the large goals or concerns of a society (PCIP, 2002). Citizens should be included in the e-government vision. For example, government support and assistance should be anywhere-anytime available to aid the citizen as a valuable customer, reflecting the fact that a government respects the citizen. In addition, businesses on the demand side should also be in the e-government vision. For example, government support and assistance should be available anywhere and at anytime to aid businesses to succeed, to facilitate their every contact with the State and regulate the environment for a healthy electronic market economy (Stamoulis and Georgiadis,

2000). A vision is a commitment to establishing rethinking and reviewing of who we are and what we are here to do (Allen, 1995). Hitchcock (1996) indicated rules for how the vision should be framed:

- It must be phrased positively; it should be stated in terms of moving towards something that is wanted.
- It should be as specific as possible; preferably the evidence should be in a form that is sensory-based, that is what could be seen, heard or felt.
- It must be possible to have an input into the achievement of the vision, to have ownership.

E-government should not solely be a strategy for reducing the cost of government, though this can be one valuable result. Saving money is an easy way to 'sell' e-government to political leaders and the public. However, with few exceptions, e-government applications do not lower costs in the short term for government itself, though they may reduce costs for citizens and business.

E-government must be about meeting the needs of citizens and improving quality of life. Borrowing a lesson from the private sector, e-government must be customer-driven and service oriented. This means that a vision of e-government implies providing greater access to information as well as better, more equal services and procedures for the public and businesses. Even when e-government projects seek to improve internal government processes, the end goal should be making government serve citizens better (PCIP, 2002).

According to Heeks (2001b) it is important to develop vision for the national e-government initiative in different areas. For the administration: improving government processes by cutting costs, by managing performance, by making strategic connections within government, and by creating empowerment. For the citizens and services area: connecting citizens to government by talking to citizens and supporting accountability by listening to citizens and supporting democracy, and by improving public services. Finally, society: building interactions beyond the boundaries of government by working better with business, by developing communities, by building government partnerships, and by building civil society.

The e-government may not materialise without an explicit vision for the civil agencies. The vision gives direction, magnitudes and the destination in the provision and improvements of services to the public. Vision includes the roadmap on how to reach the intended objectives, which becomes the goal for all decisions and plans in the whole agency. In clarifying the vision for change or the introduction of new idea, Kotter (1996) identified six important characteristics:

- Imaginable: indicates what the future will look like.
- Desirable: appeals to all stakeholders. This includes all employees in the agency, other agencies, concerned partners and the general public.
- Feasible: attains realistic and accomplishable goals.
- Focused: helps provide guidelines in the decision making process.
- Flexible: allows individuals to provide their initiatives and alternative responses in light of changing conditions.
- Communicable: is easy to be communicated to others in a short period of time.

By the end of 2001, Singapore managed to get 92% of all public services deliverable online. Singapore's success in providing public services online can be attributed to their commitment and persistence to fully turn a promising vision into reality (Ke and Wei, 2004). The need for a clear vision is important at all levels, from entire organisations to each individual in those organisations. It is fair to ask why it is so important to establish a clear vision. Research and practical experience answers that by telling us that vision (Allen, 1995):

- inspires and motivates;
- provides direction and fosters success;
- is essential to the organisation of the future; and
- enables us to benchmark our progress and evaluate our outcomes.

Furthermore, the results of non successful previous projects were blamed on the failure of the agency to communicate its vision to the concerned parties. Generally, in the civil agencies the vision is implicit and is known only to the senior management. Communicating the vision of e-government to all employees involved in the implementation process is vital. Once the vision for e-government is established, the vision and key objectives should be communicated across government and to the public.

Establish a communications strategy to ensure that people understand the vision, the changes that will occur and the tangible benefits for them from e-government (PCIP, 2002). The vision has to be established within each agency to enable employees to work towards realising the goals and objectives of the agency and has to be recognised at the national level to ensure that all agencies work towards achieving the essential goal of reducing the cost and improving the delivery of services to the general public (Ke and Wei, 2004).

Policy and legal issues in e-government adoption

Since the concept of e-government is radically changing the way the public sector is doing business, new legal issues are starting to arise (Akomode, Taleb-Bendiab, Evangelidis & Taylor, 2002). The very nature of e-government is that all governmental services should be carried out electronically. Most of such services do require the joining of some kind of contract, but unfortunately since everything is being done electronically the absence of paper is evident. Such deficiency needs to be addressed as it is argued that contracts in electronic form may not be valid (Pattison 1997).

E-government requires a range of legislative changes including electronic signatures, electronic archiving, data matching, freedom of information, data protection, computer crime, and intellectual property rights legislation. Regulatory changes are required for a host of activities from procurement to service delivery (Heeks, 2001b). Research conducted in a collaborating public establishment (Hagen *et al.*, 2000 p.23; Cavazos, 1994) shows that there is a strong need to update changes the current legislation.

Undoubtedly new modern legal frameworks have to be developed, without having to introduce 'radical' inappropriate laws (Hutchinson *et al.*, 2001; Agren 2001). Failing to do so, e-government progress will be severely hindered (Akomode *et al.*, 2002). The Audit Office of New South Wales developed legal principles that would help them with e-government adoption (AONSW, 2001):

- A legal framework supporting e-government is in place.
- Legal developments affecting e-government are monitored and necessary action is taken.
- Agency legislation is reviewed to determine and address possible e-government impediments.
- E-government business practices comply with statutory requirements.
- The legal standing of electronic transactions is assured.
- Legal liability is defined and made known to all parties involved in e-government.

E-government needs a source of access policy that can be applied at the global government level. This is when the legislation based access policy comes into play. It is a norm in modern governments that a comprehensive legal framework should be in place to provide the legal basis for all government activities, and in particular the interaction between government bodies and citizens or among different government bodies. The formulation of access policy beyond the provider's domain can and should thus be based on legislation relevant to the government service provided.

In addition, to apply the policy by a web service access control mechanism a mapping between the security subjects and the legal subjects is necessary. This mapping can be many-to-many, which means that multiply legal rules can apply to a single web service and one rule can apply to more than one web service. The task of working out the mapping for all security subjects is a complicated task requiring significant efforts from both technical and legal experts.

Since e-government projects are inheritably technology driven, many potential legal risks lie within the very nature of the technology that is used or in the way it is used. Technical-specific risks can potentially expose public sector organisations to serious liability (Watts, 2001). Typical examples of such risks are 'deep linking' and 'framing' on governmental websites.

The associated risk with deep linking is the fact that the user may bypass the home page of a website and 'jump' to another page within the website, without having to agree or disagree with the terms and conditions of that website. On the other hand 'framing' occurs where governmental websites are designed to use frames, thus offering the possibility for the user to misrepresent the contents of such websites by 'mixing' it with other websites (Akomode *et al.,* 2002).

A serious legal risk, which has to be addressed when implementing any e-government strategy, is unwillingness from traditional bureaucracy to reform legal frameworks in order to rearrange power (Hagen, 2000: 23). Research shows that some civil servants may not wish to cooperate in order to reform legislation, mainly because of fear of redundancy (Klee-Kurse 2000: 213). The existence of a government wide policy and legal framework will positively affect local agency participation in electronic information sharing with state agencies (Akbulut, 2002).

Motivation and reward system in e-government adoption

The way employees are rewarded is starting to alter rapidly. For many years, pay systems remained relatively stable while the world about them was dramatically changed. E-government project managers particularly need help with managing the human components of projects and change. They need a greater capacity to manage the issue of motivation; of internal rewards and punishments (Heeks, 2001b). An intrinsic and extrinsic reward system may render incremental developments. Furthermore, there must be a reward strategy in place. It must be derived from and contribute to corporate strategy and be based on corporate values and beliefs.

Social technology or institutional organisations foster knowledge generation, application and diffusion. These organisations succeed in increasing worker productivity by offering job promotions, benefits and monetary incentives. An e-government initiative is the creation of a positive working environment for employees. Similarly, a reward system is likely to increase employees' energy, creativity and productivity which will help the implementation of e-government initiatives. While rationally grounded motives play an important role in electronic government; motivations such as personal, departmental, economical, and political may influence the launch of electronic government projects.

According to London and Higgot (1997) the reward and recognition process consists of the following elements:

- Categories for awards

- Nominations
- Review of nominations
- Recognition of successful nominations
- Review of successful nominations
- Final selection
- Awards
- Annual quality award.

There is a substantial body of theoretical literature that links organisational strategy, human resource (HR) practices, and performance (Balkin and Gomez-Mejia, 1987; Hambrick and Snow, 1989; Lawler, 1986a; Lawler, 1986b; Ulrich and Lake, 1990; Waldman, 1994). The reward system should be aligned to motivate employee performance that is consistent with the firm's strategy, attract and retain people with the knowledge, skills and abilities required to realise the firm's strategic goals, and create a supportive culture and structure (Galbraith, 1973; Kilmann, 1989; Nadler and Tushman, 1988).

The reward system, with organisational strategy, helps to determine organisational effectiveness. Gomez-Mejia and Balkin (1992) conclude that modern organisations must align their reward system practices with their organisational strategy in order to achieve higher levels of performance at both the individual and organisational level.

However, Scholtes (1995) has listed five reasons to explain why reward and recognition systems do not work:

- No data to show long term benefits.
- They set up internal competition.
- Reward systems undermine teamwork and co-operation.

- They often reward those who are lucky and pass by those who are unlucky.
- They create cynics and losers.

An effective reward and recognition process provides a clear and visible statement to all employees of the organisational values and the commitment to employee involvement (London and Higgot, 1997). Although, some believe that motivation is an intrinsic property of human nature rather than a behaviour to be instilled by management (Scholtes, 1995). People are not likely to change their behaviour unless they are rewarded for it. A key principle of compensation is to link more of it directly to performance.

Training in e-government adoption

In general terms, priority human capacities for e-government are 'hybrids': those who understand the technology *and* the business of governance *and* the role of information in governance. It is they – as individuals or small teams – who can most successfully champion e-government in the target organisations. Furthermore, IT professionals for e-government need to be hybridised into broader change agents who combine IS and ICT skills with an understanding of the public sector context, of the civil society context and of change management. Public sector managers need to be hybridised towards a broader skill set that includes an understanding of information systems and ICTs (Heeks, 2001b).

Learning is the focal element for the current and prospective initiatives of the e-government in Saudi Arabia. One primary aspect is training. Training is a structured, formalised approach to human factors technology transfer. The success of training depends critically on producing a program that is effective and efficient (Grimes, 1983).

In developing countries, indigenous information systems development capacity for e-government must be strengthened, both within user organisations in the government and public sectors, and within private sector vendor organisations. Furthermore, for almost all developing countries, there will be a need to build basic computer literacy skills for users in the public sector and other governance-related organisations (Heeks, 2001b). Norris (1999) posited that local governments argued that their employees were not very well trained in using information technologies and this inadequate training resulted in resistance to change, resistance to use, and underutilisation of computers.

Training is necessary to meet and maintain e-government skills (AONSW, 2001). In addition, the reengineering of work processes also needs to be well managed, as well as retraining and educating the relevant staff members (Jupp, 2001). The importance of training, hands-on support and a proactive stance towards adjusting the technology to the work have been identified as important both by practitioners (Lloyd & Whitehead, 1996; Smith, 1996; Keselica, 1994) and researchers (Karsten *et al.*, 1997; Bullen & Bennett, 1990; Rogers, 1994; Orlikowski *et al.*, 1995).

Rothwell and Kazanas (1989) propose an intriguing classification of human resource development (HRD) strategies that can encompass formal training. Within such an organisational strategy for HRD they identify the following strategies, each of which may necessitate separately prepared objectives, policies, and activities:

- Employee training: short term efforts that enable individuals to have the skill competencies to carry out their existing jobs.
- Employee education: intermediate efforts for helping individuals achieve their career objectives, keep abreast of changes in their occupations, and gain new insights about themselves. It prepares people for future work.
- Employee development: long-term efforts for matching up the collective skills of a work group and the responsibilities assigned

to the group by the organisation. Employee development makes individuals agents for organisational and group change.

- Organisation development: long-term efforts for changing the culture of an organisation or group.
- Non-employee development: long-term effort for improving relations between a business, the general public, and external stakeholders.

Training content would need to pick up and disseminate the lessons of best practice, such as the need to adopt an integrated approach to e-government, the need to adapt solutions to developing country realities, and the need for better communication with key stakeholders (Heeks, 2001b). In addition, according to Oakland (1993), training should have strategy which should be addressed early with the other strategies. Another issue involves funding training events for use as curriculum development mechanisms which should be considered as an e-government initiative input.

Furthermore, LeRouge and Webb (2003) indicate potential strategic challenges for training such as: the high cost of training, selecting training processes, balancing the organisation's best interests with the individual's, and how to select, implement, develop, update and design these courses in a coordinated way. There are many different ways technologies can be utilised to further education and training in e-government. The key is to strike a balance between the costs and benefits associated with these technologies (Hayes and Jamrozik, 2001).

The currently used support systems or tools in e-learning programmes can be divided into two broad categories: (1) traditional tools: which include, but are not limited to, videotape (S-VHS), cable/public television, satellite video conferencing, teleconferencing, whiteboard; and (2) computer-assisted and network tools: which include, but are not limited to, CD-ROM titles, web browsers, chat rooms, real player, QuickTime, Windows media player, broadband video conferencing, WebCT, Blackboard, and Learning Space (Bose, 2004).

In a different area, equal training concern should be given to: choosing the correct instructors; maintaining consistency in training courses; determining the prerequisite skills and knowledge students must have before training; using appropriate teaching modes; and motivation (Grimes, 1983). Furthermore, it is important to seek funds for internal and external e-government training programmes in two directions:

- Training of e-government professionals on computer operations, system development, databases, and communication and other areas of information technologies and systems.
- Training of e-government users on general computer knowledge and use.

One of the main goals is to increase e-government literacy which will therefore create awareness among the government's public sector.

Technical staff in e-government adoption

Organisations with knowledgeable employees about e-government will be better equipped to deal with the issue of implementation. Government agencies with qualified technical expertise demonstrate a willingness to participate with other government agencies to establish projects that will enable the government agencies to share information. Technical experts are responsible for the day-to-day maintenance and updating of the system (Folstad, Jorgensen and Krogstie, 2004). They have the ability to provide their agencies with the required knowledge that can help the agency participate in e-government initiatives without hesitation or reluctance. The government has to ensure that all government agencies have access to technical personnel to assist in the adoption and implementation of e-government projects.

Though companies specialised in e-government development may be available in developing countries, the rates they charge may not be affordable for many developing countries. Even if affordable, without appropriate understanding of IT, many government officials of developing countries will find it difficult to specify requirements and resources to devote for the projects to be outsourced.

According to Heeks (2001b: 99), there is a danger of e-government being too external: this is particularly problematic given often conflicting objectives between vendors and government, and the poor quality of some vendors. Therefore, it may cause the failure of e-government initiatives. In terms of the danger of e-government being too internal: for some ruling elites in developing countries, it seems that government is seen as a tool for serving personal, then ethnic, then social affiliations, and lastly, national interest. E-government initiatives will be just the same: if senior public officials do come to see e-government as being in their interests and are able to take control of those initiatives, they are likely to steer projects towards their self-interest, and potentially away from broader goals. It is very difficult, but a balance must be struck between external and internal interests. An independent project team is required so that government cannot intimidate team members and hijack the project for their own benefit.

Government agencies which rely completely on outsourcing the implementation of their IT projects encounter difficulties in upgrading their systems and are reluctant to participate in e-government initiatives. On the other hand, government agencies which rely on their staff for the development and implementation of IT projects are more confident to accept change in technology and, therefore, accept adoption of e-government initiatives in their daily operations. College and entry level recruiting is necessary to bring in young staff. In addition, training programmes need to be improved to allow inexperienced staff to be technically able to support the existing applications and to deliver enhancements. The staffing requirements need to be regularly evaluated to ensure the agency has a sufficient number of personnel with the right competencies for the e-government operating environment (AONSW, 2001).

Funding in e-government adoption

In order to implement e-government programmes, the government needs to develop specific and reasonably attainable goals and understand what resources are available to achieve those goals. Only then will they be able to formulate a plan that can be implemented in full, rather than being cut short before any gains are realised due to lack of resources.

E-government is mainly related to lack of funding (Akomode *et al.*, 2002). In the US, over half (57.1%) of city and county governments view a lack of financial resources as a barrier to providing e-government (ICMA, 2002). In a similar study of only county governments, funding was listed as the greatest obstacle to moving county government services to the internet; as reported by 70% of respondents (NACO, 2000). Financial resources express an agency's capital available for participation in electronic information sharing. Damanpour (1991) state that organisations that have slack resources can afford costly innovations, can absorb failure, and can explore new ideas in advance of the actual need. However, funding will result in a faster response from government agencies.

Keller (2001) argued that government funding models are currently not set up to fund many of the e-government projects that are cross-agency or cross jurisdictional in nature. Therefore e-government managers who have a holistic vision towards implementing e-government see their dreams shattered since some public sector departments have the resources to develop e-government, whilst others do not. In addition, there is no additional internal funding; most e-government project plans start from the politicians, the people who run the governments. They are the ones who initially agree to invest public money into the concept of electronic government. Unfortunately, it has been observed that after the initial enthusiasm, many local politicians are not capable or willing to understand the need for further investments in IT (Akomode *et al.*, 2002).

Furthermore, research reveals that in some cases of local government establishments initiating e-government, financial support from external sources proves to be difficult to obtain. Consequently, e-government projects do not develop properly (Akomode *et al.,* 2002).

Change management in e-government adoption

There must be some degree of organisational change that an e-government system introduces. Indeed, a greater degree of change may bring greater organisational improvements (Heeks, 2002). On the other hand, the greater the degree of change the greater the risk of failure (Dodd and Fortune, 1995; Sauer, 1999). The public sector in particular has been poor at managing e-government projects and at managing change. That capacity needs to be strengthened (Heeks, 2001b).

For modern organisations the ability to manage change successfully has become a competitive necessity (Peters & Waterman 1982; Kanter, 1989; Burnes, 1996). Organisational change is usually required when changes occur to the environment in which an organisation operates. Environmental variables which influence organisations may be political, economical, sociological and technological (Jury, 1997).

Papantoniou *et al.*, (2001) indicate that change management is one of the critical factors in e-government implementation. Such restructuring of the public sector may entail three closely related levels: a) redefinition of goals and tasks of the state; b) rationale of public sector action; and c) efficiency and effectiveness of structures, processes and instruments (Budaus, 1998). Although lessons learned from e-commerce change management can be applied to e-government perspectives (Csetenyi, 2000), there are some exceptional challenges presented by e-government compared to e-commerce because of the strict and committed nature of relationships of government-to-citizen, government-to-government, government-to-business and government-to-employee (Papantoniou *et al.*, 2001). Such challenges are magnified by the socio-cultural issues in countries such as the Kingdom of Saudi Arabia where the interaction is overwhelmingly face-to-face between public service providers and users.

The acceptance process will be affected by the extent to which the changes are incremental or radical/strategic for the organisation. Incremental changes represent a series of continual progressions that maintain the organisation's equilibrium, and often affect only a part of the organisation. Radical change breaks the frame of reference and creates a new equilibrium. Incremental change occurs through the established management structure and processes, while radical change results in different structures, or processes (Hodgson & Aiken, 1998). Change may fail due to what is often termed 'resistance to change' (Mabin, Forgeson, & Green, 2001).

According to Mabin *et al.* (2001) resistance to change is acknowledged as being a fundamental block to change, and a prime reason why change does not succeed or get implemented. Resistance to change is ubiquitous in nature. It can be defined as an expression of reservation which normally arises as a response or reaction to change (Block, 1989). In most cases, resistance is seen to be problematic – something to be managed and overcome. Some authors (e.g. Schermerhorn, 1989) have suggested strategies for 'dealing with' resistance, consistent with this view of resistance as being undesirable (Mabin *et al.,* 2001). There are many reasons why people inside organisations resist change; indeed, it is possible for the entire system which the organisation represents, to be resistant to change if the preparation for change has not been carried out in a manner that correctly prepares the organisation for it. According to Luke (1982), the following factors cause resistance to change: (1) resistance to something that interrupts comfortable routine; (2) reluctance to take time out to learn something new; (3) fear of doing one's job poorly because of new, technical demands; (4) competition to be among the first to own new devices, despite some trepidation to learn; (5) lack of clear understanding of the capabilities and uses of new equipment; (6) work disruption that leads to frustrations; and (7) over-emphasis on the notion of 'improved productivity', a robot-society syndrome that leads to apprehension about the emphasis on statistics of improvements in quantity and quality of output.

In addition, Kanter (1985) indicates the factors that lead to resistance to change:

- Fear of the unknown
- Loss of control
- Loss of face
- Loss of competency
- Need for security
- Poor timing
- Force of habit
- Lack of support
- Lack of confidence
- Lingering resentment.

It is not difficult to address the human element, using thought-out plans, open communications techniques, and a reliable feedback/follow through programme to avoid risking costly investments in equipment and training (Luke, 1982). In addition, successful change management programmes need well-balanced teams, with complimentary skill sets – not only from a technical perspective, but also in the style and psychological makeup of the team members (Cauldwell, 2004).

Furthermore, According to Mabin *et al.* (2001), the theory of constraints (TOC) is a systems methodology dealing largely with change management. TOC provides tools and an overall framework to utilise resistance, breaking down resistance into layers, and ensuring the layers are addressed in sequence, thus harnessing its potential. Also it is well equipped to address leadership and change management issues: to reveal hidden assumptions and resolve conflict; to help identify new solutions to problems; and to plan and implement such changes. Change management can be handled within the TOC framework, and goes a long way to providing practical steps to achieving the prerequisites for successful change. Finally, change management takes time since it involves new roles, relationships, ways of thinking, behaviours, and approaches to work (Rideout, 1991). Therefore, one of the basic rules of successful change management must be that it requires a beginning and an end. But this fundamental principle is often forgotten (Cauldwell, 2004).

Business process re-engineering in e-government adoption

Heeks (2001) shows the scope of e-government to include improving government processes by reducing costs and managing performance. Governments at all levels and across all branches have been urged to become leaner and smarter, providing better and faster services at lower cost. Such fundamental change, however, inevitably impacts the business processes governments work by. So far, though, business process reengineering has mostly been studied in the private sector.

E-government appears as a potent enabler when reinventing the way government is doing business. When government began using telephones as a new technology, the old processes and organisational formats did not immediately disappear. They were gradually and then increasingly rapidly and radically replaced by new formats and processes that greatly enhanced the immediacy of government action and reaction. Similar patterns, it appears, underlie the changes in the context of e-government. Government has been criticised for its slow adoption of new technologies and innovative practices (Mohan & Holstein, 1990). With respect to the high number of reengineering disasters in the private sector during the 90s, governments may have even acted quite wisely by sticking to the slow adoption scheme (Champy, 1995; Hammer, 1996).

Change processes cannot completely be controlled. Change is dynamic, unpredictable, and full of surprise. Organisational systems have a tendency to return to their original state, such that relatively long periods of time are necessary for the change to take a hold. The organisation's leaders have to master the challenge of developing and maintaining a shared vision of the process from the outset to its completion (Gunasekaran & Nath, 1997). If business processes change fundamentally, then those changes cannot be planned in the traditional and incremental fashion, because fundamental change entails more than just business process and workflow mapping. Social networks and informal organisations will be affected too. Change, hence, needs to be more loosely coupled and supposedly relies on coordination by feedback rather than formal planning (Zmud & Mitchell, 1999).

This directly applies to the context of electronic government, which requires both long-term view and flexible planning due to the iterative and disruptive nature of the change process. Some authors have shown that more radical and far-reaching BPR projects expose a higher failure rate than those less ambitious projects (Kallio *et al.*, 1999). Since the number of variables involved is greater, the complexity of the change project may rise to overwhelming levels in the more radical projects (Gunasekaran & Nath, 1997).

Electronic government may help converting government toward the orientations of 'customer' needs, enterprise, prevention, decentralisation, and markets as Osborne and Gaebler (1992) foresee them. Current working processes are redundant. Such redundancies are common in the paper-based information systems of developing countries. In implementing e-government, there is a risk of replicating the same into a transformed shape. The government needs to address the redundancy and overlap of responsibilities that exists in most of the services delivered to the public by government agencies.

Citizens communicate through the internet, telephone, etc in order to access government information and services instantly, 24 hours a day, seven days a week from home, work or any other location. Citizens are not concerned about which government agency provides the information and services. Government is expected to provide access to its information and services from a single integrated gateway (one-stop-shop). Reforming the work process involves changing the way an agency performs its daily tasks in an effort to increase its employees' productivity, reduce cost, and improve service delivery to consumers. The reforms include reduction of red tape and elimination of overlapping responsibilities. There are processes that need to be changed in government agencies in order to improve service delivery to the general public. Automation alone will not improve deficient work processes.

While, in principle, business processes could be streamlined without the use of ICT. The designs of both business rules and information systems are and should be carefully integrated (Giaglis, 1999), especially considering the rare match of life cycles of information systems and those of business-relevant information (van Wingen *et al.*, 1999). Mismatches between business strategy and ICT strategy typically result in organisational frictions (Beaumaster, 2002). When using the general BPR literature within an e-government context the following insights emerge:

- For aligning business process re-engineering projects with organisational strategies and objectives, a holistic view of the organisation, systems, processes, and stakeholders seems to be required, which in turn facilitates a long-term perspective paired with flexible planning.
- Modest objectives and project scope, when defined within the long-term perspective, seem to yield better prospects for success than aggressive objectives and wide scope.
- It appears that e-government and general ICT strategies need to be tightly coupled for electronic government adoption.

A challenge in major change projects has reportedly been the organisation's inertia and the stakeholders' active and passive resistance to change. Business process reengineering appears as highly problematic under circumstances of organisational crisis (Mallalieu, Harvey & Hardy, 1999), which is characterised by loss of control over important variables. A change project may unduly and untimely add to the number of variables out of control. Decision makers, on the other hand, may question the necessity of burdensome, proactive change, if the business is humming.

In addressing those concerns, mainly effectiveness- and efficiency-oriented arguments of: (1) expected or desired cost savings, (2) speedups of the processes, and (3) customer service improvements have been used for making the case for business process reengineering (Ranganathan & Dhaliwal, 2001). Although projected cost savings remain an attractive and appealing line of argument presented to decision-makers when justifying change projects, including technology-based projects, due to unanticipated or hidden costs those projections rarely materialise. Tarn (1998) points out, that ICT investments, although they may indirectly add to shareholder returns, do not necessarily produce above-normal profits. Hitt (1999) finds evidence for the reduction of external coordination costs through ICT. By and large, the cost savings argument for justifying BPR and related ICT investments increasingly appears as a supplemental argument.

Cost savings, however, may eventually result from speeding up processes through streamlining and via improving customer service, although such savings cannot be projected in advance with any credible accuracy nor can they reliably be measured from hindsight. Decisions in favour of major change projects therefore are of relatively high risk, made on the basis of incomplete information and under high outcome uncertainty. Long and unnecessary transactions need to be cut down in processes to allow users to quickly access documents and print them or fill them out online. Transactions need to be simplified and a decision-making process must be determined. By simplifying transactions, citizens will be more likely to access sites.

Soft Q-factors in e-government implementation

Leadership in e-government adoption

Leadership is one of the critical factors upon which the e-government success hinges. A critical pre-condition in e-government adoption is a strong leadership with vision (Heeks, 2002). A transformational leadership can precipitate the augmentation of other resources required to formulate, implement and advance e-government set-up. Visionary, firm and persuasive leadership is one of the critical factors for e-government implementation. Empirical examples of the governance system and how to articulate vision and motivate all stakeholders to share that vision can be seen with reference to two cases:

First is Singapore, which has become a hallmark for research and practice. Singapore provides great a variety of dynamically integrated public services online. By the end of 2001, Singapore managed to get 92% of all public services deliverable online. The other example is of Hong Kong, which is still comparatively far behind Singapore. Hong Kong, another developed Asian economy, had 80% of its public services online by the end of 2002. Hong Kong joined the bandwagon later, even though its IT infrastructure is as advanced as Singapore's, and its government as highly computerised. Singapore's success can be attributed to the commitment and persistence of its government leadership to the strategies that it has adopted (Ke & Wei, 2004).

Following these premises, it is asserted that leaders should focus on collective issues rather than pursuing their personal agendas and developing the vision and defining the mission for their organisations (Drucker, 1990). Oakland (1993) emphasises the five requirements about which effective leadership should be clear and firm:

- Beliefs and objectives in the form of a mission statement.
- Effective strategies and supporting plans.
- Critical success factors and critical processes.
- An appropriate management structure.
- Employee participation through empowerment, and the EPDCA (evaluate, plan, do, check, amend) helix.

Armstrong (1990: 165) suggests that leadership happens when there is an objective to be achieved, or a task to be carried out, and when more than one person is needed to do it. All managers are by definition leaders in that they can only do what they have to do with the support of their team, who must be inspired or persuaded to follow them. Leadership is therefore about encouraging and inspiring individuals and teams to give their best to achieve a desired result. Leadership is required because someone has to point the way and 'ensure that everyone concerned gets there'; a leader's aim is to get people to do what he wants by obtaining willing cooperation, not grudging submission.

The leadership is responsible for developing a vision. Furthermore, the vision should be communicated across government and to the public (in case of the e-government) and ensuring that people understand the vision. E-government adoption needs a leader who puts e-government onto the agenda, who sets e-government within a broader reform agenda, and who makes it happen (Heeks, 2002).

Top management support in e-government adoption

In the UK e-government initiatives are initiated under the supervision of the office of a special envoy, which retains a cabinet position in the British government. Membership of the cabinet position ensures appropriate political support and the ability to enforce the adoption of e-government initiatives throughout the United Kingdom. In the US, the e-government act, which was introduced by the Senate in May 2001 and signed by president Bush into law in 2002, established a Chief Information Officer (CIO) position in the Office of Management and Budget to provide leadership, vision and coordination between agencies at the federal level. The e-government initiative was one of the five management reforms on President Bush's management agenda. In Singapore the government earmarked $932 million for the years 2000 to 2003 to ensure that the programme objectives of the E-Government Action Plan became a reality.

Top management needs to publicly and explicitly identify the project as a top priority (Wee, 2000). Senior management must be committed with its own involvement and willingness to allocate valuable resources to the implementation effort (Holland *et al.*, 1999). This involves providing the needed people for the implementation and providing an appropriate amount of time to get the job done (Roberts and Barrar, 1992).

Managers should legitimise new goals and objectives. A shared vision of the organisation and the role of the new system and structures should be communicated to employees. New organisational structures, roles and responsibilities should be established and approved. Policies should be set by top management to establish new systems in the company. In times of conflict, managers should mediate between parties (Roberts and Barrar, 1992).

The e-government initiatives need the organisation's top management support. Also, middle management can play a major role in the adoption of e-government initiatives. Finally, the development of e-government requires a political decision from top management. Governments need to set up objectives in realising their e-government.

Awareness in e-government adoption

The rapid growth of electronic government technologies and practices has created a tremendous need for awareness creation for organisations which seem to lack the necessary information about technology (Papazafeiropoulou, Pouloudi and Doukidis, 2002). Awareness is communicating e-government initiatives to the appropriate stakeholders and providing means for individuals to realise e-government projected benefits.

One part of awareness is recognising the importance of improving the way the government provide services to its citizens and businesses and acknowledging that e-government is the appropriate approach for this reform. Another is knowing of the importance of implementing e-government and believing that their agencies would realise the benefits of e-government initiatives. The benefits include reducing the time and cost of providing services to the general public; empowering employees, reducing bureaucracy and increasing the efficiency and effectiveness of civil agencies.

It is important to increase people's awareness regarding the merits of e-government to ensure its acceptability during the adoption process. This can be done through educating the civil agencies' work force and providing technical training to increase people's familiarity of computer operation and internet usage. According to Kotter (1996), individuals are willing to accept change (e.g. e-government initiatives) if the potential benefits are outlined and they believe that the transformation is possible.

By indicating the benefits of e-government and defining the relative advantage that can be gained from adopting e-government, it is possible to solve several problems, such as resistance to change, and it should be in the awareness programme. Relative advantage encompasses several different types of benefits such as economic gains and social prestige as well as the different types of costs or risks associated with the adoption of an innovation (Kwon and Zmud, 1987; Rogers, 1995). According to Tornatzky and Klein (1982) relative advantage is to be an important factor in determining the adoption of new innovations.

In general, the perceived relative advantage of an innovation is positively related to its rate of adoption (Rogers, 1983). Likewise, as e-government services allow citizens to access from any location, at any time of the day, it provides tremendous advantage and convenience to users. However, the reasons for a big lack of awareness seem to be two-fold: the variety of existing media creates a division and uncertainty of which media to use for a specific situation; and there can be problems with the physical location (Tollmar, Sandor and Schomer, 1996).

Furthermore, e-government budgets must include funds to raise awareness and publicise projects through various media channels (e.g. newspapers, radio, posters). Without awareness, the target audience may not learn about the project or use it; and without a large number of people benefiting from the project, the benefits will not be sufficient to justify the costs (PCIP, 2002).

Digital divide in e-government adoption

Governments should take into account the digital divide because research indicates that the wealthy are more likely to take part in internet transactions with their governments. Governments should place kiosks in public places in order to provide access to their online services for citizens who do not have internet access (Reddick, 2004). The potential digital divide is clearly a concern, and yet it applies to many types of public infrastructure, be it roads, airports, or schools.

In fact, information and communication technologies (ICT) may offer more hope in this respect than other infrastructures, as technology and communication costs are continuously dropping, and energy for computers can be provided through small power generators or solar cells. As such, a local village may not have roads, a school house, or telephone landlines, but with a satellite dish and a telecenter, it may still be connected to the world (Wagner, Cheung, Lee and Ip, 2003).

Some initiatives have focused on increasing ownership as a solution to the digital divide. For example, governments purchasing home PCs for poor families. Other governments have used tax breaks or subsidies as ways to try to increase the numbers of those who actually own IT systems, or IT may be placed in a variety of locations such as: public spaces (common areas within shopping malls); semi-public spaces (libraries or sport facilities); and dedicated spaces (community telecentres housing a room full of internet-linked PCs. However, such placement of IT only addresses technology barriers, not skills barriers (Heeks, 2000).

Internet users account for only 6% of the world's population and out of that, 85% are in developed countries where 90% of all internet hosts are located. This is the essence of the global digital divide that needs to be transformed into a global digital opportunity. In addition, in a developing country, the gap between educated and under-educated people can be large. The educated population will already have good opportunities to use ICT. This 'digital divide' between those that already have access and those that do not gain access for a long time may result in long-lasting and widening economic gaps between the ICT haves and have-nots.

Blumenfeld and Thickett (2003) add that in addition to the existence of a technological gap, the digital divide may exacerbate socio-economic divisions or gaps within society. As such, the digital divide can be seen in terms of race and gender, as well as access to training and education. As a result, the provision of e-government services would be biased, favouring educated, urban residents (Wagner *et al.*, 2003). Because of those costs, there is a very uneven profile of those who own and use information technology; the rich not the poor; the graduate not the school leaver; the ethnic majority not the ethnic minority; the urban not the rural citizen; the young not the old; men not women (Heeks, 2000).

The benefits that new ICT brings can only be reaped if the excluded population has access to ICT and the internet. As discussed above this is a key problem: many have no access to a computer, or lack the skills to use one. To a large extent, the digital divide reflects gaps already present in society between the rich and the poor. In other words, 'information poverty' is closely associated with other forms of poverty (Norris, 2001). In general, this perimeter requires deliberate attention for any countries taking e-government initiatives. Be the initiatives physical or social, institutional or system based, the success of e-government squarely relies on the users. If the users are unwilling to or unable to access the e-government technologies, there is little point in setting up any kind of network system. Therefore, a system level approach may ultimately enhance the positive impact of and prevent the adverse aspects related to other issues discussed above. Concisely said, the policy approach hinges upon technological, organisational and institutional reforms and developments.

According to Cahill and Cornish (2003) an essential part of bridging the gap between the information rich and information poor is ensuring that no-one is denied access to these services because of a disability, or because equipment that exists in order to broach such difficulties is not available at their point of access to ICT services. This is especially important in public libraries, which are open to all members of the community.

Citizen relationship management (CzRM) factor

Customer relationship management (CRM) is defined by Jon Anton (2000) as:

> *The seamless accessibility by internal and external customers to their mission-critical company information by the integration of a company's telephone system, web-site and e-mail touch points resulting in satisfying customer self service for initial product purchases, followed by targeted intelligent up-sells and cross sells, and finally the creation of customer loyalty, value and profitability.*

Furthermore, Bose (2004) defines CRM as an integration of technologies and business processes used to satisfy the needs of a customer during any given interaction. More specifically, CRM involves acquisition, analysis and use of knowledge about customers in order to sell more goods or services and to do it more efficiently. Bose also defines CRM in IT terms, as an enterprise-wide integration of technologies working together such as data warehouse, website, intranet/extranet, phone support system, accounting, sales, marketing and production. These definitions are centred on three basic concepts:

- Technology centric
- Customer lifecycle centric
- Strategy centric.

Seeing citizens parallel to the customers, further implications emerge. In e-government, there is citizen relationship management (CzRM) which is related to customer relationship management, and focuses specifically on how governmental bodies relate to their constituents (Xavier, 2002; Jha & Bokad, 2003). Governmental agencies, in their arrangement find that citizens expect the same level of service given at the civilian business level.

Unlike a private organisation, one of the government's missions is to make the services available to all citizens. To meet this goal, e-government systems are required to provide equal accessibility to all citizens in an easy-to-use way. Putting all government services on the web is a major step toward this end, which provides around-the-clock access to the government services in any location via the internet. Usually the portal provides grouping of government services by 'life events': few people visit government sites for information surfing and citizens usually use e-government for a purpose; the 'life events' grouping provides a means for a citizen to locate the required service quickly. Building such a portal should be much easier if all the required legacy functions have been exposed as web services. The term 'joined-up government' is sometimes used to describe a holistic government structure in which the citizens requiring government services do not need to care about which department does what.

CzRM in e-government adoption

All government agencies are required to follow the same guiding principle: that every service that can be delivered electronically shall be electronically available and that all services shall be designed on a 'customer-centric' and not an 'agency-centric' basis. Along these aspects, the literature comments on gaining more services users and retaining them. Drawing on the business oriented perspectives, this, however, depends on how customers are treated in order to win their loyalty, commitment and reuse of the services (Kannabiran & Xavier & Anantharaaj, 2004).

According to Piercy and Lane (2003), CRM is currently revolutionising the company customer relationship. CRM introduces the concept of managing customer relationships across the different points of customer contact and is widely being adopted by local authorities as an integral part of e-government implementation. CRM is often implemented successfully by installing and utilising CRM technology and by developing an effective customer relationship strategy (Bradshaw and Brash, 2001).

According to an article in Europe Intelligence Wire (2003), the UK government is spending 4.25m on a national advice service to help local authorities implement their CRM systems. Another example is Singapore. The E-citizen, Singapore's e-government portal, is 'the most developed example of integrated service delivery in the world'. It generates approximately $14.5 million in savings for the Singapore government annually and was rated second in Accenture's 2001 e-government survey. This implies that customer relationship management (CRM) initiatives are more important than what the government can offer. In other words, it requires a business philosophy that aligns a government activity with customer's needs. The CRM is an enterprise approach to understanding and influencing customer behaviour through meaningful communications in order to improve customer acquisition, customer loyalty, and customer profitability (Evans and Laskin, 1994). Heeks (2001a) shows the scope of e-government to include connecting citizens to government by consulting with citizens, supporting accountability, listening to citizens, and improving public services.

Hence, e-government activities today are aimed at achieving efficiency in creating and delivering services to citizens. However, citizens need to be differentiated from business customers; Nowlan views the citizen as a consumer of public goods and services

(Nowlan, 2001). Reduction in cost of delivery, improved ease of delivery and many other internal benefits, ultimately with less commitment or obligation to citizens, are the main aims. Although, applications are more inward looking in terms of benefits to government and do not consider the service expectations of citizens.

This inward looking phase supports the argument that some governments are setting up websites to provide basic information to their citizens. Increasing technological sophistication, coupled with demand for quality services has forced governments to get more citizen-centric. It is at this stage that governments typically use multi channels to deliver their services and develop networking capabilities with different departments to provide seamless services to their citizens. In this regard, the government needs to be evaluated based on the governance perspectives – that is, citizens should be treated as customers of business organisations, where serving citizens is the sole purpose of governments.

The CzRM equally serves the public administration. For instance, development in citizen's understanding and needs opens new venues for e-government. In the conventional manner, governments view citizens as fragmented individuals, scattered across different departmental databases. Accordingly, employees can't access the information in a timely and usable form. In the wake of e-government, such issues can be easily tackled. Providing a single source to answer all queries in one visit or one call requires new computer applications and integration between existing applications and legacy systems. From the users' dimension, citizens' interaction with a one-stop-shop like scenario and engagement in online transactions enables respective governments to understand their customers' behaviour.

This argument does not support the idea that through CzRM, public administrations have a golden opportunity to access and manipulate data to gain an accurate picture of citizen behaviour and requirements. CzRM is about making better use of the considerable amounts of information that government already collects (Smith, 2003). It is a method for public authorities to use to reorient their service operations around citizens rather than around self-serving administrative processes. Thus in this phase, most governments start off with automation for cost minimisation, effective governance and efficient administration. And typically the government website is used to provide basic information. Nevertheless, the learned and connected citizens, who indulge into e-government, are likely to propel the demand for quality services for customer-oriented deliveries.

As highlighted in reference to the case of Singapore, the core of the e-government paradigm is the transformation of citizen relationships and the processes and mediums that support them. An effective CzRM strategy raises citizens above traditional departmental and bureaucratic lines and makes them the centre of service activities. Hence CzRM is a cross-functional, multi-application undertaking based on the integration of specific public sector components, such as electronic processing of records with full-text search, document imaging and archive interfaces, and workflow. Rather than employing compartmentalised, programme-driven budgeting and customer service methods, a successful CzRM strategy transforms disparate government budgets and processes into an integrated, citizen-centric service culture, one that aims to maximise lifetime relationship value.

Furthermore, customer relationship management (CRM) aims at managing the interactions between an organisation and its existing and potential customers as a relationship, instead of individual unrelated transactions. CRM software enables the organisation and its employees to 'know' its customers via their profile (pattern of past transactions), and to provide them with the most fitting services. Leading CRM systems embed analytical solutions (Barlas, 2003; Maoz *et al.,* 2001), that facilitate performance tracking of customer-facing processes across the enterprise. Therefore, CRM software can help e-government better recognise citizen demands, create citizen profiles, and in turn serve citizens accordingly, for example, Singapore and the e-Citizen services (Wagner, Cheung, Lee and Ip, 2003).

Selecting the right CRM system requires some amount of work due to its board nature. The CRM product is typically 'wrapped' with a layer of integration tools. These tools provide a powerful, high performance framework for the integration of the CRM and bespoke applications to both internal systems. This would involve data warehousing, wireless applications, supply change management and enterprise resource planning (Chou *et al.,* 2002).

There is a general acknowledgement that the public sector can be far more complex than many private sector organisations. This is demonstrated by Arnott (2002) who says, 'Most CRM systems are aimed at a limited range of facilities because private companies have a fairly narrow portfolio, but Local Authorities have a wide portfolio of services from street sweeping to paying university grants'. Norris and Pang (2002) reveal a number of issues and challenges related to applying CRM in government that need to be addressed:

- Citizen privacy concerns.
- The gap between technology have and have-nots.
- Integration of systems: different government organisations need to establish similar approaches.
- Network bandwidth and reliability.
- Equality of service.

Integrating hard and soft Q-factors for e-government implementation

The hard and soft Q-factors pertinent to e-government policy formulation, implementation and execution were reviewed in the sections above. The hard factors for e-government initiatives include, amongst others, focusing on a clear vision, change management, training, clear strategy, reward systems, business process re-engineering, technical skills and knowledge, funding, and legal policies. The soft Q-factors for e-government adoption are support from top management, awareness, reduction of the digital divide, proactive and strong leadership and citizen relationships management (CzRM). In terms of CzRM, it is possible to emulate the successful strategies and software of the private sector which can be transposed upon e-government.

The following model depicts how the enabler factors for e-government adoption can be put to work together in harmony (Figure 5.3).

Figure 5.3 Enabler factors for e-government adoption model

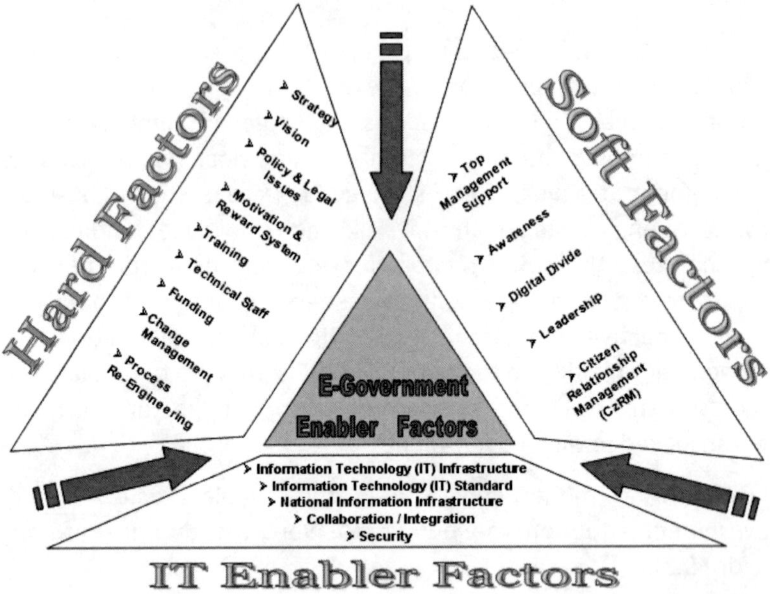

References

Accenture (2001) E-Government Leadership Rhetoric vs. Reality Closing the Gap, *Accenture Consulting*, 1-61.

Agren, P. (2001) Is Online Democracy In The EU For Professionals Only? *Communications of the ACM*, 44, 1, 36-38.

Akbulut, A. (2002) An Investigation of the Factors that Influence Electronic Information Sharing between State and Local Agencies, *Eighth Americas Conference on Information Systems,* 2454-2460.

Akomode, J., Taleb-Bendiab, A., Evangelidis, A. and Taylor, M. (2002) UML Approach to Risk Assessment Modelling for eGovernment, *Proceedings of the Second European Conference on e-Government, ECEG 2002*, 187-214, St. Catherine's College, Oxford, England.

Allen, R (1995) On a clear day you can have a vision: a visioning model for everyone, *Leadership and Organization Development Journal*, Emerald Group Publishing Limited, 16, 4, 39-44.

Anton, J. (2000) The past, present and future of customer access centres, *International Journal of Service Industry Management*, 11, 2, 120-130.

Armstrong, M. (1990) *How to Be an Even Better Manager*, Kogan Page, London.

Arnott, D.C. and Bridgewater, S. (2002) Internet, interaction and implications for marketing. *Marketing Intelligence and Planning, 20*, 2, 86-95.

Audit Office of New South Wales (2001) *E-ready, e-steady, e-government: e-government readiness assessment guide for government agencies.*

Balkin, D. and Gomez-Mejia, L. (1987) Toward a contingency theory of compensation strategy, *Strategic Management Journal*, 8, 169-182.

Barlas, D. (2003) Gartner's CRM Rankings, available at http://www.line56.com!articles/default.asp? Article ID=4510.

Beaumaster, S. (2002) Local government IT implementation issues: A challenge for public administration, paper presented at *The Proceedings on the 35th Hawaii International Conference on System Sciences; Hawaii*, 175-181.

Block, P. (1989) Flawless consulting, In R. McLennan, (ed.) *Managing Organisational Change*, Prentice-Hall, Englewood Cliffs, N.J.

Blumenfeld, S. and Thickett, G (2003) Surfing the Knowledge Wave: The Impact of Information and Communication Technology (ICT) on Decent Work in New Zealand, *New Zealand Journal of Industrial Relations*, 28, 1.

Bose, R. (2004) Information Technologies for Education & Training in E-Government, *International Conference on Information Technology: Coding and Computing,* IEEE, 49-61.

Bradshaw, D. and Brash, C. (2001) Managing customer relationships in the e-business world: how to personalise computer relationships for increased profitability, *International Journal of Retail & Distribution Management,* 29, 12, 520-530.

Budaus, D. (1998) Von der burokratischen Steuerung zum New Public Management - Eine Einfuhrung, In D. Budaus et al., (eds.) *Managementforschitng*, De Gruyter, Berlin; New York.

Bullen, C. and Bennett, J. (1990) Learning from User Experience with Groupware, In *Proceedings of the CSCW'90,* ACM Press, Los Angeles, C.A., 17-25.

Burn, J. and Robins, G. (2003) Moving towards e-government: a case study of organisational change processes, *E-government Logistics Information Management*, 16, 25-35.

Burnes, B. (1996) *Managing Change: A Strategic Approach to Organisational Dynamics,* Pitman.

Cahill, K. and Cornish, S. (2003) Assistive technology for users in the Royal Borough of Kensington and Chelsea public libraries in the UK, *Program: electronic library and information systems*, 37, 3, 190-193.

Cauldwell, B. (2004) All Change, Manufacturing Engineer, 83, 2, 16-17.

Cavazos, E. (1994) *The Legal Risks of Setting Up Shop In Cyberspace*, available at http://cism.bus.utexas.edu/ravi/ed_paper.html.

Champy, J. (1995) *Reengineering management: The mandate for new leadership,* (1st) Harper Business, New York.

Chou, D., Xu, Y., Yen, D. and Lin, B. (2002) Adopting customer relationship management technology, *Industrial Management & Data Systems*, 102, 8, 442-452.

Comptroller and Auditor General (2002) Better Public Services through e-government, *HC*, 704, 1, 1-10.

Csetenyi, A. (2000) Electronic Government: Perspectives from E-commerce, *Proceedings of the 11th International Conference on Database and Expert Systems Applications,* London.

Damanpour, F. (1991) Organizational Innovation: A Meta-Analysis of Effects of Determinants and Moderators, *Academy of Management Journal,* 34, 3, 555-590.

Das, A., Soh, C. and Lee, P. (1999) A Model of Customer Satisfaction with information technology Service Providers: An Empirical Study, *ACM*, 190-193.

Dawes, S. (1996) Interagency Information Sharing: Expected Benefits, Manageable Risks, *Journal of Policy Analysis and Management,* 15, 3, 377-394.

Dodd W. and Fortune, L. (1995) An electronic patient record project in the United Kingdom: can it succeed? In R. A. Greenes, H. E. Peterson and D. L. Protti, *Medinfo 95*, Healthcare Computing and Communications Canada, Edmonton, 301-304.

Dow, N., Teicher, J. and Hughes, O. (2002) E-government: a new route to public sector quality, *Managing Service Quality*, 12, 384-393.

Drucker, P. (1990) *Managing the Non-profit Organization*, Butterworth-Heinemann Ltd, Oxford, UK.

Europe Intelligence Wire (2003) *Government aims to help Local Authorities install CRM.*

Evans, J. and Laskin, R. (1994) The relationship marketing process: a conceptualization and application, *Industrial Marketing Management*, 23, 5, 439-452.

Folstad, A., Jorgensen, H. and Krogstie, J. (2004) User Involvement in e-Government Development Projects, *ACM*, 217-224.

Galbraith, J. (1973) *Designing Complete Organizations*, Addison-Wesley, Reading, MA.

Gant, J. P. and Gant, D. B. (2002) Web portal functionality and State government E-service, paper presented at *The Proceedings on the 35th Hawaiian International Conference on System Sciences; Hawaii.*

Gartner Group (2000) *Gartner's Four Phases of E-Government Model*, available at http://www.gartner.com.

Giaglis, G. (1999) Integrated design and evaluation of business processes and information systems, *Communications of AIS*, 2, 1, 1-33.

Gibson, C. and Nolan, R. (1974) Managing the four stages of EDP growth, *Harvard Business Review*, 52, 1, 76-88.

Gomez-Mejia, L. and Balkin, D. (1992) *Compensation, Organizational Strategy, and Firm Performance*, Southwestern Publishing Company, College Division, Cincinnati, OH.

Gouscos, D., Mentzas, G. and Georgiadis, P. (2001) Planning and Implementing e-Government Service Delivery: Achievements and Learnings from On-line Taxation in Greece, the Workshop on e-Government in the context of the *8th Panhellenic Conference on Informatics*, Nicosia, Cyprus.

Government Online Project Service Center (2000) *Government Online Project White Paper*, Beijing.

Grimes, D. (1983) Human Factors Training and Awareness, *ACM*, 73-78.

Gunasekaran, A. and Nath, B. (1997) The role of information technology in business process reengineering, *International Journal of Production Economics*, 50, 91-104.

Hagen, M. and Kubicek, H. (2000) *One-Stop-Government in Europe: Results from 11 National Surveys*, University of Bremen, Bremen, Germany.

Hambrick, D. and Snow, C. (1989) Strategic reward systems, In C. C. Snow, (ed.) *Strategy, Organizational Design and Human Resource Management*, JAI Press, Greenwich, CT, 929-964.

Hammer, M. (1996) Beyond reengineering: How the process-centered organization is changing our work and our lives, (1st) Harper Business, New York.

Hayes, M. and Jamrozik, M. (2001) Internet distance learning: The problems, the pitfalls, and the future, *Journal of VLSI Signal Processing Systems for Signal, Image, and Video Technology*, 29, 63-69.

Heeks, R. (2001a) Understanding e-Governance for Development, *I-Government working paper series*, Institute for Development Policy and Management, University of Manchester, Manchester, UK, 1-25.

Heeks, R. (2001b) Building e-Governance for Development: A Framework for National and Donor Action, *I-Government working paper series*, Institute for Development Policy and Management, University of Manchester, UK, 1-31.

Heeks, R. (2002) Government in Africa: Promise and Practice, *I-Government working paper series*, Institute for Development Policy and Management, University of Manchester, Manchester, UK, 1-26.

Hitchcock, P. (1996) The practical use of vision in small teams, *Health Manpower Management,* Emerald Group Publishing Limited, 22, 2, 28-31.

Hitt, A. (1999) Information technology and firm boundaries: Evidence from panel data, *Information Systems Research*, 10, 2, 134-149.

Hodgson, L. & Aiken, P. (1998) *Organizational Change Enabled By The Mandated Implementation Of New Information Systems Technology: A Modified Technology Acceptance Model*, Boston, MA, USA, 205-213.

Holland, P., Light, B. and Gibson, N. (1999) A critical success factors model for enterprise resource planning implementation, *Proceedings of the 7th European Conference on Information Systems*, 1, 273-287.

Howard, M. (2001) E-Government Across the Globe: How Will "e" Change government? *Government Finance Review*, 6-9.

Huang, C. and Chao, M. (2001) Managing WWW in public administration: uses and misuses, *Government Information Quarterly*, 18, 357-373.

Hutchinson, W. and Stoney, M. (2001) The Implications of the United Kingdom's Terrorism Act on Cyberspace, *1st European Conference on E-Government (ECEG 2001)*, Trinity College, Dublin, Ireland.

ICMA (2002) Electronic Government, *International City/County Management Association*, Washington, D.C

ISEC (2001) *Government IT Projects, Parliamentary*, available at http://europa.eu.int/information_society/programmes/egov_rd/about_us/text_en.htm.

Jha, B. and Bokad, P (2003) Managing Multiplicity of Citizens' identity - A Taluka level case study, *International conference on e-governance*, 1, 5, 24-31.

Joia, L. (2002) *Electronic government in search of a conceptualization*, available at http://www.ebape.fgv.br/e_government/asp/dsp_oquee.asp

Jupp, V. (2001) Government portals - the next generation of government online, *In the Proceedings of the European Conference on E-Government,* 217-223.

Jury, G. (1997), "Managing technology: the environment in which technology is managed", *IEEE Engineering Management Journal*, Vol. 7, No. 1, pp. 27-32

Kallio, J., Saarinen, T., Salo, S., Tinnila, M. and Vepsalainen, A. J. (1999) Drivers and tracers of business process changes, *Journal of Strategic Information Systems*, 8, 125-142.

Kannabiran, G., Xavier, M. and Anantharaaj, A. (2004) Enabling e-Government through citizen relation management-concept model and application, *Journal of Social Research*, 4, 2, 1-18.

Kanter, R. (1985) Managing the human side of change, *Management Review*, 74, 52-56.

Karsten, H., Lyytinen, K., Heilala, V. and Tynys, J. (1997) The Impact of User Support in Successful Groupware Implementation: Case Tasman to Support Paper Machinery Delivery, *ECIS'97, The 5th European Conference on Information System,* Cork, Ireland.

Ke, W. and Wei, K. (2004) Successful E-Government in Singapore: How did Singapore manage to get most of its public services deliverable online? *Communications of the ACM*, 47, 95-99.

Keselica, M. (1994) The 'People' Part of Groupware, *Online*, 18, 2, 104.

Kilmann, R. (1989) *Managing Beyond the Quick Fix*, Jossey-Bass, San Francisco, C.A.

Klee-Kurse, G. (2000) One-Stop-Government in Finland, In M. Hagen, and H. Kubicek, (eds.) *One Stop-Government in Europe: Results from 11 National Surveys*, University of Bremen, Bremen, Germany.

Kotter, J. (1996) *Leading Change*, Harvard Business School, Boston.

Kwon, T. and Zmud, R. (1987) Unifying the Fragmented Models of Information Systems Implementation, In R. J. Boland, Jr. and R. A. Hirschheim (eds.) *Critical Issues in Information Systems Research,* John Wiley and Sons Ltd, Chichester, Chapter 10.

Lawler, E. (1986a) *High Involvement Management*, Jossey-Bass, San Francisco, C.A.

Lawler, E. (1986b) Reward systems and strategy, In J. Gardner, R. Rochlin, and H. Sweeney, (eds.) *Strategic Planning Handbook*, Wiley, New York, N.Y.

Lenk, K. and Traunmuller, R. (2002) Preface to the focus theme on e-government, *Electronic Markets*, 12, 145-147.

Lerouge, C. and Webb, H. (2003) Managing Training in a Technology Context, *SIGMIS Conference,* Philadelphia, Pennsylvania, ACM.

Lieber, A. (2000) *E-Government initiatives meeting,* available at ostiwebmaster@osti.gov.

Lloyd, P. and Whitehead, P. (1996) *Transforming organisations through groupware,* Springer.

London, C. and Higgot, K. (1997) An employee reward and recognition process, *The TQM Magazine,* 9, 5, 328-335.

Luke, A. W. (1982) Office Automation and the Management of Change, *ACM*, 104-106.

Mabin, V., Forgeson, S. and Green, L. (2001) Harnessing resistance: using the theory of constraints to assist change management, *Journal of European Industrial Training,* MCB University Press, 168-191.

Mallalieu, G., Harvey, C. and Hardy, C. (1999) The wicked relationship between organizations and information technology (industry trend and event), *Journal of End User Computing*, 11, 4, 40-50.

Maoz, M., Close, W. and Herschel, G. (2001) *CRM Suites Magic Quadrant 2001: Only One Leader*, Gartner Research Note.

Mitretek Systems (2002) *E-Government*, Mitretek Systems Inc., available at http://www.mitretek.org/EGovernment.htm.

Mohan, L. and Holstein, W. (1990) EIS: It can work in the public sector, *MIS Quarterly*, 14, 4, 434-448.

Munson, K., Wolfe, E. and Raca, N. (2001) CRM Implications for Government, *White Paper Series*, People Soft, USA.

NACO (2000) *National Association of Counties: 2000 E-Government Survey*, National Association of Counties, Washington, D.C.

Nadler, D. and Tushman, M. (1988) *Strategic Organization Design, Scott*, Foresman, Glenview, IL.

Nolan, R. (1979) Managing the crisis in data processing, *Harvard Business Review*, 57, 2, 115-126.

Norris, D. (1999) Leading Edge Information Technologies and Their Adoption: Lessons from U.S. Cities, In G. D. Garosn (ed.) *Information Technology and Computer Applications in Public Administration: Issues and Trends*, Idea Group Publishing, Hershey, P.A.

Norris, D., Fletcher, P. and Holden, S (2001) Is Your Local Government Plugged In? *Highlights of the 2000 Electronic Government Survey*, ICMA, Washington, D.C.

Norris, R. and Pang, L. and (2002) Applying customer relationship management (CRM) to government, *The Journal of Government Financial Management*, 51, 1, 40-45.

Nowlan, S. (2001) *cCRM in the Public Sector*, Pricewaterhouse-Coopers, USA.

Oakland, J. S. (1993) *Total Quality Management*, Butterworth-Heinemann, Oxford.

Orlikowski, W., Yates, J., Okamura, K., and Fujimoto, M. (1995) Shaping Electronic Communication: The Metastructuring of Technology in the Context of Use, *Organization Science*, 6, 4, 423-444.

Osbourne, D. and Gaebler, T. (1992) *Reinventing Government: How the Entrepreneurial Spirit is Transforming the Public Sector*, Addison Wesley, Reading, MA.

Pacific Council on International Policy (2002) *Roadmap for E-Government in the Developing World*, 1-29.

Papantoniou, A., Hattab, E., Afrati, F., Kayafas, E. and Lournos, V. (2001) *Change Management, a Critical Success Factor for e-Government*, IEEE.

Papazafeiropoulou, A., Pouloudi, A. and Doukidis, G. (2002) A framework for best practices in electronic commerce awareness creation, *Business Process Management Journal*, 8, 3, 233-244.

Pardo, T. (2000) *Realizing the promise of digital government: It's more than building a Web site*, unpublished manuscript, Albany, N.Y.

Pattison, M. (1997) Legal Implications of Doing Business on the Internet, *Information Management and Computer Security*, 29-34.

Peters, T. and Waterman, R. (1982) *In Search of Excellence: Lessons from America's Best Run Companies,* Harper and Row, London.

Piercy, N. and Lane, N. (2003) Transformation of the Traditional Salesforce: Imperatives for Intelligence, Interface and Integration, *Journal of Marketing Management*, 6, 3, 563.

Ranganathan, C. and Dhaliwal, J. (2001) A survey of business process reengineering practice in Singapore, *Information and Management*, 39, 125-134.

Reddick, C. (2004a) A two-stage model of e-government growth: Theories and empirical evidence for U.S. cities, *Government Information Quarterly*, 21, 1, 51-64.

Reynolds, M. and Regio, M. (2001) E-Government as a Catalyst in the Information Age, Microsoft E-Government Initiatives, *E-Government 2001*, available at www.netcaucus.org/books/egov2001/.

Rideout, T.B. (1991) Changing Your Methods from the Inside, *IEEE*, 8, 99-111.

Roberts, H. and Barrar, P. (1992) MRPII implementation: key factors for success, *Computer Integrated Manufacturing Systems*, 5, 1, 31-38.

Rogers, E. (1983) *Diffusion of Innovations*, Free Press, New York.

Rogers, Y. (1994) Exploring Obstacles: Integrating CSCW in Evolving Organizations, *CSCW'94*, ACM, Chapel Hill, NC, New York, 67-77.

Rogers, E. (1995) *Diffusion of innovations* (4th) Free Press, New York.

Rothwell, W. and Kazanas, H. (1989) *Strategic Human Resource Development*, Prentice-Hall, Englewood Cliffs, N.J.

Saanen, Y., Sol, H. and Verbraeck, A. (1999) Snapshots of e-commerce's opportunities and threats, *Electronic Markets*, 9, 3, 181-189.

Sauer, C. (1999) Deciding the future for IS failures: not the choice you might think, In R. Galliers and W. L. Currie, *Rethinking Management Information Systems,* Oxford University Press, Oxford, UK, 279-309.

Schermerhorn, J. (1989) *Management for Productivity*, John Wiley & Sons, New York, N.Y.

Scholtes, P. (1995) Do reward and recognition systems work? *Quality Magazine,* December, 27-29.

Sharifi, H. and Zarei, B. (2004) An adaptive approach for implementing e-government in I.R. Iran, *Journal of Government Information*, 30, 5-6, 600-619.

Smith, E. (1996) A study of the penetration of competency-based training in Australia, *Research in Post-Compulsory Education*, 1, 2, 169-186.

Smith, A. (2003) *Opinion: Citizen Relationship Management*, available at http://www.crm-forum.com.

Stamoulis, D. and Georgiadis, P. (2000) Vision, Roles and Steps for Governments in Transition to the Digital Age, *Proceeding in the 11th international workshop on 4-8 September*, 143, 1, 41-50.

Tambouris (2001) European cities platform for online transaction services: The euro city Project, *In the Proceedings of the European Conference on E-Government.*

Tapscott, D. (1997) *The Digital Economy*, Makron Books, Sao Paulo.

Tarn, K. (1998) The impact of information technology investments on firm performance and evaluation: Evidence from newly industrialized economies, *Information Systems Research*, 9, 1, 85-98.

Tollmar, K., Sandor, O. and Schomer, A. (1996) Supporting Social Awareness @Work Design and Experience, *Proceeding of the 1996 ACM conference on Computer Supported Cooperative Work*, United State, Boston, 298-307.

Tornatzky, L. and Klein, K. (1982) Innovation Characteristics and Innovation Adoption-Implementation: A Meta-Analysis of Findings, *IEEE Transactions on Engineering Management*, 29, 1, 28-45.

Ulrich, D. and Lake, D. (1990) *Organizational Capability*, Wiley, New York, N.Y.

United Nations - ASPA (2002) *Benchmarking e-government: A global perspective: Assessing the progress of the UN member states*, United Nations American Society for Public Administration, New York.

Van Wingen, R., Hathorn, F. and Sprehe, J. (1999) Principles for information technology investment in US Federal Electronic Records Management, *Journal of Government Information*, 26, 1, 33-42.

Wagner, C., Cheung, K., Lee, F. and Ip, R. (2003) Enhancing E-government in Developing Countries: Managing Knowledge through Virtual Communities, *The Electronic Journal on Information Systems in Developing Countries (EJISDC)*, 14, 4, 1-20.

Waldman, D.A. (1994) Designing performance management systems for total quality implementation, *Journal of Organizational Change Management*, 7, 2, 31-44.

Warkentin, M., Gefen, D., Pavlou, P. and Rose, G. (2002) Encouraging Citizen Adoption of e-Government by Building Trust, *Electronic Markets*, 12, 3, 157-162.

Wassenaar, A. (2000) E-Governmental Value Chain Models - E-government from a business (modelling) perspective, *DEXA conference, Workshop on Electronic Government*, IEEE Press, Greenwich, England, pp. 289-293.

Watts, D. (2001) Managing Legal Risks Online: A Guide for Victorian Government Web Sites, *Multimedia Victoria*, State Government of Victoria, Australia.

Wee, S. (2000) Juggling toward ERP success: keep key success factors high, *ERP News*, available at http://www.erpnews.com/erpnews/erp904/02get.html.

West, D. (2001a) *Urban E-Government: An Assessment of City Government Websites*, Brown University.

West, D. (2001b) E-Government and the Transformation of Public Service Delivery, *paper presented at the American Political Science Association Annual Meeting*, San Francisco.

Xavier, M. (2002) CRM–Concepts, Tools and Applications, *South Asian Journal of Management*, 9, 2, 23-31.

Zmud, R. and Mitchell, V. (1999) The effects of coupling IT and work process strategies in redesign projects, *Organization Science*, 10, 4, 424-438.

Zweers, K. and Planque, K. (2001) Electronic Government, From the Organizational Based Perspective Towards the Client Oriented Approach, In J. E. J. Prins (ed.) *Designing E-Government*, Kluwer Law international, 92.

Chapter 6

Quality online: The real customer experience

Introduction

Over a short period of time, the internet has become fundamental to the global economy with more than a billion users worldwide (OECD 2008). It has turned into a major economic and social force that has almost substituted some of the traditional communication forms and has continued to affect a broad range of other important activities of people's everyday lives.

Online environments differ in multiple ways from conventional environments. Emerging research points out those online customers are more empowered and more engaged in online self-driven activities.

Today's business world is not only affected by the change in customers' roles as a result of technological facilities and advancements. The attention of today's business world is moving from offering products and services to building great customer experiences, reviving by that some early contributions from consumer behaviour literature on experiential motives of customers.

The internet economy

The internet has grown over the past three decades from an experimental research network to a network that underpins a range of new economic activities along with functions and infrastructures that support today's economy, from financial markets and energy to health services to transport (OECD, 2008).

The ever-changing technological advancements on the internet, the increasing growth in electronic commerce size and scope, as well as continuing growth in the popularity of blogs, online video and news websites is changing the ways in which people are entertained and informed, and is making internet access and use an increasingly ubiquitous convenience (Britton and McGonegal, 2008).

Jonathan Carson, President of Nielsen Online stated:

> *The Internet is no longer a niche technology, it is mass media and an utterly integral part of modern life. Almost no aspect of life remains untouched by online media. As our lives become more fractured and cluttered, it isn't surprising that consumers turn to the unrivalled convenience of the Internet when it comes to researching and buying products.* (Nielsen, 2007)

Although the growth of internet usage differs from one country to another, the most apparent and dominating note is that it is growing everywhere, despite being at varying speeds. Figure 6.1 outlines the growth of internet users in a selection of countries during 1999, 2002 and 2006.

Figure 6.1 Internet users per 100 population for a selection of countries

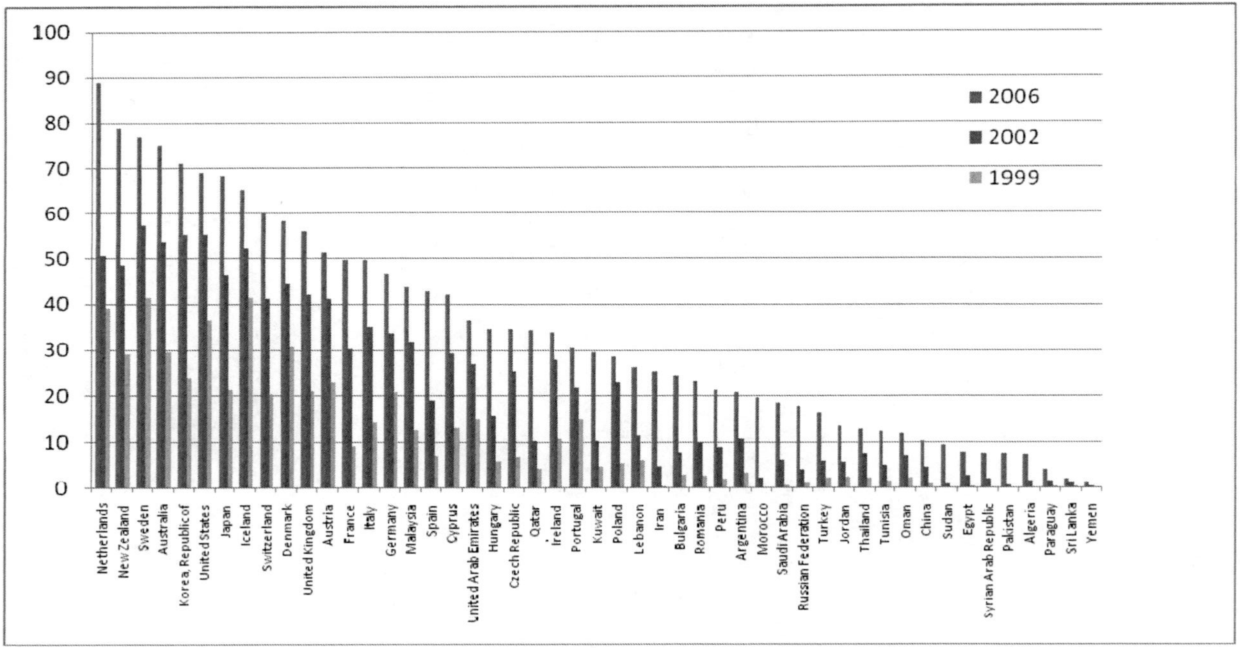

Source: UNData

Another indicator of internet growth and total usage of the internet comes from looking at the number of host computers connected to the internet (Britton and McGonegal, 2008). The number of hosts has shown a growth from 1.25 million hosts in Jan 2002 to round 5.5 million hosts in Jan 2008 (ISC, 2008).

The internet has brought substantial economic advantages to the world. Businesses have used the internet, not only as a new delivery channel to customers, but also as a means to introduce efficiency gains to business. Nestlé, the multinational food giant receives all of its orders from supermarkets over the internet for quicker and cheaper transactions. Similarly, UPS, the shipping company, used online networks in 2006 to optimise its delivery routes, and saved around 12 million litres of fuel. Healthcare systems are increasingly making use of the internet through remote patient monitoring and electronic record management to increase affordability, quality and efficiency (OECD, 2008).

The internet is also impacting upon public policy areas. At the public sector level for instance, e-government has become the prime tool for delivering and supporting government services and managing interactions with citizens and businesses (OECD, 2008).

At the customer level, the internet is permeating all economic and social domains. It has made consumers' and citizens' activities more efficient, faster, and cheaper, and has also extended social interaction possibilities in different ways. It has empowered consumers and citizens by allowing greater access to information, and turned them into active players who have the platform to create new content and interact in new ways (OECD, 2008).

The emergence of 'Web 2.0', which refers to websites that feature user-generated content, allows for activities such as blogging, podcasting, and tagging. A blog is an online diary or journal that is usually accompanied by pictures, links, and other content. A podcast is a recording of audio, available on the internet for downloading and typically released in a serial format like an audio version of a newspaper opinion column or daily news broadcast. Tagging is the labelling of blog posts so that the content can be categorised and organised with other related items (Britton and McGonegal, 2008).

In a report analysing the trends around blogs and bloggings, it was reported that as of mid 2007, there were over 70 million weblogs, 120,000 new weblogs being created worldwide each day and about 1.4 blogs created every second of every day (Sifry's Alerts, 2007).

Blogs are found to have a positive impact on the economy. According to a report published by (eMarketer, 2008a), blogs are becoming a preferred way to get information about products; 50% of surveyed blogs readers do trust blogs for purchase decisions.

Consequently, and as a result of electronic advancements, consumers are becoming more informed about product attributes, availability, and pricing, a 2007 survey reported that 92.5 percent of adults in the United States regularly or occasionally go online before they make a purchase (Mahoney, 2007).

Bringing more information to customers through the internet seems to pay back. Britton and McGonegal (2008) state that as the internet gradually is relying more on online product information and reviews, more people become regular internet shoppers for an expanding variety of goods.

Thirty-four percent of all adults in the USA use the internet for personal shopping, indicating an increase of 57.7% between autumn 2002 and autumn 2006; this is the third growing activity after use of emails and obtaining news (ClickZ, 2006). A recent report published by OECD revealed that over 25% of the adult population of all OECD countries shopped online in 2007 for goods or services (OECD, 2007). An average of 30% of the adult population use the internet for banking services, 25% use the internet for music purchases and downloading, 24% use the internet for online travel services, 20% for formalised educational activities, 30% for interacting with government authorities, while 43% of business firms used the internet to process government services.

Online shopping is constantly growing; the Global Online Survey on internet shopping habits published by Nielsen Online in Jan 2008 revealed some stunning statistics. The report revealed that globally, more than 50% of internet users had, in the previous month, made at least one purchase online, indicating a dramatic increase of online shoppers worldwide with the highest percentage of shopping online being found in South Korea (99% of adults with internet access), followed by the UK (97%), Germany (97%), Japan (97%) then the US (94%). The same study revealed an increase of 40% between 2005 and 2007, reaching a total of 875 million online shoppers (Nielsen, 2007) which is almost 20% of the total world population. According to a Forrester research project, online retail sales increased from $74 billion in 2002 to $172 billion in 2005 and are estimated to grow $329 billion in 2010. The same study also reported that internet users' ability to shop online has significantly improved from 16% to 32%, since March 2001 (Forrester, 2005).

Although the size and scope of online business is growing dramatically, there seem to be some particularly popular goods and services. Research by Nielsen Online reported that the most purchased items via the internet over a period of three months were books (41%) making an increase of 7% against a similar survey that took place a number of years earlier. Some of the biggest buyers came from developing countries, such as China, Brazil, Vietnam and Egypt which are considered fast-growing markets for online business. This was followed by clothing, accessories and shoes (36%) making an increase of 16%, followed by videos, DVDs and games (24%), airline tickets (24%) and then electronic equipment (23%) (Nielsen, 2007).

According to this report, travel was found by customers to be a category extremely suited to the internet due to the efficient accessibility of an extremely wide range of comparable information, with more than 70% of Indians, 60% of Irish and UAE internet users reserving their airline tickets online (Nielsen, 2007).

Online shopping is making big steps in some sectors. Fashion shoppers, for instance, are well accustomed to using the net for window-shopping prior to making in-store purchases, nevertheless, through the use of more recent technologies such as visualisation tools and personalising services or more liberal shipping and return policies, the market of online apparel shopping is growing (eMarketer, 2007). US online apparel sales, which include footwear and accessories, reached $18.3 billion in 2006 making an increase of 31% compared to 2005.

Growth of the online music industry witnessed dramatic increases too during the last few years. Purchases of online music increased by 56% between 2005 and 2006 with the sales of 500 million music files (The NPD Group, 2007)

Online sales are expected to grow over the coming years, According to a report by eMarketer, online sales will continue to rise steadily in the UK business-to-consumer market during the next few years: business-to-consumer e-commerce sales in the UK will total $116.6 billion with an increase of more than 28% over 2007, and it is expected to reach $169.6 billion by 2012. The percentage of online buyers from the total number of internet users reached 76.6% in 2007 (with 26.2 million buyers aged 14 and above) and is expected to steadily increase over the coming years to reach 78.8% in 2012 (eMarketer, 2008b).

Characteristics of online web-based business environments

Upon the advert of the World Wide Web, firms started to make their products and services available to customers online, opening up the traditional communication and delivery channels to online (electronic), web-based environments.

The interaction between customers and firms on the internet is mediated through the technology, where customers rely entirely on sight and sound, instead of sight, sound, texture and smell as in traditional experiences (Dawes and Rowley, 1998).

The World Wide Web (WWW) is defined by (Hoffman and Novak, 1996) as an 'Internet-based global information initiative' that was first proposed by Tim Berners-Lee at the European Laboratory for Particle Physics (CERN) in Geneva, Switzerland and was released to the internet community in 1991. According to the authors, it was the first example of a hypermedia computer-mediated environment that made it possible for people on the internet to search, retrieve, browse, and add information to the environment based on a body of software and group of protocols and conventions.

Dawes and Rowley (1998) argue that service delivery through the online environment is very different from service delivery through any other channel, be it physical stores, post and mail order, telephone, or 'on location'. They believe that the main differences between service delivery online and other channels, is the interactivity which allows consumers to add their information and allows organisations use this as a basis for customisation. Online environments are different as they integrate marketing with operation through exchange of information.

Demangeot and Broderick (2007) also argue that online environments are too different from offline environments; online environments are virtual, small and flat, comprise two sensory representations, while offline environments are real, large and comprise four sensory representations.

Online environments may lack some of the qualities that traditional stores may offer, such as the ability to interact with a salesperson face-to-face, touching or trying the merchandise, or perhaps some of the sensory attributes of a store such as the smell. Those attributes when important to customers, will cause consumers to choose conventional settings over online settings (Monsuwe and Dellaert *et al.*, 2004).

Nevertheless, the technological revolution of the internet and its advert as a new environment for customers has brought more opportunities for service consumption (Laukkanen, 2006).

Consumers have also responded to this expansion of environments, and have become more receptive to new electronic channels, becoming more sophisticated and demanding, especially for more service quality and more service availability (Coelho and Easingwood, 2003). Instead of dealing with whatever is pushed by organisations, the customers' role has changed from isolated to connected, from unaware to informed and from passive to active (Prahalad and Ramaswamy, 2004).

According to Monsuwe and Dellaert *et al.* (2004), online environments fulfil customer needs more than conventional environments, due to the following reasons:

- The ability to browse the whole product assortment with minimal efforts.
- Consumers have increased competency in making better shopping decisions due to their ability to obtain critical knowledge about firms, products and brands.
- Consumers can compare products' features, prices and availability in a more effective and efficient manner.
- Shopping can take place with a level of anonymity especially with sensitive products.
- Online shopping saves time to consumers and offers high level of convenience.

Therefore, the way businesses understand their online environment's dynamics is very important. It is believed that the ability of a business to create and maintain its online presence through a website that fulfils the needs of customers will become a distinguishing feature of it success (Huang, 2003).

In an attempt to understand the dynamics of online environments, some of its main characteristics are discussed below.

Convenience and web-mediated control

Technology as a mean of communication between customers and organisations is found to have better convenience and control over conventional environments.

Convenience is reported in the literature as one of the most important relative advantages for the internet (Wolfinbarger and Gilly, 2001; Mäenpää and Kanto *et al.*, 2006; To and Liao *et al.*, 2007). It refers to the degree of comfort and ease in customers' personal effort and in savings of time (Lawler and Joseph, 2006) . Availability of technology round the clock diminishes the time and distance constraints applied by traditional settings (Dawes and Rowley, 1998), provides 24/7 access, and allows customers to go online according to their own schedule and comfort (Mäenpää, Kanto *et al.*, 2006). It also eliminates frustrations resulting from fighting traffic or looking for a parking space, or waiting in long checkout lines, and offers a single 'stop' shopping that eliminates travel to and from stores (Childers *et al.*, 2001)

Linked to convenience is customer control (Dawes and Rowley, 1998) where customers are presented with defined choices in relation to the service experience they wish to engage in. Online customers can choose the channel they prefer to acquire a product, the product mode of delivery, product degree of customisation, and the extent they wish to be engaged in the design and delivery of the product, or even take control of service delivery to other customers.

The interaction between the customer and the organisation is largely led and controlled by the consumer (Wolfinbarger and Gilly, 2001). The web is believed to give consumers the power to become a central player who exerts increased control in the online environment, instead of being a passive recipient of marketing and selling activities (Hoffman and Novak, 1996).

Communication

Communication throughout the online environment is also different from that in conventional settings, it is interactive in a two-way direction and replaces face-to-face interactions.

Chang (2006) believes that one of the reasons why electronic technology makes the online shopping experience different from its counterpart in the traditional store setting, is that the human-human interaction has been replaced by human-computer interaction, where communication activities that usually occur in physical stores, are converted into text, pictures and video clips.

Choi *et al.* (2004) argue that the online environment is fundamentally different from conventional environments because of the possibility of bi-directional many-to-many communication in online shopping. The many-to-many interactive communication model allows customers to interact not only with business and other customers, but also with the tools and content themselves (Hoffman and Novak, 1996). The communication is a two-way communication where consumers to provide content, often outside the firm's control, to the environment in a radical departure from conventional media (Novak and Hoffman *et al.*, 2000).

Information services

Several scholars have argued that information is one of the most important benefits of the web and one of the distinguishing characteristics from traditional businesses. When compared to conventional shopping channels, information availability and content are considered key benefits of online shopping (Wolfinbarger and Gilly 2001; Zeithaml, Parasuraman *et al.*, 2002;

Prahalad and Ramaswamy, 2004; Kim, Ma *et al.*, 2006). Korgaonkar and Wolin (1999) argue that one of the reasons for the usage of internet is to gratify the need for information. Consumers can make more informed decisions due to availability of unprecedented information (Prahalad and Ramaswamy, 2004)

Online environments have been characterised by the high reach and richness of information (Evans and Wurster, 1999). Information reach refers to the number of products and people that are reachable quickly and cheaply in online environments despite geographical boundaries, and richness refers to the detail and depth of information that can be accumulated, offered, and exchanged between participants within the environment.

Consumers today have a global view, the variety of information they can access is almost unlimited, be it firms, products, performance, technologies, prices, or consumer actions and reactions (Prahalad and Ramaswamy, 2004).

Another form of information provided by the internet, unlike conventional stores, is through use of software agent websites. Such websites provide online customers with a huge variety of products and comparative prices on products from different integrated sources. Among the information provided on such websites there are displays of multiple customer online post-shopping evaluations on each linked store. The availability of such information allows customers to make better and more informed decisions on which internet store to choose based on what they think they will trust and feel comfortable with when conducting their online shopping (Wang and Huarng, 2002).

One of the many advantages provided by availability of large amounts of rich information on the internet, is that it provides a vast potential for exploration (Demangeot and Broderick, 2007). At any one point in time, customers 'can only display one page, but can carry in the form of hyperlinks, clickable images or search engines, the promise of thousands more pages to explore'.

Self-service

Online consumers are expected to help themselves during the experience, they have to figure out how to reach for information they require, how to select and compare between products, and how to complete the product purchase transaction by themselves. The internet allows consumers to experience self-service which 'can be conceptualised as the transference of control to the customers' (Dawes and Rowley, 1998). The author argues that one distinguishing factor of service delivery on the web is that customers must learn from the interface, or from other friends and family who have experienced it, and that customer experience may be significantly influenced by customer performance, which could have unpredictable consequences for customer expectations and evaluation of service quality.

This is why self-service technology may create reasons for customer frustration and irritation when their skills (i.e. computer skills) and the challenges (i.e. the task) are not equally matched (Moon and Frei, 2000).

New types of products

The web has also introduced a new type of product to customers, i.e. digital or information products (Wang *et al.*, 2001). Examples of such products include digital books, papers, music, online transactions, etc. The author argues that traditional methods of measuring customer satisfaction seem conceptually and operationally inappropriate for such products.

Experience-intense involvements

The advanced and more sophisticated technologies provided now on the web allow for a differentiated experience that is richer and requires a high level of consumer involvement.

Mascarenhas *et al.* (2006) argue that many internet-based companies show a clear example of customer-value-chain involvement, where the active interaction and participation of customers' involvement at various touch points in the service or product value chain, adds value to customers, not only through the more useful, convenient and state-of-the-art product, but also through the competitive experience of co-creating the product with the company.

Lawler and Joseph (2006) stipulate that beyond the basic catalogue content of apparel products, more sophisticated features are being brought to this business through tools such as 'try clothing on' virtual dress models or dressing rooms which involve advanced functionality such as: (3D) dynamic images that can be manipulated by customers; consumer personalised 360-degree models; contrasted product colours; rich information text; zooms of pictures of products with high resolution; product simulations; 3D navigational shopping tools; and speedy 'one-click express checkouts', etc. Such features are enriched by customised tips and guides such as 'great get together' product recommendations and personalised buying guides. Therefore the authors argue that the high level of customer involvement indicates that experience is richer on self-service and shopping virtual dress model sites.

Klein (2003) argued that experience-intense environments affect positively the intensity of consumer attitudes and beliefs towards advertised products.

Online communities

One of the differentiating attributes of internet environments is also its ability to support the emergence of virtual communities around users (Hagel and Armstrong, 1997). Such communities of customers, including hobbyists and enthusiasts, allows for experiential e-commerce (Wolfinbarger and Gilly, 2001).

Customer needs and motivations in online business environments

As discussed above, online environments differ in multiple ways from conventional environments. New internet technologies have empowered customers (Prahalad and Ramaswamy, 2004), allowed for their engagement in self-driven activities (Dawes and Rowley, 1998), and provided platforms for customers to become part of a social group and enjoy control over the experience in online environments (Hoffman *et al.*, 2000).

Since the early studies of marketing around the 1950s, academics and businesses have been on a continuous quest to understand the factors involved in identifying and meeting consumers needs and delivering value to the consumers (Yu, 2006).

Traditionally, customers approach consumption activities with a specific set of possible motivations (Tauber, 1972). Originally, motivation occurs because of unfilled needs (Schiffman and Kanuk, 2004). Pooler (2003) argued that consumer needs are of several layers, each layer stacked upon the other, where the hierarchy of customer needs are satisfied in a succession process, one level at a time, starting from physical survival needs, security needs, belongingness and social acceptance, esteem needs and ending with self-actualization.

Similarly, consumer behaviour scholars have argued that customers are motivated by a range of psychosocial needs that go beyond the need for buying a product or service (Tauber, 1972; Westbrook and Black, 1985; Arnold and Reynolds, 2003; Pooler, 2003).

Tauber (1972) outlined that shopping, for instance, occurs to meet a variety of needs, only some of which involve spending money. Customer motivations according to the author include a set of personal and social aspects.

Personal motives consist of role playing, recreation, self-gratification, physical activity, learning about new trends and sensory stimulation. While social motives consist of social experiences, communication with others who have a similar interest, affiliation with peer groups, obtaining status and authority, and gaining pleasure from bargaining and negotiation. Table 6.1 outlines the definition of each of those motives.

Table 6.1 Personal and social types of customer motivations

Consumer needs and motivations		Definition
Personal motives	Role playing	The different roles a customer needs to fulfil in the course of daily activities and the certain activities that must be carried out in order to fulfil this role, be it a father, a mother, a career woman, etc.
	Recreation	Diversion from the problems and stresses of the daily life routine.
	Self gratification	A need for reward after a long hardworking job for instance, where emotional states and moods lead to rationalisation of shopping behaviours.
	Physical activity	
	Learning about new trends	The enjoyment of seeing new items and getting new ideas, new products, new trends.
	Sensory stimulation	Colour, sound, and scent are all critical dimensions that motivate consumers to shop and enhance consumption experience.
Social motives	Social experiences	Social activities create an exciting shopping experience through talking, watching people and meeting friends.
	Communication with others	Communicate and form affiliations with people who share the same interests or enjoy the same thing.
	Peer group attraction	The desire to be like peers or to model a reference group.
	Status and authority	
	Pleasure of bargaining	Bargaining for a lower price or getting better value, provides a unique form of enjoyment for some.

Source: Tauber (1972)

Sheth (1983) has suggested that there were two classes of motives underlying shopping patronage: functional and non-functional, of which Tauber's (1972) motivations were the non-functional (Parsons, 2002).

The contribution of Tauber's study brought to the attention of researchers the fact that customers are motivated not only by the need to acquire a desired product, but also a need to gain satisfaction for various non-product-related needs, and finally a need to satisfy non-acquisition-related wants or needs (Westbrook and Black, 1985). In other words, this means that customers are not motivated by the utilitarian value of the products, they are also motivated for the satisfaction obtained during the experience, resulting from non-product related needs and non-acquisition related needs. The authors however emphasised that product acquisition needs and choice optimisation needs are two additional important motivation attributes missed by Tauber's study, and argued that they lead to satisfaction resulting from self-actualisation and achievement.

One of the breakthrough studies in this area is the study of Holbrook and Hirschman (1982). Hirschman (1984) introduced the concepts of customer hedonic motivation in relation to utilitarian motivation, expanding the thinking around shopping motivation to include factors such as pleasure, feeling, aesthetics, emotion, and enjoyment as additional motivations, compared to product acquisition motivations.

Utilitarian motivation advocates that customers start from a mission or task which is the need to acquire a product/service, and the acquired benefit depends on whether the mission is completed or not, or whether the mission is completed efficiently and more effortlessly (Holbrook and Hirschman, 1982; Batra and Ahtola, 1991; Babin *et al.*, 1994; Hirschman, 1984). Utilitarian motivation relates therefore to mission critical, goal oriented and rational needs

(Hirschman, 1984; Holbrook and Hirschman, 1982; Babin *et al.*, 1994).

Customer utilitarian motivation is transaction-oriented with the intention to purchase what is needed as quickly as possible and without distraction and is evaluated by the terms 'success' and 'accomplishment' (Thompson *et al.*, 1999).

Hedonic motivation on the other hand refers to consumption behaviours in fulfilment of happiness, fantasy, awakening, sensuality, and enjoyment needs (Hirschman, 1984). Values gained from hedonic motivation are experiential and emotional. According to this perspective, what triggers customers is the need to enjoy the experience by itself, and not the mere need of obtaining a product, or completing a mission. The study of hedonic motivation is seen to be a study of shopping enjoyment (To *et al.*, 2007).

Table 6.2 Synthesis of customer needs and motivations in conventional business settings

Type of needs	Customer needs	Studies
Functional (utilitarian) needs	Convenience	(Buttle, 1984)
	Selection, choice optimisation	(Westbrook and Black, 1985)
	Product/service functional attributes, anticipated utility	(Westbrook and Black, 1985)
Experiential (emotional) needs	Role playing	(Tauber, 1972; Arnold and Reynolds, 2003)
	Diversion from daily routine, relaxation, time-killing	(Tauber, 1972; Buttle, 1984)
	Self-gratification	(Tauber, 1972; Arnold and Reynolds, 2003)
	Physical/mental activity	(Tauber, 1972; Buttle, 1984)
	Learning about new trends, idea shopping, acquire information	(Tauber, 1972; Arnold and Reynolds, 2003; Buttle, 1984)
	Sensory simulation	(Tauber, 1972)
	Social experience (positive sociality)	(Tauber, 1972; Buttle, 1984; Arnold and Reynolds, 2003)

	Communication with others	(Tauber, 1972)
	Affiliation with peer groups	(Tauber, 1972)
	Obtaining status and authority	(Tauber, 1972)
	Bargaining hunting and negotiation	(Tauber, 1972; Pooler 2003)
	Compare alternatives	(Buttle, 1984)
	Self-expression	(Buttle, 1984)
	Adventure	(Arnold and Reynolds, 2003)
	Fun, fantasy, feelings	(Holbrook and Hirschman, 1982)

Similarly, studies of customer needs and motivations in online environments have also included the same types of needs, affirming that customers approach the internet as a new business channel to satisfy both their functional and experiential (emotional) needs.

Table 6.3 Synthesis of customer needs and motivations in non-conventional business settings

Type of needs	Customer needs	Studies
Functional needs	Convenience	(Wolfinbarger and Gilly, 2001)
	Product /service customisation	(To *et al.,* 2007)
	Transaction efficiency (time saving)	(Mäenpää *et al.*, 2006)
	Selection, choice optimisation	(Wolfinbarger and Gilly, 2001)
	Information acquisition, information availability	(Wolfinbarger and Gilly, 2001)
	Lack of sociality	(Wolfinbarger and Gilly, 2001)
	Cost saving	(To *et al.*, 2007)
	Product/service functional attributes, anticipated utility	(Mäenpää *et al.*, 2006)
	Ease of use	(Childers *et al.*, 2001; Monsuwe *et al.*, 2004)
	Usefulness	(Childers *et al.*, 2001;

		Monsuwe *et al.*, 2004)
Experiential needs (emotional)	Role playing	(Parsons, 2002)
	Diversion from daily routine, relaxation, time-killing	(Parsons, 2002)
	Self-gratification	(Parsons, 2002)
	Physical/mental activity	(Parsons, 2002)
	Learning about new trends, idea shopping, acquire information	(Parsons, 2002)
	Sensory simulation	(Parsons, 2002)
	Social experience (positive sociality)	(Mathwick *et al.*, 2001; Parsons, 2002; Wolfinbarger and Gilly, 2001)
	Communication with others	(Parsons, 2002)
	Affiliation with peer groups	(Parsons, 2002)
	Obtaining status and authority	(Mathwick *et al.*, 2001; To *et al.*, 2007; Parsons, 2002)
	Bargaining hunting and negotiation	(Parsons, 2002; Wolfinbarger and Gilly, 2001)
	Compare alternatives	
	Self-expression	
	Adventure	(To *et al.*, 2007)
	Sensory stimulation	
	Competition needs	
	Aesthetics , auxiliary features	(Mathwick *et al.*, 2001; Mäenpää *et al.*, 2006)
	Exploration, browsing	(Mäenpää *et al.*, 2006)
	Tele-presence	(Mäenpää *et al.*, 2006)
	Fun, fantasy, feelings	
	Enjoyment	(Childers *et al.*, 2001; Monsuwe *et al.*, 2004)
	Involvement with product class	(Wolfinbarger and Gilly, 2001)
	Positive surprise	(Wolfinbarger and Gilly, 2001)

The study of Hirschman and Holbrook (1982) not only provided clear definitions of customer motivations by shifting from the utilitarian only paradigm to the conceptual hedonic viewpoint but added fun, fantasy and feelings to function. It also broke new grounds for future studies on consumer behaviour models and intentions (To *et al.*, 2007) and in highlighted the experiential aspect of consumer behaviour.

The following sections are dedicated to addressing the customer experience concept, starting from early theories of consumer behaviour and moving to more recent literature from the marketing discipline.

Traditional and evolving consumer behaviour models

Traditional models that explain consumer behaviour have evolved to address the new changing attitudes of today's consumer who is becoming more sophisticated and demanding (Yu, 2006).

Utilitarian and hedonic customer perspective

Traditionally, consumer behaviour research has emphasised the importance of utilitarian performance of goods as the primary value to consumers, where utility is a function of product tangible attributes. This is perhaps understood from the economic view of products as objects, for which consumers desired to maximize utility (Hirschman, 1984).

According to Holbrook (2000), marketing and consumer researchers awoke two decades ago to the importance of hedonic consumption and the experiential aspects of consumer behaviour (Holbrook and Hirschman, 1982). The unit of emphasis at the time was consumption experience which was described by the headings of fantasies, feelings, and fun or the 'three Fs' (Holbrook, 2000). Whereas consumption here refers to two major phases: (1) the transaction between the consumer and the firm including a range from discrete transaction to relationship building; and (2) the use of the product transacted (Addis & Holbrook, 2001).

Holbrook (2000) argues that customers do value the consumption experience and did always, it is however, our understanding of their behaviour that has evolved to become closer to reality:

> *Consumers still sensuously savor their food. They still daydream about their summer vacations. They still feel sad in tear-jerking movies and happy when their team wins the championship. They still play tennis or golf for fun and derive esthetic pleasure from a Bruckner symphony or a Dickens novel. So consumers themselves have not changed. Rather, our own understanding of them has been radically revised.*

Resulting from this shift in paradigm, consumers have increasingly been viewed less as computer-like decision makers who focus on buying in the form of purchasing outcomes to more subjective flesh-and-blood humans who respond emotionally to consumption situations and use products in various playful leisure activities (Holbrook, 2000).

The previously popular utilitarian view, advocates that consumers are concerned with purchasing products in an efficient and timely manner to achieve their goals with a minimum of irritation; desired outcomes of this experience will be achievement of pre-identified end goals (Hirschman, 1984).

In an attempt to expand the traditional theories of consumption, Holbrook and Hirschman (1982) and Hirschman (1984) were first to focus on what they termed, the hedonic perspective of consumption. A more general approach would suggest that hedonic consumption refers to the aesthetic, intangible, and subjective aspect of consumption, and considers also the potential entertainment and enjoyment resulting from the fun and play arising from the experience itself.

Hedonic consumption designates 'those facets of consumer behavior that relate to the multi-sensory, fantasy and emotive aspects of the consumption experience' (Hirschman, 1984). Multi-sensory refers to 'the receipt of experience in multiple sensory modalities including tastes, sounds, scents, tactile impressions and visual images'. It is important to mention here, that according to the authors, consumer experience is generated not only by responding to multi-sensory impressions from external stimuli through encoding these inputs, experience is also generated from internal imagery of sights, sounds, and tactile sensations which can be historic imagery of a past event evoked and recalled by a stimuli or a fantasy imagery produced not based on a previous experience. All are experienced by the consumer.

Emotions, or emotional arousal relate to feelings such as joy, love, hate, jealousy, fear, rage, etc. According to the authors, seeking emotional arousal is a major motivation for the consumption of products, ranging from sporting events and plays to cloths and food.

Although the traditional models of consumer behaviour stipulate that consumers differ from each other by their demographic and socio-economic backgrounds, the hedonic perspective emphasises the fact that consumers are distinct individuals with emotions and different personalities (Mäenpää *et al.,* 2006).

It is important to understand that the hedonic perspective of consumer behaviour does not replace the traditional perspective; it represents an important extension of the latter and aims to offer a complementary perspective for conceptualising some neglected yet important phenomena in the area (Hirschman, 1984).

Table 6.4 Comparison between the hedonic and traditional perspectives of consumer behaviour

	Traditional perspective	Hedonic perspective
Mental construct	Emphasis on the belief (cognition) component of mental activities.	Focuses also on the different sensory channels used by consumers to perceive and experience products.
	Focus on verbal information processing.	Supplements verbal data with data supplied by sensory modalities.
	Emotion is represented by the construct of affect as a consumer's evaluation of a product attribute.	Explores the boarder dimension of emotions such as strong feelings of aguish and rapture in response to products.
	Suitable for goods whose tangible qualities and utilitarian performance serves as primary value determinant.	Appropriate for products whose selections are based also on satisfying emotional wants.
	Utilitarian motives dominate in the choice of a product.	Emotional desires dominate in the choice of a product.
	Product is perceived as a concrete object.	Product is imbued with a subjective meaning or symbol that supplements the concrete attributes it possesses.
	Tied to actual reality.	Tied to imaginative (self-constructed) reality.
	Based on information cognitive seeking dimension.	Focused on sensory-emotive seeking with acknowledgment of existence of two dimensions.
Product class	Low involvement experienced products.	All products can be hedonically experienced by consumers. Study emphasised more intense and involving products.
	Focus on packaged goods (toothpaste, cereal, detergent, cigarettes) and major durables (appliances, automobiles) as objects for study.	Investigates aesthetics products/services that generate unusually strong emotional involvement and potentially more important in the life of consumers. Such as the performing art (opera, ballet, dance, theatre), the plastic

		art (painting, photography, sculpture, crafts) and high-culture products such as movies, concerts, sporting events, fashion and apparel.
		The consumption of products requires and generates substantial mental activity from the consumer due to the inspiration of multi-sensory imaginary and consumption of emotional resources. The brain activity is most likely to be predominately right-brain oriented.
	Patronage decisions are based primarily on the product tangible features.	Patronage decisions regarding hedonically consumed products are based primarily on the symbolic elements of the product.
Product usage		Hedonic perspective includes the psychological experiences that accompany product usage. Hedonic responses is the essence of the usage experience.
		Emphasises the importance of the dynamic interaction between the consumer and the product (dynamic usage experience) which may have reciprocal effects on both.
	Allocation of resources is exclusive to money.	During product usage, mental energies are exerted to create emotional and imaginary responses. Resources allocation extends to emotional-imaginary type too.
Individual differences	Takes a post-hoc approach to sources of interpersonal variances in which consumers adopt certain behaviours such as brand loyalty, satisfaction, etc.	Consider that individual differences in ethnic background, social class and gender cause products to vary in the emotions and fantasies or even the amount of emotions and fantasies they inspire in consumers.

Source: Hirschman (1984)

Consumers can be hedonic or utilitarian or both hedonic and utilitarian (Hirschman, 1982). Hedonic consumers seem to value experience and enjoyment, and approach the consumption activity with no substantial plan in mind, while utilitarian consumers are rational information processors who approach the consumption activity with a substantial plan in mind.

The weight of the consumption experience depends also on the difference between the subjective and objective types of responses a product/service receives by a customer. For instance, if the technical performance of a product has more influence on the consumer his objective response was greater than his subjective response, this is called a utilitarian type of experience (Addis and Holbrook, 2001).

Figure 6.2 Utilitarian products vs. hedonic products

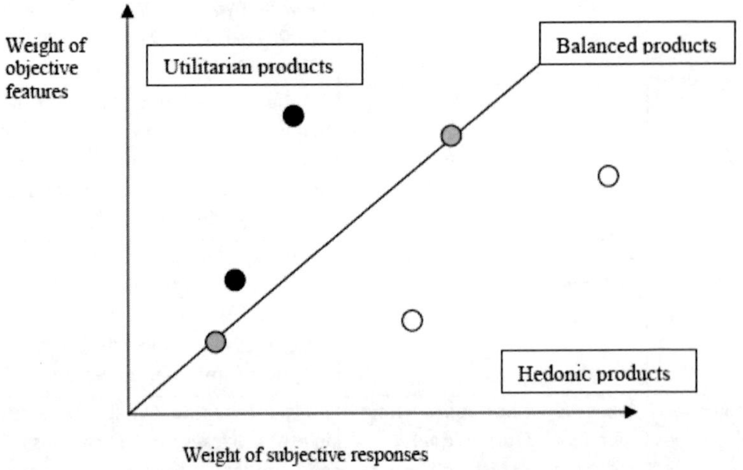

Source: Addis (2001: 45)

Following the Hirschman and Holbrook studies (Holbrook and Hirschman, 1982; Hirschman, 1984), hedonic dimensions of consumption have been well recognised by consumer behaviour researchers (see for example, Babin *et al.,* 1994; Havlena and Holbrook, 1986; Westbrook and Black, 1985 Richins, 1997; Holbrook, 1986; Holbrook, 1994; Holbrook and Corfman, 1985; Oliver, 1999; Hirschman, 1984; Firat, 1987). Thus generating more interest in the broader concept of experiential consumption and distinguishing between the consumer behaviour models, the information processing and the experience seeking models (Yu, 2006).

Information-processing model

The information processing model emphasises the rational choice of consumers and regards them as logical thinkers who make purchase decisions through problem solving and information processing (Holbrook and Hirschman, 1982).

Holbrook and Hirschman (1982) outlined that the origins of this theory started in early microeconomics and classical decision theory which emphasised that decision making is based on pure rational choice; this moved towards the largely irrational buying needs based on motivation research and ended up with a bounded rationality approach and use of logical flow models: the 'information processing model'.

According to this model, consumer behaviour can be presented in logical flow models where various inputs (some environmental and some from the consumer) are processed by an intervening response system (which consists of three elements; cognition, affect and behaviour) which in turn generates output consequences. The model is closed with a learning feedback loop which results when output consequences are appraised against certain criteria, such as individual differences, search activity, type of involvement, and task definition (Holbrook and Hirschman, 1982).

Figure 6.3 Information processing paradigm of consumer behaviour

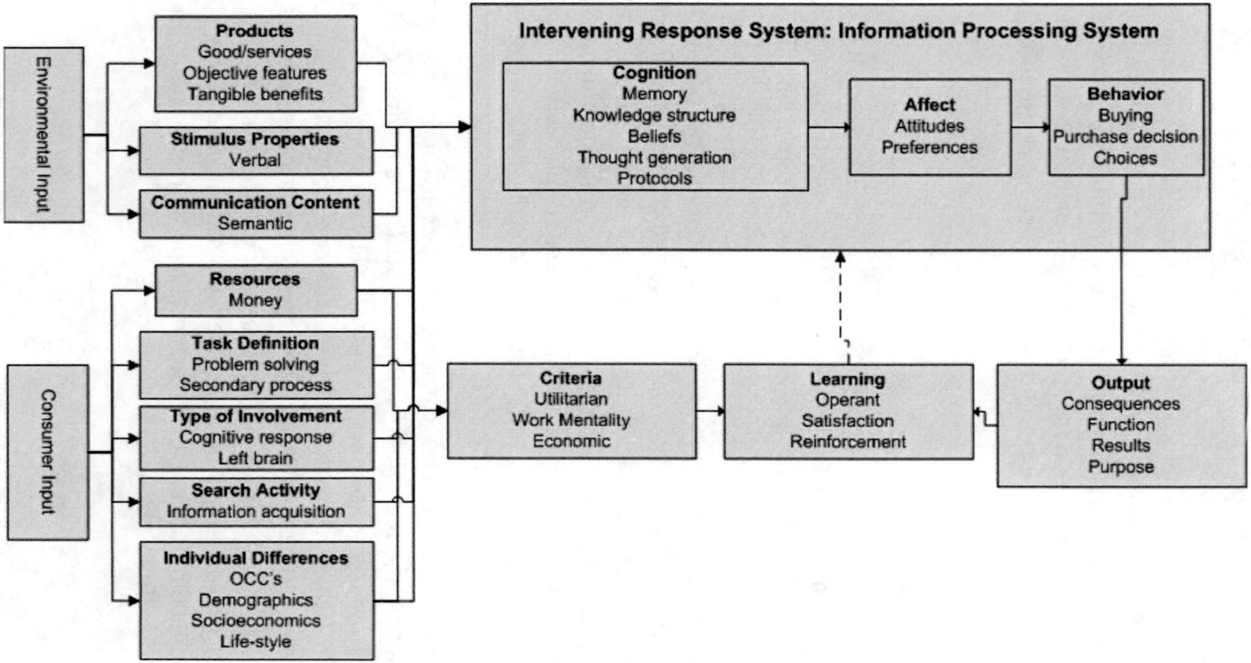

Source: Hirschman (1984)

The cognition variable in this model outlines that customers' memory, knowledge structure, beliefs, thought generation and protocols determine their affective responses in terms of attitudes and preferences which in turn guide behavioural effects such as buying, purchase, decision and choice making. The three variables relate in a causal flow with a feedback loop of satisfaction to present learning effects (Hirschman, 1984).

The model may be found more appropriate with low-involvement, frequently-purchased consumer non-durables, such as detergents or canned peas, for which consumers may be unable to make valid perceptual or affective distinctions among more than a few different brands (Holbrook and Hirschman, 1982).

The model has been extended and reviewed by many researchers resulting in more refined models. Nevertheless, although the refinements touched base with different aspects (including but limited to, product feature effects, attitude toward the ads, attitude toward the brand, feedback loops, changes in process order, etc. or separating key parts of the model) the refinements brought slight modifications to the model and preserved its foundation spirit emphasising product acquisition and choice as the ultimate outcome of the model (Yu, 2006).

One of the main limitations of this paradigm that is does not count for the role of emotions; on the contrary, it views consumers exclusively as thinkers and rational information-seeking decision makers, at the same time, products are viewed according to the model as collections of functional and tangible attributes (Hirschman, 1984).

The model also focuses on brand choice and/or purchase decisions emphasising only the economical aspect of the buying behaviour with product choice and acquisition as the ultimate outcome (Holbrook, 1986). According to the author, this is not surprising, as the model is presented from the view of marketing managers whose major concern is the determinants of sales or market share.

Experience-seeking model – value-oriented paradigm

Morris Holbrook and Beth Hirschman contributed to driving a paradigm shift in the understanding of consumer behaviour. The authors published two papers on the consumption experience (Hirschman, 1984), and the experiential aspects of consumption (Holbrook and Hirschman, 1982) to challenge the original model explained above and its several refinements and they introduced a new outlook on the consumption process overall. The new model looks at consumption as a complex process that 'entails multi-way interactions among physiological, cognitive, behavioral, and experiential components' and involves a steady flow of fantasies, feelings, and fun. The consumers of this process are not cognitive thinkers only, on the contrary, the model is based on the argument that the difference between machines and consumers is that human beings experience emotions (Holbrook and Hirschman, 1982), (Hirschman, 1984).

In their paper, Holbrook and Hirschman (1982) highlighted the neglected importance of the experiential aspect of consumption and urged for further research in this area: According to the authors:

> *The behavior of people in general and of consumers in particular is the fascinating and endlessly complex result of a multifaceted interaction between organism and environment. In this dynamic process, neither problem-directed nor experiential components can safely be ignored.*

They also added:

> *By focusing single mindedly on the consumer as information processor, recent consumer research has tended to neglect the equally important experiential aspects of consumption, thereby limiting our understanding of consumer behavior.*

Experiential consumption or hedonic consumption, addresses playful leisure activities, sensory pleasures, daydreams, aesthetic enjoyment and emotional responses (Mäenpää *et al.,* 2006), experiential consumption expands consumer behaviour literature by emphasising the 3Fs 'fantasies, feelings and fun' or the 4Es 'experience, entertainment, exhibitionism and evangelising' (Holbrook, 2000).

In order to better understand the experiential perspective of customer behaviour, components of the experience seeking model (Figure 6.4) are explained in detail, as outlined by Holbrook and Hirschman (1982).

Environmental input

- Explores the symbolic meanings (which all products carry no matter how mundane) of more subjective characteristics of the product, such as its cheerfulness, sociability, elegance, etc. in contrast with the conventional model which focuses on the tangible benefits and its utilitarian functions which are usually based on objective features and characteristics.
- It emphasises the nature of experiential stimuli as multi-sensory and psychophysical, in contrast to the stimuli generated by product attributes and verbal descriptions.
- The experiential view of consumer behaviour should focus on the effect of external messages sent to the consumer (syntactic structure) instead of studying consumer responses to the semantic aspects of communication content.

Figure 6.4 Experience seeking paradigm of consumer behaviour

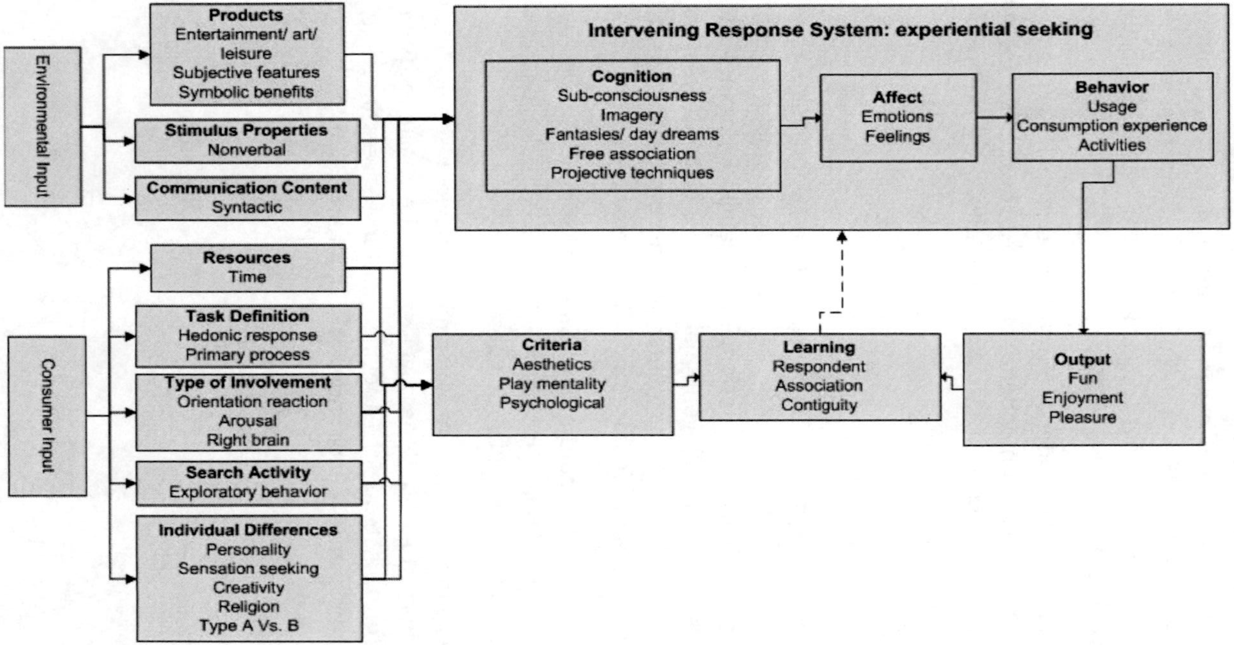

Source: Hirschman

Consumer input

- The experiential view of consumer research emphasises the importance of considering consumers' time as another resource invested, in addition to the monetary resources.
- It involves primary process thinking which means that consumers are engaged in the activity in pursuance for immediate pleasure or gratification. Experiential consumption seeks fun, fantasy, amusement, arousal, sensory stimulation, and enjoyment. This is in contrast with the information processing view which regards consumers as secondary-process thinkers (resulting from socialisation) and problem-solvers who consider the purchase process as goal-directed activities of searching for information, retrieving memory cues, weighing evidence, and arriving at carefully considered judgmental evaluations.
- Consumer involvement in the experiential view of consumer behaviour exceeds the typical personally relevant multiplicity of cognitive responses to include attention, interest and excitement, by emphasising degree of activation or arousal. Involvement is therefore more emotional and is associated with the right brain. This is instead of it being a left-brain phenomenon that relates to cognitive responses associated with analytic, logical, problem-oriented activities.
- Activity searching is related heavily to exploratory behaviour, where stimulus ambiguity and working through arousal are the determinants of the search activity.
- Consumer input offers considerable attention to consumers' individual differences and the revival of personality and allied variables of consumers, such as subculture and personality constructs. This is mainly due to the relative inability of typical customer classifications such as demography, socio-economic status, etc to predict consumer behaviour.

Intervening response system

- Focuses on subconscious and private cognitive processes such as fantasies, fun, daydreams, etc. instead, the information processing model focuses on memory and views consumers as a complex knowledge structure embodying intricately interwoven subsystems of beliefs referred to as 'memory schemas' or 'semantic networks'.
- The experiential perspective recognises a full scale of relative emotions that includes diverse feelings of love, hate, fear, joy, boredom, anxiety, pride, anger, disgust, sadness, sympathy, lust, ecstasy, greed, guilt, elation, shame and awe. This is in contrast to the conventional information processing model that emphasises only one subset of consumers' emotions, i.e. like or dislikes a brand.
- At the behavioural level, the purchase (brand choice) process is perceived as the ultimate and most important behavioural outcome according to the information processing model. According to the experiential view, this is only a small fraction of the phenomenological data that comprises the entire experience of consumption. According to the authors, research and investigation in this area is vital for consumer behaviour research.
- The conventional model views the consequences of consumer choice in terms of functionality and usefulness of the product, leaving the criteria for evaluation purely utilitarian. By contrast, in the experiential view, the consequences of consumption are viewed in terms of fun, enjoyment and pleasure that it offers or evokes. Therefore the criteria for evaluation are aesthetic in nature and depend on the consumer's type of involvement, search activity, and personality.
- Learning according to the conventional model views brand satisfaction as a strong reinforcement of future behavioural

responses and repeat purchases. The experiential view considers that although brand satisfaction constitutes one important experiential component that affects repeat purchase, the stream of associations that occur during consumption, including emotions, may be equally important.

It is important to mention that the experience-oriented paradigm does not advocate abandoning the information processing approach, it was intended to supplement and enrich it (Holbrook and Hirschman, 1982).

Despite the fact that consumer behaviour studies tend to emphasise products that arouse strong emotions or perhaps extreme states of feelings, such as games, adventure and sports, performing arts and music, it is not possible to emphasise more that *all* products involve goods that perform services that provide consumption experiences (Holbrook, 2000).

Hirschman (1984) argued that looking at the consumption experience from a subjective view suggests that almost all acts that involve the consumption of products have stimulation of our thoughts and/or our senses as their outcomes and therefore people consume products for the overall phenomenon of 'experience seeking'.

Experience seeking according to the author is divided into four types:

- Cognitive experience seeking, where the objective of the experience sought is to stimulate cognitive activity and stimulate a thought process, such as taking a course to gain knowledge. Information seekers are individuals who may share some characteristics, they are largely affluent, highly educated, highly exposed to the mass media, difficult to satisfy, influential but not innovative and politically liberal.
- Sensory experience seeking is where the objective of the experience is to stimulate sensory activity and activate one or

multiple sense organs, example of this type of experience seeking includes purchasing a music CD to listen to. Sensory seekers are usually innovative and risk takers.

- Novelty seeking is where the objective is the desire of the individual to seek out novel stimuli. Novelty experience seeking taps only into the cognitive or sensory experience that a consumer may desire to have.
- Experience seeking is where the objective of the consumption experience consists of the three above types of experiences collectively.

Following on from early contributions in the area of experiential consumer behaviour, the literature witnessed substantial support for the model and associated subjects (see for example, Hirschman, 1984; Westbrook and Black, 1985; Havlena and Holbrook, 1986; Holbrook, 1986; Firat, 1987; Oliver, 1993; Holbrook, 1994; Holbrook, 1997; Richins, 1997; Holbrook, 2000; Carù and Cova, 2003a; Caru and Cova, 2003b).

In addition to the early grounding contributions in this field, marketing literature has witnessed a stream of recent research and publications embracing the original thinking of initial studies and highlighting the importance of customer experience (Berry and Carbone *et al.,* 2002; Gilmore and Pine, 2002; Milligan and Smith, 2002; Shaw and Ivens, 2002; Smith and Wheeler, 2002; LaSalle and Britton, 2003; Schmitt, 2003; Shaw, 2007).

The following sections are dedicated to discussing the more recent contributions in the area of customer experience.

Customer experience

Following on from early research by consumer behaviour scientists and marketers in the 1980s, which advocated that every consumption event provides some form of experience (Hirschman,

1984), the concept of customer experience has been increasingly perceived in the literature as a fundamental factor in today's economy (Gilmore and Pine, 2002), a central element of consumers' lives (Carù and Cova, 2003a) as well as an understanding of customer needs and motivations (Holbrook, 2000).

Carù and Cova (2003a) summarised the evolvement in the literature by saying:

> *The notion of experience entered the field of consumption and marketing with Holbrook and Hirschman's pioneering article of 1982. Twenty years later, this notion has become a key element in understanding consumer behavior, and, in some views, a foundation for the economy and marketing of the future.*

This perhaps is owed to the constantly increasing external challenges that organisations are facing (Gilmore and Pine, 2002). Globalisation and technological advancements have put firms face-to-face with more sophisticated and demanding customers (Coelho and Easingwood, 2003) who are connected, informed and active (Prahalad and Ramaswamy, 2004). Customers of today are in the driving seat and are given millions of options that are only one click away from them with the minimal switch cost.

Customer experience has been perceived as a strategic and competitive advantage to firms. An IBM research project conducted in 2005 concluded that 'to create a new and lasting source of competitive advantage, businesses must manage the customer experience'. Senior business leaders agree that differentiating solely on the traditional physical elements such as price, delivery and lead times is no longer a sustainable business strategy, differentiating through customer experience is today's rescue for companies when differentiation in goods and services is becoming almost impossible (Thompson *et al.,* 1999).

Gilmore and Pine (2002) wrote that 'experiences are the fourth economic offering [after commodities, services and goods] and as distinct from services as services are from goods'. According to the authors, the progression in economic offerings is moving the emphasis of companies from fungible materials extracted from the natural world (commodities), to tangible products that are standardised and then inventoried by companies (goods), to intangible activities performed for a particular client (services), to events that engage individuals in a memorable and personal way (experiences) (Gilmore and Pine, 2002).

Figure 6.5 The progression in economic value

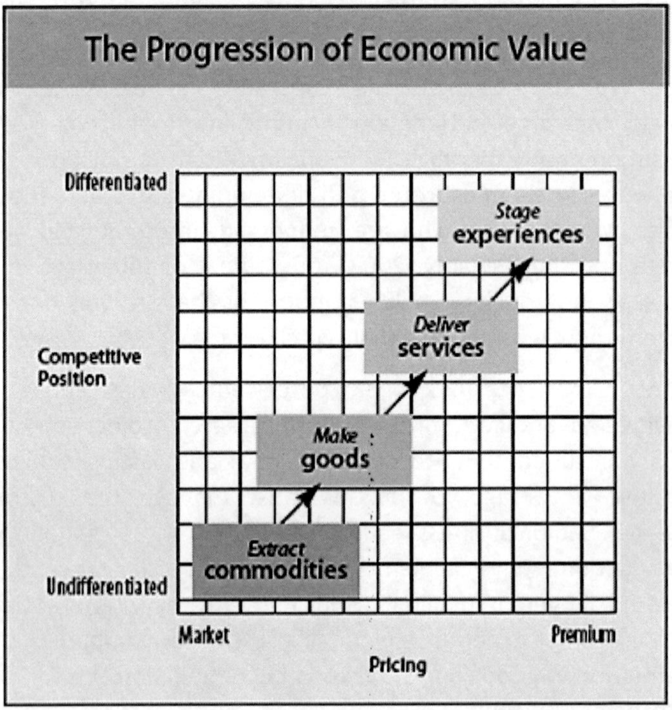

Source: (Gilmore and Pine, 2002)

Characteristics of the experiences as the new economy offerings are very different from what companies are accustomed to. They are usually revealed over a duration and involve sensations as the factors of demands. Table 6.5 outlines differences between experiences and other economic offerings.

Table 6.5 Economic distinctions

Economic offering	Commodities	Goods	Services	Experiences
Economy	Agrarian	Industrial	Service	Experience
Economic function	Extract	Make	Deliver	Stage
Nature of offering	Fungible	Tangible	Intangible	Memorable
Key attribute	Natural	Standardised	Customised	Personal
Method of supply	Stored in bulk	Inventoried after production	Delivered on demand	Revealed over duration
Seller	Trader	Manufacturer	Provider	Stager
Buyer	Market	User	Client	Guest
Factors of demand	Characteristics	Features	Benefits	Sensations

Source: Gilmore and Pine (2002)

Definition of customer experience

To start with a definition for the term 'customer experience' it is perhaps useful to understand what is meant by the term 'experience' in general. Carù and Cova (2003a) illustrated that disciplines define experience differently.

One of the earliest definitions for the term customer experience appeared in the consumer behaviour literature by Holbrook and

Hirschman (1982) who refer to it as a personal event or occurrence that is associated with important emotional significance and founded in the interaction with the consumed product or service. This definition limits the customer experience to the consumption process and refers to the experience generated during the course of service or product consumption.

One of the most recent definitions for the term 'customer experience' was laid out by Colin Shaw (2007) in his recent book *The DNA of customer experience*. The author illustrates that:

> *A customer experience is an interaction between an organisation and a customer. It is a blend of an organisation's physical performance, the senses stimulated and emotions evoked, each intuitively measured against customer expectations across all moments of contract.*

Customer experience has also been defined as an added value to the product or service that originates from customers' interactions with each touch point with the brand. Shawn Smith defines customer experience in contrast to customer service, by stipulating that customer service is driven by the perception of the organisation, it is basically what the organisation does to the customer (expression), however, customer experience, is what the customer receives at every touch point with the brand (impression) (GCCRM, 2007).

It is perhaps interesting to know how consumers define 'customer experience'. CRMguru carried out research to define customer experience from an expert and consumer point of view. Results of the survey showed that customer experience relates to interactions with an organisation's people, processes or systems and products. Experience also relates to the feelings or emotional responses generated by the interactions according to other expert respondents (Thompson *et al.*, 1999).

Customer respondents preferred the definition: 'The sum of all my interactions with a brand's products, services and people'. Another highly selected definition was: 'The feelings and thoughts resulting from all impressions, tangible and intangible, from anyone or anything representing, directly or indirectly, an organisation, brand or product'. The study therefore concluded that customer experience is a customer's perception of interactions with a brand; where experience is about what the interaction incited in a customer, including thoughts and feelings and where the brand relates to the organisation as a symbol and not a logo or marketing or advertising communication.

One of the most comprehensive definitions for the term customer experience was suggested by Yu (2006) and regards customer experience as 'the synthesis of the affective and cognitive actions and reactions that consumers have during their interface with products, services, and the marketplace environment'.

> *The Customer Experience originates from a set of interactions between a customer and a product, a company, or part of its organisation, which provoke a reaction. This experience is strictly personal and implies the customer's involvement at different levels (rational, emotional, sensorial physical and spiritual). Its evaluation depends on the comparison between a customer's expectations and the stimuli coming from the interaction with the company and its offering in correspondence of the different moments of contact or touch-points.* (Gentilea *et al.* 2007)

Unlike the definition of Holbrook and Hirschman (1982), recent definitions for 'customer experience' expanded the scope of the term to include not only the consumption process but also all touch points with the brand, including pre-purchase advertising, enquiring, etc.

To conclude, customer experience is seen as a new economical offering (Gilmore and Pine, 2002) or a value added to services or products (Shaw, 2007), that represents customers' affective and cognitive actions and reactions (Yu, 2006) resulting from customers' interactions with the firm in each touch point. Customer experiences are unique (Addis and Holbrook, 2001; Gilmore and Pine, 2002), can be more utilitarian, hedonic or balanced according to the respective weights of the contributions by the objective product-based and subjective consumer-related component (Addis and Holbrook, 2001)

This definition takes us to our next level of discussion, what drives customer experience.

How customer experience is generated

As laid out above, customer experience relates to the reaction generated by a customer during his interaction with the product or service or the brand at large. The question now is what drives this reaction? How are customer experiences generated? What happens during the interaction process to create a desired customer experience?

There are two views on how customer experience is generated. The first view considers that customer experience results from a staging process carried out by the company which not only performs a function but competes on the basis of engaging customers in memorable, personal and unique experiences. According to the Gilmore and Pine (2002), this view assumes that companies 'intentionally use services as the stage and goods as props to engage an individual' on a physical, intellectual, emotional or even spiritual level.

The second view considers that the creation of a unique and compelling customer experience occurs through involving customers in the formation of a co-created and co-owned customer experience that suits his/her own personalised needs (Prahalad and Ramaswamy, 2004; Mascarenhas *et al.*, 2006).

Whether staged by the company (Gilmore and Pine, 2002), or co-created with the customer (Prahalad and Ramaswamy, 2004), Shaw (2007) draws our attention to the fact that 50% of customers' experiences are driven by customers' emotions. The author believes that customer experience is a blend of two experience categories: physical customer experience and emotional customer experience, each category has a different type of driver.

- Customer rational experience: driven by product or service specific physical features, such as price, location, opening times, channel used for delivery including phone, online, stores, etc.
- Customer emotional experience: driven by customers' emotions and how they feel during their interaction with all touch points with the organisation. A separate section is outlined later for types of the emotional component of customer experience

In another and perhaps more comprehensive perspective Berry *et al.* (2006) stipulated that there are three types of clues that drive or generate customer experience. Experience clues are initiated by the organisation and sent to the customer. Those clues incite or evoke perceptions, reactions or an impression by the customer.

Functional clues – basic and minimal requirements

Functional clues relate to the so called technical quality of offerings, reliability and competence of the service. In other words, this component of the experience is generated from fulfilment of minimal requirements of the product/service.

In order not to underestimate the importance of functional clues, it is very important to remember that functional clues relate to the core of any service, in other words, the main reason for customers approaching a company for a product or a service.

Additionally, research into the main reasons for switching between companies and leaving one service provider to another one resulted in core service failure, such as a service mistake or billing error, being ranked as a top rated reason for switching; this was according to 44 percent of respondents who had switching experience. (Keaveney, 1995)

However, it is also important to mention that customers who switch between suppliers for the reason of failing to fulfil basic functional requirements are unlikely to be surprised when the service is performed completely.

Mechanic clues – sensory impression

The mechanic component of the experience refer to sensory presentation of the service such as smells, sounds, sights, textures, etc.

Mechanic clues come from inanimate objects to offer a physical representation of the intangible service. Accessories of a graduation ceremony and a certificate hanging on the wall are among the mechanic clues a student would receive to feel more than the core service itself which is learning. The tablecloths on a restaurant tables, the design and layout of the restaurant, its equipments, furnishings, signs, colours, textures, sounds, lighting and smells are all among the mechanic clues that the customer receives about the service, all without a single word spoken. According to the author, mechanic clues not only attract customers to do business with the company, they also help attract the right type of customers.

Mechanic clues are also important because they are used to make a positive first impression on the customer even before he makes his purchase decision. They also provide customers with information about what they can expect during a service performance, and therefore affect their perception of the service quality.

Humanic clues – exceeding customer expectations

The humanic component is generated from the behaviour and appearance of service providers – choice of words, tone of voice, level of enthusiasm, body language, neatness, and appropriate dress, etc.

Humanic clues according to this classification are created by employees and provide personal and enduring customer-provider interaction. Humanic clues are sent to cultivate emotional connectivity with the customer to strengthen their trust and deepen their loyalty.

Humanic clues, especially in interaction-intense services, are of highest importance and have impacts on service satisfaction and loyalty. Other clues are not expected to overcome poor humanic clues.

Conceptual basis for experience clues

In summary, customer experiences are driven by clues that are responsible for creating customer experience by influencing customers' thoughts, feelings and behaviour.

In an article by Berry *et al.* (2002) the three types of clues were classified under two categories, not according to their source this time, but according to how they are processed in customers' minds.

- Functionality clues which relate to the actual functioning of the product/service and the promise it was supposed to deliver. Such clues are interpreted primarily by the logical circuitry of the brain.
- Emotions clues which relate to all types of mechanic and humanic clues coming from the smells, tastes, textures, sights of the product/service and, tastes and textures of the good or service, the environment in which the service/product was

offered as well as clues resulting from interactions with employees.

Figure 6.6 explains how customer experience is generated and how experience affects consumers' perception of quality.

According to this model, functional clues primarily influence customers' cognitive or calculative perceptions of service quality. Mechanic and humanic clues primarily influence customers' emotional or affective perceptions.

The carry off from this is that fulfilling technical requirements of a product or service or the technical competence of a product or service does not compose the whole perception for customers of a product or service.

Figure 6.6 Experience clues

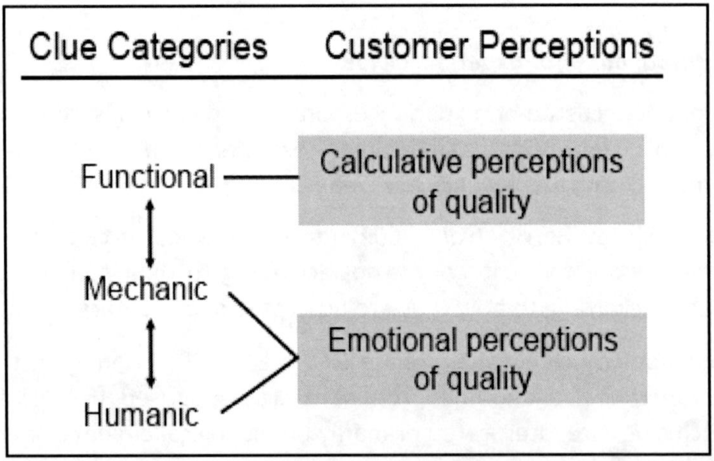

Source: Berry *et al.* (2002)

Customer experience is believed to have the following dimensions or components (Gentilea *et al.,* 2007). Knowing which can also help identify what drives and generates customer experience.

- *Sensorial component*: stimulation of this component affects the senses. A good sensorial offering addresses sight, hearing, touch, taste and smell so as to arouse customers' aesthetical pleasure, excitement, satisfaction and sense of beauty.
- *Emotional component*: this component involves one's affective system through the generation of moods, feelings and emotions. Generally, an offering that can generate emotional customer experience creates an affective relation with the company, its brand or products.
- *Cognitive component*: this component is connected with thinking or conscious mental processes and generates by engaging customers in using their creativity, problem solving skills, revision of the usual idea of a product or some common mental assumptions, etc.
- *Pragmatic component*: a component coming from engaging the customer in the practical act of doing something.
- *Lifestyle component*: a component that results from the affirmation of the system of values and the beliefs of the customer often through the adoption of a lifestyle and behaviours. For example, the offering itself and its consumption/use become a means of adhesion to certain values that customer shares with the firm.
- *Relational component*: a component that involves the customer and his/her social context, relationship with other people or his/her ideal self. Offerings encourage the use/consumption together with other people, or are the core of a common passion. This component is related to the lifestyle component as it represents a means of affirmation of a social identity, inducing a sense of belonging or of distinction from a social group.

(Schmitt, 2003: 105)

The process of customer experience: when does it occur?

To understand the process of customer experience, let's discuss first when customer experience occurs?

As explained above, early contributions from the consumer behaviour research argued that customer experience generates mainly from the consumption process, using the term 'consumption experience' (see for example, Holbrook and Hirschman, 1982; Hirschman, 1984; Holbrook, 1997).

Nevertheless, customer experience has been seen since then as much more than the consumption experience. The shopping experience, for instance, encompasses customer service, the provision of information and guidance, the chance to try out, and the search for the new (Parsons, 2002).

Schmitt looked at customer experience from a broad perspective and outlined the fact that customer experience generates from different sources according to the experience type (Schmitt, 2003) and referred to that as the experiential world.

- The experience provided by the brand, which relates to the look and feel and special features of the brand when you touch it and first use it.
- The experience provided by the product category, which relates to the functionality of the product itself in general and what the product/service is supposed to deliver.
- The experience provided by the usage or consumption situation of the brand.
- The board-based experience associated with the customer's socio-cultural contexts; this relates to the broader social and cultural aspects of the brand consumption experience, which relates usually to consumers' lifestyles and the impression they wish to leave.

According to Schmitt, customers receive stimuli through different means that trigger experience along the four experiential layers; stimuli according to the above classification can be received during the consumption process itself as in the third layer or through media tools such as magazines, movies, advertisements, etc. (Schmitt, 2003). The mechanism of how each experience type is generated in the different layers of the experiential world is similar to the 'experience clues' theory stipulated by Berry *et al.* (2006).

Another classification of the stages of customer experience was made by Arnould *et al.* (2002):

- Pre-consumption experience which includes searching for, planning, foreseeing and imagining the experiences, including day-dreaming about it.
- Purchase experience which includes the actual choice, payment and any encounter with the service and the surrounding environment during that.
- Core consumption which includes the actual sensation, the satiety, the satisfaction/dissatisfaction, the irritation/flow, and the transformation.
- Remembered consumption experience which incorporates past experiences that are based on accounts of stories and on arguments with friends about the past and which move towards the classification of memories.

Experience and emotions

Originally, consumption experience was associated with strong emotional significance (Holbrook and Hirschman, 1982; Holbrook, 1986; Holbrook, 1997). Consumption emotions are defined by (Phillips, 1999) as 'the set of valenced, directed affective responses that the consumer experiences as a result of engaging in consumption of a product or service'. Havlena and Holbrook (1986) refer to consumption emotions as the set of emotional responses elicited specifically during consumption experiences or product usage.

Recent studies that broadened the scope of customer experience to include all touch points with the brand have also emphasised its emotional component (Berry *et al.,* 2002; Gentilea *et al.,* 2007; Shaw, 2007). Shaw's (2007) research, for instance, proved that more than 50% of customer experiences are about emotions. Experience can be rich in value if it offers the right emotional benefits. He therefore outlined that there are three clusters of emotions that drive value and that organisations should focus on when they design their desired customer experiences.

The three value driving clusters of emotions are: the attention cluster, the recommendation cluster and the advocacy cluster

The attention cluster includes the feelings of being stimulated, interested, exploratory, energetic and indulgent at the beginning of an experience with a product or service, whether by seeing an ad, or making the first few visits to a place, etc. According to Shaw's research, these types of emotion have a direct impact on short-term spend.

The attention cluster includes the type of emotions that decline gradually over a period of time from 'strongly felt' to 'not felt at all' if nothing is done to alter the experience and the type of emotions evoked.

The recommendation cluster of emotion includes feelings of being valued, cared for, trusted, focused, and safe. The advocacy cluster of emotion includes feelings of being happy and pleased. Both recommendation and advocacy clusters build long-term relationships with customers and incite customers to recommend a brand and therefore create loyal customers.

According to Shaw, once an organisation has been successful in attracting a customer by evoking the attention emotions it must work to retain them and create loyal customers who keep coming back again and again. This is where organisations need to evoke the recommendation cluster and then create advocates by inciting the advocacy clusters.

The significant difference between the two clusters is that the recommendation cluster is reactive, where a consumer may only recommend a brand if they are asked, whereas advocates are proactive in advocating the use of the organisation's brand without even being asked.

Table 6.6 Types of emotional clusters associated with customer experience

Emotional cluster	Types of feelings
Attention cluster	Feelings of being stimulated, interested, exploratory, energetic and indulgent at the beginning of an experience with a product or service whether by seeing an ad, or making first few visits to the place, etc.
Recommendation cluster	Include the feelings of being valued, cared for, trusted, focused, and safe.
Advocacy cluster	Include the feelings of being happy and pleased.

Source: Shaw (2007)

Customer experience management (CEM)

Increased attention towards the concept of customer experience was associated with a rise in literature on how to manage and reengineer customer experience. The term CEM was defined by Bernd Schmitt as 'the process of strategically managing a customer's entire experience with a product or company' (Schmitt, 2003).

The degree to which the organisation is oriented towards delivering a great experience to its customer should be key to any organisational strategy and the way its drives its vision. CEM can be a very strategic concept that helps shape the strategy of an organisation and the way it delivers it vision (Schmitt, 2003).

Shaw (2005) classified organisations according to their orientation towards customer experience and divided them into four categories using the Naïve to Natural Model. Each category represents the strategic position or stand of an organisation.

The Naïve to Natural Model™ is claimed to be a very high level measure that determines the direction of a firm's strategy. It allows organisations to use the CEM concept as a strategy to help understand their orientation, or decide on one.

Figure 6.7 The Naïve to Natural Model

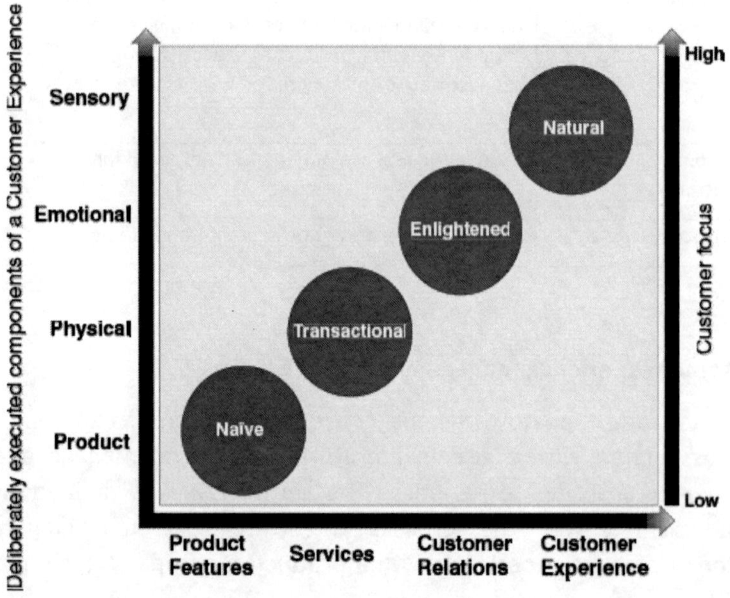

Source: Shaw (2005)

As the model suggests orientation for customer experience starts from the top and plays a key role in determining the organisation's strategy and the way it intends to deliver its vision. Determining the orientation of the organisation or its strategy in other words, may move the organisation from the naïve position to the natural position. What now follows is an explanation of all four strategic positions of an organisation in relation to customer experience management.

Naïve orientation

By definition, this is the type of organisation that focuses on itself (product, service and processes) to the detriment of the customer. It is 'inside out' rather than 'outside in'.

Obviously, these organisations are mostly unaware of the importance of understanding customer needs and driving the organisation around that, or unaware of how to do that. In some cases, organisations in this position do not lack awareness, yet they do not care because their customers are a nuisance.

Transactional orientation

These are organisations that have recognised the importance of customers, and have largely paid attention to some areas of interaction with the customer during the customer/company transaction. However they only focus on the physical aspects of the customer experience. Similar to the naïve orientation organisations adopting this approach are only reactive to customer demands.

Core measures that matter to transactional organisations relate to accessibility of services, reliability, delivery times, responsiveness, etc. Any other aspects (non-physical) of customer experience may appear but not as a result of deliberation or pre-planning.

It is also common to see management claiming that customer centricity is among their values, however, this is not really evident in the strategy or how the business is running.

Enlightened orientation

As the name suggests, enlightened organisations are those who appreciate the impact of managing customer experience, including the emotional aspect of it. Such organisations recognise the need for a holistic, coordinated, and deliberate approach to the customer experience. Organisations who adopt this position take a proactive approach towards customer needs by orchestrating emotionally engaging customer experiences.

In such organisations, customer experience has been brought to the forefront of the agenda by the management and board. Time has been spent to agree on a customer experience statement or policy, which has then been communicated to employees. Processes have been revised or new processes added, not only to deliver great physical experience but also to stimulate customers' emotions and therefore deliver great emotional experience too.

Enlightened organisations do also appreciate the importance of employee experience and undertake actions to account for it.

Natural orientation

Looking at the discussion above, one may think that enlightened organisations occupy the highest rank among organisations who wish (and should) deliver a differentiated service by adopting the CEM strategy.

Natural organisations focus on the complete customer experience naturally. They are very proactive when it comes to customer needs.

This type of organisation understands first the DNA of their customers' experience, and builds the whole organisation around that by looking at the product or service as a secondary offering. It therefore uses specific senses to evoke planned emotions and therefore deliver memorable customer experiences. It involves the customer in the design of the customer experience.

Customer experiential world

Understanding and enriching the experiential value offered to customers can be achieved by identifying the customer experiential world through the following structured steps (Schmitt, 2003). According to Schmitt this is only possible by obtaining as much as possible from customer insights including customers' values, lifestyles, self-concepts, work styles, etc.

Identify the precise target customer for the planned experience.
An analysis of the target customer that a company serves is very important, whether they are business customers (distributors, wholesalers, retailers), or individual customers.

Although this concept is not new, and identifying target customers is basically one of the old management rules, the emphasis here is oriented around understanding the different target customers from an experience point of view. Obviously, the experience desired by the individual customer who buys to directly consume by himself, is different from the desired experience of a business client who has pre-determined goals which need to be met.

Schmitt has highlighted under this area, that in understanding the customer target from an experience point of view it is also important to consider usage rate and loyalty. According to him, consumers buying for the first time have different expectations from a product/service than those of repetitive purchases. Similarly, expectations and experiences of consumers who have been loyal to a brand are different from those who have not been sticking to one brand and move from one brand to another. This is perhaps due to awareness gained through switching and comparisons that come along. 'Experiences depend on frequency of usage and loyalty.'

Define the experiential world of customers
As mentioned above, the experiential world of consumers consists generally of four layers, the experience of the product or the brand,

the product category experience, the usage and consumption situation and the socio-cultural context.

Respectively, each company has to layer the experiential world of its customers, starting with lifestyles, and funnelling it down to understanding customer usage situations, including the usage nature and users themselves, ending up with an understanding of the nature and users of the product category and then the brand.

The main purpose of this process is to understand the context that surrounds the customer experience and how the customer perception is affected by more than the product in his/her hand.

Track customer experience along all the touch-points between the company and the customer. This includes awareness of the brand too.

The emphasis of Schmitt throughout the touch points was to develop an understanding of customer experiences and how they can be enriched throughout the decision making process of customers. This is why the touch points are exclusive to the need recognition for the product, information search, information processing, choice, purchase, usage, disposal, etc. Interestingly, the focus of Schmitt in tracking the customer experience touch point was through emphasis on the decision making process

Survey the competitive landscape and examine how competition can affect the customer experience

Understanding the experiences offered by competitors and using what can be learnt to shape the company's next moves is essential. Schmitt referred to this as experiential benchmarking. Analysis of a competitive landscape includes direct competitors in the same industry and product/service category. It also includes new entrants to the market and even players outside the company industry whose experiences offered to customers can be of inspiration.

Customer experience management project

CEM can be a very strategic concept that can help shape the strategy of an organisation and the way it delivers its vision. Introducing CEM into an organisation can be done as a project that follows several sequential or parallel steps (Schmitt, 2003):

Analysing the experiential world of the consumer

This is a vital step in any CEM project, the results of which form the basis of all subsequent steps. In order to understand the experimental value chain, companies have to go through an intensive exercise to determine the target customer, analyse the customer experience world, track the experience touch points and understand the competitive landscape.

Building the experiential platform

The purpose of building an experiential platform is to communicate an organisation, its brand and the value it offers to customers. Communication is carried out internally and externally.

The experiential platform consists of three strategies: the experiential positioning, the experiential value promise and the overall implementation theme.

Experiential positioning: is an image-driven depiction of the experience that the brand stands for, it must reflect relevancy to the buyers or users of the brand.

Experiential value proposition: is mainly the conversion of the experiential positioning into reality. It refers directly to what an experiential positioning will do for a customer and what the customer will get in terms of experience when dealing with the company.

It is similar to the value proposition which relates to what value the customer gets by doing business with a certain customer, given that the value can be functional and experiential.

The above two strategies will help the company identify how it would present to the customer and what experience it must deliver.

Through the overall implementation theme, the company has to determine a concrete manifestation of the platform; this is basically a concept that fits with the style and content of the brand and all of its elements.

Designing the brand experience

Upon analysing the customer's experiential world and determining the experiential value proposition and value theme, the company will need to determine its brand experience.

This refers to all the static elements that the customer encounters with the brand, such as the logo, brochure, packaging, advertising and even the product itself. In other words, the brand experience refers to the perception created within a customer when he is in direct contact with the static aspects of the brand that has been manufactured in the factory or in the marketing department, such as communication material. Therefore, this section is not involved with the dynamic experience of the customer with the company where one-to-one interaction is required through phone calls, store visits, online purchases or online searches.

Brand experience has three key aspects:

- Product experience which relates to the customer experience generated from the customer encounter with the product. This experience is generated from the following attributes:
    - The functional attribute of the product (how well the product/service works) which is of less importance now due to the availability of high quality products in almost every

sector. Customers buy cars with a default expectation that it will function. The functionality of the car may or may not affect the customer experience or his perception of the product as this feature is expected to be there.

- The experiential features generated from the real life consumption of the product or service. Products are expected to generate an interesting and engaging experience for customers during the consumption.
- The experience generated from how the product works, and this refers to elegance, simplicity, uniqueness, intricacy, etc.
- The aesthetic appeal of the product, its design, colour, shape, etc.

- The look and feel surrounding the product, or in other words the brand identity, which refers to the brand name, logo, packaging, where the product is displayed, the store design or the website design and graphics.
- The experiential communication, which refers to the experience generated within customers when receiving communication material about the brand through different media tools, including advertising. Communication material has to provide value through information and entertainment. According to Schmitt, consumers of today are different and perceive advertising differently. 'Today's consumers, especially young customers, are market-savvy and hate being manipulated'.

Structuring the customer interface

This refers to the dynamic exchange of information and/or service that takes place between the company and the customer throughout any possible interfaces, which includes face-to-face interaction, voice or written personal but distant interaction, electronic interaction on an e-commerce site through email or SMS, which takes place using a template or mass-produced communication.

It goes without mentioning that with the introduction of e-commerce, integration of all communication methods to deliver almost the same delightful experience is very important to companies.

As this type of communication between customers and the company is very interactive and dynamic, companies have to study all touch points within this interactive experience to answer at least the following questions:

- What is the actual moment of truth? What are customers' needs, expectations, and wants at the particular touch point? How does this vary from one customer segment to another?
- What is the ideal service interaction? What are the service delivery imperatives? How does the firm deliver great anticipatory service?
- How does the firm personalise the service interaction and use the critical touch point to foster relationship building? How does this vary from one customer segment to another?
- How does the firm use the critical touch point and the interaction to bring each brand's values to life? How does it make the brand more distinct and much more relevant to targeted customer and travel occasion segments?
- How does the firm create differentiated service signals that can be owned by the brand? How does the firm create barriers to switching?
- What knowledge, analysis and technology are required to make all this happen?

Similar to the static interaction presented above, dynamic interaction has different key issues to focus on. In interface design, companies should create the right mix between each pair of the following three key interfaces:

- Essence and flexibility: where essence refers to the key operations, interaction and exchanges. In other words, it relates to the operational processes the customer goes through in his contact with the company. Flexibility, on the other hand, relates to providing the customer with a living space that makes it easy for him to complete his interaction.
- Style and substance: where style refers to the manner of expressing the first two key aspects of the interface 'essence and flexibility'; the friendliness, for example, of front-liners is part of the style. The substance, by definition, refers to real tangibles delivered through a certain style. Substance can be overwhelming or just have the right balance.
- Time: refers to the duration of the experience at every contact point. Deciding on the right engagement time of customers is very important, how long the experience should last and when the customer should leave are key questions.

Engaging in continuous innovation

Typically, customer experience when designed should still be followed by revisions and improvements. Schmitt (2003) suggested that CEM initiatives have to be followed by innovations from all types that keep improving the experience of customers.

Innovations that can affect the experience can be of three types:

- Breakthrough innovations: which relate to the launch of new products. Counting for and integrating customer experience in the design process is very important. This is practically possible with prototype testing and piloting where customer feedback is taken into consideration from an experiential point of view.
- Small innovations: across any of the brand touch points.

- Marketing innovations: which relate to promoting the experience generated by the brand through new and innovative ways, such as events, brand celebrations, etc.

Total experience management

Total experience management is a term used by Berry *et al.* (2002). The authors highlighted the necessity of going through the following steps to effectively implement total experience management:

Recognising the clues and conducting the experience audit

As explained earlier, clues can be of different types and they all make up the customer experience whether coming from the product/service functional attributes, the physical settings around it, or the gestures/comments or even appearance of employees.

Managing the total customer experience highlights the need to shed light on all types of clues related to the emotional component of the experience which, according Berry *et al.* (2002) have been neglected for a long period of time, despite its crucial impact on customers' perceptions and satisfaction.

In order for companies to gain a deeper understanding of the clues processed by customers during their encounters with the company, companies have to initiate contact with customers through discussions or observations

The 'experience audit' tool is suggested to help companies get close to their customers in a literal sense. The tool relies on using different recording technological facilities, such as stationary video cameras as well as pinhole cameras hidden in a researcher's wristwatch or clothing, to document the actual experience with the customer. Results of such processes are expected to reveal customers' emotions at different times of the transaction according to their body language and gestures.

The experience audit also relies on conducting in-depth interviews with customers and employees to find out the perspective of both and reveal how they feel about different aspects of an experience at each transaction.

Decide on the 'experience motif' that addresses the emotional needs of customers

Once the audit has been completed, the team in charge of overhauling the customer experience should use the results to develop an 'experience motif' to address the emotional needs of customers. The experience motif refers to the organisation's core values and branding strategy; in other words, the theme of the experience which is desired to be on offer by the company. It is mainly a unifying element that acts as a reference point for the team when deciding on the clues that need to be sent to create the new customer experience.

The motif can be described in a few words to describe the desired experience or the theme of the customer experience intended to be received. Feeling 'recognised, reassured and engaged' or 'create a feeling of psychological comfort' are two suggested motifs. Other motifs can be 'extraordinary people', 'classy treatment', 'state-of-the-art' (Berry *et al.,* 2002).

A motif is 'a succinct, verbal characterisation of the desired take-away customer perception'.

According to the authors, the ultimate reason for deciding on an experience motif is to simulate a scene of mechanic and humanic clues with graphical and narrative presentation in order to leave the desired perception and hence create the intended experience.

The desired clues are then used as a road map of drawings and narratives to implement the necessary changes.

To decide on the experience motif, or in other words, select the right experience design or experience engineering, Berry *et al.* (2002) recommend the following best practices:

Assume control, with style

Companies should assume control over its customers' experiences. This establishes its style. Although the word style was not defined by Berry *et al.* (2002) in this article, a few examples were made indicating that style can be boldness or subtlety, commands or suggestions, politeness or bluntness, personal or impersonal.

Mechanics and humanics

Berry *et al.* (2002) suggest that companies have to start paying a lot of attention to humanic clues sent to customers. Training of employees is necessary:

> *Managers have a fairly good understanding of mechanics clues because they are often an important part of product design - the shape, quiet operation, colors, smells, and textures of a new car, for example. Not as obvious, perhaps, is the extent to which new technologies can enhance the range and impact of mechanics.*

They suggest that paying the same amount of attention to humanics is necessary. They argue that empowering personnel to deal with customer rising issues or problems 'on the spot' whenever they occur is not the right strategy, because it does not assure consistency in delivering the desired experience unless employees are carefully selected and trained to be equipped with highly intuitive skills that assess and sense customer reactions to service encounter clues and respond accordingly and appropriately.

Thematic 'Sticktion'

By this, Berry *et al.* (2002) mean that the company should be careful about the motive it uses to brand the offering. Some negative themes may backfire. However, no clues were really given to provide hints on what would be a good theme and what would not.

Integrate process and experience designs

Deciding on the experience motif and designing the desired customer experience should not be done in isolation. It must be intimately associated with the financial, operational, motivational, and training business processes.

Berry *et al.* (2002) argue that customer experience frameworks should be reinforced by a complementary employee motivational scheme. Customer experience and design of humanic and mechanic clues must be dealt with in the same way as any other business process in the company, and therefore it should involve objectives for desired performance, identification and sequencing of tasks, resources, decisions, and human accountabilities. The authors argue that any process design or reengineering project is half complete if it does not consider the experience design process.

According to this perspective, the following section will consider how to look at customer experience as a process and will examine what is meant by engineering customer experience.

Engineering customer experience

Engineering customer experience is also a term that has emerged in recent literature. Berry *et al.* (2002) propose a four-phase process for engineering the customer experience. They argue that those stages have proved effective in different types of situations ranging from shopping and retail to building a home.

Phase I: Acquisition of service experience design skills

The following main tasks are included in this stage:

- Assembling a cross-functional team with representatives from all the major functions and operational processes of the company.

It is important to involve a large number of representations from people who have daily contact with customers.

- Train the team on concepts and methodologies of customer experience engineering and the concept of customer experience. This should also include creating awareness and ability to recognise the different types of clues and their impact. The training conducted should be also carried out across the organisation to create clue-consciousness and customer empathy throughout the organisation with specific attention to honing employees' intuitive and perceptive skills to enable them to respond to daily issues with customers and to create a culture of treating employees as facilitators of experience architecture.
- The team will be responsible for clarifying the experience that will be delivered and evaluating it against a number of criteria to identify the motif, and isolating those places where sticktion could support this motif.

Phase II: Data collection and analysis

Collecting data about how customers evaluate the experience represents the second stage of this process. Berry *et al.* (2002) argue that using typical surveying methods that provide quantitative factual evidence may be misleading and believe that sensory impressions can outweigh factual evidence in forming perceptions about the experience. They therefore recommend the following stage:

- Recruiting customer panels as customer representations and exposing them to either the existing experience or a realistic mock-up of a planned experience.
- Monitoring and recording what they see, hear, taste, touch, smell, and feel in detail at each phase of the experience and in response to each designed clue.

- If possible, and in order to benchmark for what Berry *et al.* called 'best of breed' clues, a comparable study at a competitors' location is recommended.

Phase III: Service clue design

The second stage of this process requires gathering as much input as possible before the assigned team unleash their imagination to generate a detailed index of additional clues, their impact to enhance or detract from the desired 'takeaway perception'. This phase however, is led by an 'experience architect' who is responsible for the process of analysing, creating, categorising and modifying humanics and mechanics clues.

The ultimate goal is to eliminate the negative service clues and or to move them into the 'commodity zone', and to insert highly differentiated clues to build preferred experience.

Evaluation of the impact of experiences and the sequencing of them is carried out technically using a tool called an engineered Experience Blueprint.

The Experience Blueprint is a set of blueprint drawings that include graphic depictions of the service clues at all phases of a particular experience; each phase is referred to as a layer. For each one of the experience layers, a set of specifications that summarise the ranking of the clues, their impact, estimated financial costs and the operational impact is prepared on a corresponding page. This process of evaluating layered clues helps build a commutative perception of the aggregate effect of certain clues in establishing a composite experience impression for customers.

Berry *et al.* (2002) believe that clues should then be organised in three groups: those 'that should have been implemented yesterday' – obviously, this includes immediate fixes and removal of negative clues; the second group includes the set of clues that 'we can implement today' to create a preferred experience; and those 'to be done in the future' for reasons that prevent them from taking place now, such as technology constraints.

Ultimately, at the end of this stage, the team is required to find those combinations of clues that have the highest impact for the target customer they have studied.

Phase IV: Implementation and verification

This stage includes prototyping as many constituencies of clues as possible, with a subset of clues being chosen to validate costs, specifications, and impact.

The same tool 'graphic depiction' is used then to communicate the design to the entire organisation in order to promote understanding and buy-in.

Customer experience in online business settings

Wolfinbarger and Gilly (2001) divided online customers into experiential oriented and goal-oriented. Experiential customers have an ongoing, hobby-type interest, and enjoy auctions, involvement with a hobby/product class and bargains. Experiential consumers are interested in the excitement and community created by bidding sites and they enjoy surprises such as new products and features.

Goal-oriented customers

Goal-oriented customers are interested in freedom and control as much as the outcome of the experience. They are interested in finishing the task as quickly as possible with the fewest clicks without wasting any time, and with maximum ease of use; they would like to do the job themselves and to receive immediate responses to their questions. Goal-oriented customers enjoy control over the experience in terms of the information they receive, the sites they visit, and the time they choose to make the purchase. They also enjoy the freedom provided by the online experience, where they do not need to interact with a salesperson, or wait in lines to receive a service.

This type of customer is motivated to shop online only when they have a specific purchase in mind. They use the online environment largely because of planned purchases, which they can complete at a convenient time, indicating that they like the less committed experience compared with offline settings and the low level of pressure they feel due to a facility that allows them to pick up their purchase where they left it, which in turn increases their feeling of control, an outcome Wolfinbarger and Gilly (2001) found to be valued among goal-oriented customers. Goal-oriented consumers emphasise accomplishment, and therefore start with a purpose in mind, go to a specific site, look for a specific product, find the best price for a specific item and make repeat purchases.

Goal-oriented customers were found to appreciate the convenience, informativeness, selection and lack of sociality in online environments, which contributed to their increased feelings of freedom and control.

Experiential-oriented customers

Experiential shoppers, on the other hand, are interested in fun as the ultimate outcome of the experience. They would like to be engaged in a site that draws them in, allows them to interact with other consumers, and shows them a lot of choices. They would like to browse sites that are related to their hobbies and give them a unique experience. Experiential shoppers enjoy the fun provided by reading reviews, getting drawn into a site, the excitement of bidding, window shopping and surprises.

Experiential customers were found to value some specific benefits of the online environment, such as the opportunity for surprise/

uniqueness/excitement, the positive sociality, online deal searching and involvement with a product class. Online consumers associated the experience with fun and were interested in ongoing hobby-type searches which allowed for many experiential benefits where products change often, are unique or collectable and where consumers' activities involve an element of risk or gaming. Consumers enjoy chatting with other customers about their shared hobbies, checking out sites of interest, and looking for new items, updated information and new deals.

In conclusion, experiential customers emphasise enjoyment through surfing/trying new sites, looking for new things, looking for ideas, checking favourite sites regularly, bargain hunting for what's on sale and killing time.

Compelling online experience

Hoffman and Novak (2007) argue that despite the efforts of marketers over the past decade to gain some understanding of marketing strategies that attract visitors to the wide range of commercial websites, less is known about the factors that make using the web a compelling experience for its users and the impact of that on consumer behaviour.

Rather than addressing customer perceived quality per se, Hoffman and Novak's focus was flow as a means to establishing a 'compelling online experience'. Flow or (experiential flow as it was called by Huang, 2003) is a construct that has been highly emphasised in the marketing literature related to online environments (Novak and Hoffman *et al.,* 2000; Novak and Hoffman *et al.,* 2003; Hoffman and Novak, 2007).

Traditionally, flow or experiential flow has been defined as the optimal experience through which we feel 'in control of our actions, masters of our own fate...we feel a sense of exhilaration, a deep sense of enjoyment' (Csikszentmihalyi, 1975).

According to Hoffman and Novak (1996) online flow is 'the state occurring during network navigation which is characterised by a seamless sequence of responses facilitated by machine interactivity, intrinsically enjoyable, accompanied by a loss of self-consciousness, and self-reinforcing'. They also argue that 'creating a commercially compelling website depends on facilitating a state of flow'.

Flow relates to users' complete engagement and immersion in web activities so that there is little attention left to consider anything else (Hoffman and Novak, 1996). Accordingly, flow creates a compelling experience through congruence of skill and challenge, interactivity, vividness, and motivation.

Flow is both cognitive and affective (Huang, 2003). It is also believed to consist of the following four components: a sense of control over the computer interaction, the degree to which the user's attention is focused on the interaction, the curiosity aroused during the interaction, and the extent to which the user finds the interaction intrinsically interesting (Trevino and Webster, 1992).

According to Novak and Hoffman *et al.* (2000), flow is a cognitive state that creates compelling online experiences which are positively correlated with fun, recreational and experiential uses of the web, expected use of the web in the future as well as the amount of time consumers spend online.

As a result of the flow, self-consciousness disappears, the consumer's sense of time becomes distorted, and the state of mind arising as a result of achieving flow on the web is extremely gratifying.

They identified flow as 'the state occurring during network navigation which is characterized by a seamless sequence of responses facilitated by machine interactivity, intrinsically enjoyable, accompanied by a loss of self-consciousness, and ... self-reinforcing'.

Flow during online navigation is determined by (Hoffman and Novak, 1996) as:

- High levels of skill and control.
- High levels of challenge and arousal.
- Focused attention.
- Enhanced by interactivity and telepresence.

According to that, to experience flow while engaged in online interactive environments, consumers must perceive a balance between their skills and the challenges of the interaction, which both must be above a critical threshold. Enough challenge is necessary to arouse consumers, too much challenge or too little challenge can cause consumers to log off out of frustration or boredom. Similarly, Pearce, Ainley and Howard (2005) define flow as a difference measure between skill and challenge. Along these lines, Mathwick and Rigdon (2004) identified a 'flow cluster', referring to individuals with high internet search skills and high navigational challenges of the search task.

Flow was also reported in utilitarian and hedonic online shopping (Sénécal *et al.,* 2002; Bridgesa and Florsheimb, 2008). Not only was this contrary to expectations, it was found that reported flow experiences were actually more prevalent among goal-directed users (Novak and Hoffman *et al.,* 2003).

Despite the fact that the construct has been widely studied over the past decade in marketing and related fields, it has proven to be an elusive construct to measure and model (Hoffman and Novak, 2007).

Components of the online customer experience

Minocha *et al.* (2006) provided a useful classification of a total customer experience (TCE). According to them, TCE consists of six stages; expectations setting, pre-purchase, e-purchase, post-purchase, consumption and post (TCE) evaluation.

- Expectations setting: during this stage the customer draws upon a number of influences to create his/her personal benchmark of service quality expectations which are going to play a vital role in the decision made later on. Influences can be social, organisational or individual influences and they include the customer's motivations, his needs along with the benefits and costs of shopping online, recommendations, word-of-mouth, advertising, brand, his own experiences of interacting with off-line business channels of that and other organisations, etc.
- Pre-purchase stage: during this stage, the customer chooses a website, carries out the necessary searches for a product or service and makes a decision about whether or not to make a purchase. Such decisions are influenced by several factors, such as website usability, information provided, the price, the credibility of the website, delivery mechanisms and refund policies, etc.
- E-purchase: during this stage, the customer selects the product/ service and completes the transaction; this usually involves entering personal details, billing and delivery information, and payment details.
- Post-purchase: this stage involves tracking the order and the receipt of the products/services. During this stage, the customer may need to query an order, complain about the state of the delivery, or question his payment handling. He might need to contact the organisation at a touch point other than the website.
- Consumption.
- Post TEC evaluation: at this stage, the customer will review his online experiences and compare that with his benchmark of expectations that were set during stage one, and therefore

assess whether or not he/she has received value from this experience.

Minocha et al. (2006) argue that unpleasant or unsatisfactory experiences across any of the stages may render a negative TCE and make it unlikely that the customer will return to the site for future business.

Figure 6.8 The total customer experience in online environments

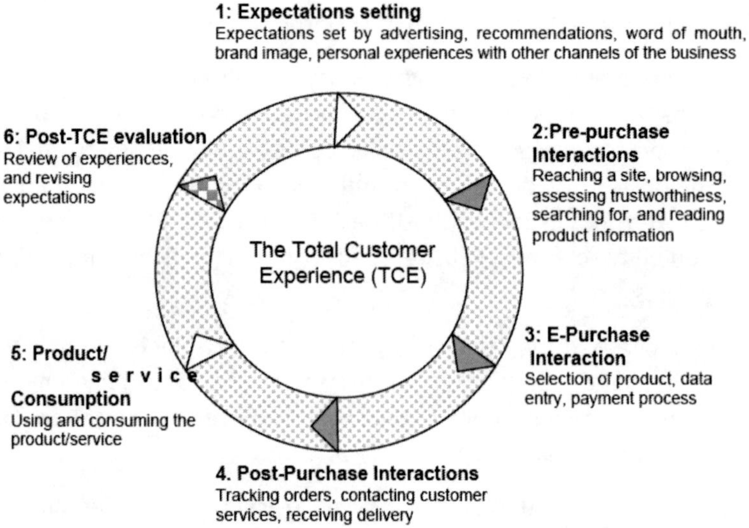

Source: Minocha *et al.* (2006)

Conclusion

Online environments may lack some of the qualities that traditional business have (Monsuwe *et al.,* 2004), nevertheless, the technological revolution of the internet has brought more opportunities to the overall customer experience (Laukkanen 2006).

New internet technologies have empowered customers (Prahalad and Ramaswamy, 2004), allowed for their engagement in self-driven activities (Dawes and Rowley, 1998), and provided the platforms for customers to become part of a social group and enjoy control over the experience in online environments (Hoffman, Novak *et al.*, 2000).

Online environments differ in multiple ways from conventional environments. It is more convenient (Wolfinbarger and Gilly, 2001; Mäenpää *et al.*, 2006; To *et al.*, 2007) and provides customers with greater control over their choices and what they engage in. The online environment is fundamentally different from conventional environments because of its bi-directional many-to-many communication possibility (Choi *et al.*, 2004), the availability of wide and rich information selection (Wolfinbarger and Gilly, 2001; Zeithaml *et al.*, 2002; Prahalad and Ramaswamy, 2004; Kim *et al.*, 2006), and the offering of new types of products (Wang *et al.*, 2001).

Additionally, online consumers are expected to help themselves and drive their self-controlled experiences (Dawes and Rowley, 1998) and are provided with the facilities for differentiated experiences that are richer and require a higher level of consumer involvement (Mascarenhas *et al.*, 2006).

Studies of evolution of customer motivation and behaviour models, affirmed that customers are and have always been about the experience (Holbrook, 2000). Accordingly, and whether it is staged by companies or co-created along with the customer, the importance of paying attention to customer experience is increasingly being picked up by researchers and practitioners in traditional and online business settings.

References

Addis, M. and Holbrook, M. B. (2001) On the Conceptual Link Between Mass Customisation and Experiential Consumption: An Explosion of Subjectivity. *Journal of Consumer Behaviour* 1(1): 50-66.

Arnold, M. J. and K. E. Reynolds (2003) Hedonic shopping motivations, *Journal of Retailing,* 79: 77-95.

Arnould, E. J., Price, L. L. and Zinkhan, G.M. (2002) *Consumers*, McGraw-Hill, New York.

Babin, B. J., Darden, W. R. and Griffin, M. (1994) Work and/or Fun: Measuring Hedonic and Utilitarian Shopping Value. *Journal of Consumer Research* 20(4): 644.

Batra, R. and Ahtola, O. T. (1991) Measuring the hedonic and utilitarian sources of customer attitudes. *Marketing Letters* 12(2): 159-170.

Berry, L. L., Carbone, L. P. and Haeckel, S. H. (2002) Managing the Total Customer Experience. *MIT Sloan Management Review*, 43 (3): 85-89.

Berry, L. L., Shankar, V., Parish, J. T., Cadwallader, S. and Dotzel, T (2006) Creating New Markets Through Service Innovation. *MIT Sloan Management Review,* 47(2): 56-63.

Bridgesa, E. and Florsheimb, R. (2008) Hedonic and utilitarian shopping goals: The online experience. *Journal of Business Research* 61(4): 309-314

Britton, D. and McGonegal, S. (2008) *The Digital Economy Fact Book - 2007.* Retrieved December 2008, from www.pff.org/issues-pubs/books/factbook_2007.pdf.

Buttle, F. C. (1984) Shopping motives. *The Service Industries Journal* 4(1): 71-82.

Carù, A. and Cova, B. (2003a) *A Critical Approach To Experiential Consumption: Fighting Against The Disappearance Of The Contemplative Time.* 3rd International Critical Management Studies Conference, Lancaster University.

Caru, A. and Cova, B. (2003b) Revisiting Consumption Experience: A More Humble But Complete View of the Concept. *Marketing Theory* 3(2): 267-86.

Chang, C. Y. C. (2006) What customers perceive during their online shopping experience.

Childers, T. L., Carr, C. L., Peck, J. and Carson S. (2001) Hedonic and utilitarian motivations for online retail shopping behavior. *Journal of Retailing* 77(4): 511-535.

Choi, B., Lee, C., Lee, H. and Subramani, M. (2004) Effects of Web Retail Service Quality and Product Categories on Consumer Behavior: A Research Model and Empirical Exploration. *Proceedings of the 37th Hawaii International Conference on System Sciences:* 177–186.

ClickZ (2006) *New Online Activities Show Greatest Growth.* Retrieved December 2008, from http://www.clickz.com/3624155.

Coelho, F. and Easingwood, C. (2003) Multiple channel structures in financial services: a framework. *Journal of Financial Services Marketing,* 8(1): 22-34.

Csikszentmihalyi, M. (1975) *Beyond boredom and anxiety.* San Francisco, Jossey-Bass.

Dawes, J. and Rowley, J. (1998) Enhancing the customer experience: contributions from information technology. *Management Decision,* 36(5): 350-357.

Demangeot, C. and Broderick, A. J. (2007) Conceptualising consumer behaviour in online shopping environments. *International Journal of Retail & Distribution Management,* 35(11): 878-894.

eMarketer (2007) *Apparel E-Commerce.* Retrieved December 2008, from http://www.emarketer.com/Reports/All/Emarketer_2000423.aspx.

eMarketer (2008a) *Blogs and the Purchasing Decision.* Retrieved December 2008, from http://www.emarketer.com/Article.aspx?id=1006716.

eMarketer (2008b) *UK B2C E-Commerce: Continued Growth in Tricky Times.* Retrieved December 2008, from http://www.emarketer.com/Reports/All/Emarketer_2000527.aspx.

Evans, P. and Wurster, T (1999) *Blown to Bits: How the New Economics of Information Transforms Strategy.* Boston, MA, Harvard Business School Press.

Firat, F. A. (1987) Towards a Deeper Understanding if Consumption experiences: The Underlying Dimensions. *Advances in Consumer Research*: 342-346.

Forrester (2005) *2005 US eCommerce: The Year In Review - An Overview Of Annual And Q4 US Online Retail Sales.* Sucharita Mulpuru.

GCCRM (2007) *Defining CEM,* White Paper Retrieved May 2007, 2007, from www.gccrm.com.

Gentilea, C., Spillera, N., *et al.* (2007) How to Sustain the Customer Experience: An Overview of Experience Components that Co-create Value With the Customer *European Management Journal*, 25(5): 395-410.

Gilmore, J. H. and Pine, I.I. (2002) Customer experience places: the new offering frontier. *Strategy & Leadership* 30(4): 4-11.

Hagel, J. and Armstrong, A. (1997) *Expanding Markets through Virtual Communities*, Harvard Business School Press.

Havlena, W. J. and Holbrook, M. B. (1986) The Varieties of Consumption Experience: Comparing Two Typologies of Emotion in Consumer Behavior. *Journal of Consumer Research* 13(December): 394-404.

Hirschman, E. (1984) Experience Seeking: A Subjectivist Perspective of Consumption. *Journal of Business Research* 12: 115-136.

Hoffman, D. L. and Novak, T. P. (1996) Marketing in Hypermedia Computer-Mediated Environments: Conceptual Foundations. *Journal of Marketing*, 60: 50-68.

Hoffman, D. L. and Novak, T. P. (2007) *Flow Online: Lessons Learned and Future Prospects.* eLab Sloan Volume, DOI.

Hoffman, D. L., Novak, T. P. *et al.* (2000). *Consumer Control in Online Environments.* Elab. vanderbilt. edu, February.

Holbrook, M. and Corfman, K. P. (1985) Quality and Value in the Consumption Experience: Phaedrus Rides Again, in *Perceived Quality.* J. Jacoby and J. Olsen. Lexington, Mass, Lexington Books: 31-57.

Holbrook, M. B. (1986) Emotion in the Consumption Experience: Toward a New Model of the Human Consumer The Role of Affect in Consumer Behaviour, in *Emerging Theories and Applications* R. A. Peterson, W. D. Hoyer and W. R. Wilson. Lexington MA, DC, Heath and Co: 17-52.

Holbrook, M. B. (1994) The Nature of Customer Value: An Axiology of Services in the Consumption Experience. in *Service Quality: New directions in theory and practice.* R. T. Rust and R. L. Oliver. London, Sage Publications: 21-71.

Holbrook, M. B. (1997) Romanticism, Introspection, and the Roots of Experiential Consumption in *Consumption, Markets and Culture* 1(2): 97-164.

Holbrook, M. B. (2000) The Millennial Consumer in the Texts of Our Times: Experience and Entertainment. *Journal of Macromarketing* 20(2): 178.

Holbrook, M. B. (2001) The Millennial Consumer in the Texts of Our Times: Exhibitionism. *Journal of Macromarketing* 21(1): 81-95.

Holbrook, M. B. and Hirschman, E. C. (1982) The experiential aspects of consumption: Consumer fantasies, feelings, and fun. *Journal of Consumer Research,* 9(September): 132-40.

Huang, M. H. (2003) Designing website attributes to induce experiential encounters. *Computers in Human Behavior,* 19(4): 425-442.

ISC (2008) *ISC Domain Survey.* Internet Systems Consortium, Retrieved December 2008, from https://www.isc.org/solutions/survey.

Keaveney, S. M. (1995) Customer Switching Behavior in Service Industries: An Exploratory Study. *Journal of Marketing*, 59(2): 71-82.

Kim, W. G., Ma, X. *et al.* (2006) Determinants of Chinese hotel customers'e-satisfaction and purchase intentions. *Tourism Management*, 27(5): 890-900.

Klein, L. R. (2003) Creating virtual product experiences: The role of telepresence. *Journal of Interactive Marketing*, 17(1): 41-55.

Korgaonkar, P. K. and Wolin, D. (1999) A multivariate analysis of web usage. *Journal of Advertising Research*, (March/April): 53-68.

LaSalle, D. and Britton, T. (2003) P*riceless: Turning Ordinary Products Into Extraordinary Experiences,* Harvard Business School Press.

Laukkanen, T. (2006) Customer-perceived value of e-financial services: a means-end approach. *International Journal of Electronic Finance* 1(1): 5-17.

Lawler, J. and A. Joseph (2006) A Study of Apparel Dress Model Technology on the Web. *Journal of Information, Information Technology, and Organisations*, 1: 59-73.

Mäenpää, K., Kanto, A. *et al.* (2006) More hedonic versus less hedonic consumption behaviour in advanced internet bank services." *Journal of Financial Services Marketing,* 11(1): 4-16.

Mahoney, S. (2007) *When It Comes To Shopping, Offline Action Drives Searchers Online*. MediaPost Publications Retrieved December 2008, from http://publications.mediapost.com/index.cfm?fuseaction=Articles.printEdition&art_send_date=2007-3-26&art_type=13.

Mascarenhas, O. A., Kesavan, R. *et al.* (2006) Lasting customer loyalty: a total customer experience approach. *Journal of Consumer Marketing*, 23(7): 397-405.

Mathwick, C., Malhotra, N. *et al.* (2001) Experiential value: conceptualization, measurement and application in the catalog and Internet shopping environment? *Journal of Retailing,* 77(1): 39-56.

Mathwick, C. and Rigdon, E. (2004) Play, Flow, and the Online Search Experience. *Journal of Consumer Research*, 31(September): 324-332.

Milligan, A. and Smith, S. (2002) *Uncommon Practice: People who Deliver a Great Brand Experience*, Financial Times Prentice Hall.

Minocha, S., Dawson, L., Blandford, A. and Millard, N. (2005) Providing Value to Customers in E-Commerce environments: The Customer's Perspective, in *Contemporary Research in E-Marketing*, IDEA Group, PA, USA.

Monsuwe, T. P., Dellaert, B. G. C. *et al.* (2004) What drives consumers to shop online? A literature review. *International Journal of Service Industry Management*, 15(1): 102-121.

Moon, Y. and Frei, F. X. (2000) Exploding the Self-Service Myth. *Harvard Business Review* 78(3): 26-27.

Nielsen (2007) *Over 875 Million Consumers Have Shopped Online - the Number of Internet Shoppers Up 40% in Two Years* The Nielsen Company Retrieved December 2008, from www.earthtimes.org/articles/show/over-875-million-consumers-have-shopped-online--the-number,263812.shtml.

Novak, T. P., Hoffman, D. L. *et al.* (2003) The Influence of Goal-Directed and Experiential Activities on Online Flow Experiences. *Journal of Consumer Psychology*, 13(1&2): 3-16.

Novak, T. P., D. L. Hoffman, *et al.* (2000). "Measuring the Customer Experience in Online Environments: A Structural Modeling Approach." Marketing Science 19(1): 22-42.

Novak, T. P., Hoffman, D. L. *et al.* (2000) Measuring the Flow Construct in Online Environments: A Structural Modeling Approach. *Marketing Science*, 19(1): 22-44.

OECD (2007) *The Future of the Internet Economy - A Statistical Profile,* Organisation For Economic Co-Operation And Development, Retrieved December 2008, from www.oecd.org/dataoecd/44/56/40827598.pdf

OECD (2008) *The Future of the Internet Economy*, Organisation For Economic Co-Operation And Development Retrieved December 2008, from www.oecd.org/dataoecd/20/41/40789235.pdf.

Oliver, R. L. (1993) A conceptual model of service quality and service satisfaction: compatible goals, different concepts. *Advances in Services Marketing and Management*, 2: 65-85.

Oliver, R. L. (1999) Whence consumer loyalty? *Journal of Marketing*, 63(Special Issue): 33 - 44.

Parsons, A. G. (2002) Non-functional motives for online shoppers: why we click. *Journal of Consumer Marketing,* 19(4/5): 380-392.

Pearce, J. M., Ainley, M., & Howard, S. (2005) The Ebb and Flow of Online Learning. *Computers in Human Behavior*, 21(5), 745-771.

Phillips, D. M. (1999) *The role of consumption emotions in the satisfaction response.* The Pennsylvania State University, The Pennsylvania State University. Doctoral dissertation.

Pooler, J. (2003) *Why We Shop: Emotional Rewards and Retail Strategies,* Westport, USA Praeger Publishers.

Prahalad, C. K. and Ramaswamy, V. (2004) Co-creating unique value with customers. *Strategy & Leadership* 32(3): 4-9.

Richins, M. L. (1997) Measuring Emotions in the Consumption Experience. *Journal of Consumer Research: An Interdisciplinary Quarterly* 24(2): 127-46.

Schiffman , L., G and Kanuk, L. (2004) *Consumer Behaviour.* New Jersey, Prentice-Hall Inc.

Schmitt, B. H. (2003). Customer Experience Management. A Revolutionary Approach to Connecting with Your Customers Hoboken, New Jersey John Wiley & Sons.

Sénécal, S., Gharbi, J. E. *et al.* (2002) The influence of flow on hedonic and utilitarian shopping values. *Advanced Consumer Research*, 29(pp. 483-484).

Shaw, C. (2005) *Revolutionize Your Customer Experience*: Palgrave Macmillan, NY.

Shaw, C. (2007) *The DNA of Customer Experience*, Palgrave Macmillan, NY.

Shaw, C. and Ivens, J. (2002) *Building Great Customer Experiences*, Palgrave Macmillan, NY.

Sheth, J. N. (2003) Emerging trends for the retail industry, *Journal of Retailing*, 59, 3, 6-18.

Sifry's Alerts (2007) *The State of the Live Web, April 2007.* Retrieved December 2008, from http://www.sifry.com/alerts/archives/000493.html.

Smith, S. and Wheeler, J. (2002) *Managing the Customer Experience: Turning Customers into Advocates,* Financial Times/Prentice Hall.

Tauber, E. M. (1972) Why do people shop? *Journal of Marketing*, 36(October): 46-59.

The NPD Group (2007) *Legal Music Downloads Were Fastest Growing - Digital Music Category in 2006*. The NPD Group Retrieved December 2008, from http://npd.com/press/releases/press_0703141.html

Thompson, C. J., Locander, W. B. *et al.* (1999) The Lived Meaning of Free Choice: An Existential-Phenomenological Description of Everyday Consumer Experiences of Contemporary Married Women. *Journal of Consumer Research*, 17(December): pp. 346-361.

To, P. L., Liao, C. *et al.* (2007) Shopping motivations on Internet: A study based on utilitarian and hedonic value. *Technovation*, 27(12): 774-787.

Trevino, L. K. and Webster, J. (1992) Flow in computer-mediated communication. *Communication Research* 19 (5): 539-573.

Wang, M. and S. A. Huarng (2002) An Empirical Study of Internet Store Customer Postshopping Satisfaction. *Special Issues of Information Systems* 3: 632-638.

Wang, Y., T. Tang, *et al.* (2001) An instrument for measuring customer satisfaction toward web sites that market digital products and services. *Journal of Electronic Commerce Research*, 2(3): 89-102.

Westbrook, R. A. and Black, W. C. (1985) A motivation-based shopper typology. *Journal of Retailing*, 61(1): 78-103.

Wolfinbarger, M. and M. C. Gilly (2001) Shopping Online for Freedom, Control, and Fun. *California Management Review,* 43(2): 34-55.

Yu, L. (2006) *Cross-Shopping and Shopping Orientation: Consumer Perceived Value in Today's Dynamic Retail Environment*. Faculty of The Graduate School. Greensboro, The University of North Carolina. PhD: 206pp.

Zeithaml, V. A., Parasuraman, A. *et al.* (2002) Service quality delivery through web sites: a critical review of extant knowledge. *Journal of the Academy of Marketing Science,* 30(4): 362-75.

Chapter 7

How do customers get Fast + Simple experiences from companies like Amazon

A Survey Report Published by LimeBridge Global Alliance

Foreword

Our passion - How do we stop doing dumb things to customers? Over the last ten years we have worked on many practical approaches to developing great customer experiences. With over 300 clients in many countries, our learning has been distilled into an approach that fits the way customers and clients are interacting in maturing markets. We describe our passion as 'how do we stop doing dumb things to customers and people?' We describe what customers want as a 'fast and simple' experience. As we advocated in our 2004 white paper, businesses need to remove the frustrations that customers repeatedly experience, if they want to be trusted. They need to maximise how much time and value their customers are prepared to spend and invest with them but they can only do that if they get the basics right. We, as customers in the 21st century, want to tell companies how to improve – if only they would listen and act on what we could tell them. Loyalty, churn and frustration are inherently linked. We do not expect companies to be perfect all the time. What sets the 'excellent' out from the 'not so great' are the companies who consistently get the basics right. And when they get something wrong, they admit it and put it right. They listen and act. As we evidenced in our 2004 executive research, it is crucial to be systematic if you want to win in this environment. The system being described is a closed loop of customer/ programmes/operations. 'Closing the loop' was identified as the critical factor in optimising customer experience and in optimising the performance of people and business results.

In our 2005 executive research we have looked at how companies have been progressing from an environment of talking about customers to one where the easier things have been, or are, getting fixed. An environment in which the challenge is to perform the basics consistently well. And having started to do that, they must now join up the various parts of the loop, fixing their weakest links and bringing systematic improvement to the customer. Not just once but in consistent end to end processes.

We believe best practice companies which deliver Fast+Simple experiences:

a. Work systematically to remove their customers' frustrations.

b. Have strong leadership and are, more often than not, led by someone who has an eye for the real detail of what customers experience.

c. Have completely thought through what they do, so they can see a beginning, a middle and an end to what they do and why they do it for their customers –they have vision and joined up thinking.

d. Focus on delivering Brilliant Basics consistently.

e. Focus on their people.

f. Are systematic, wasting as little energy as possible.

g. Work in closed loops by planning, monitoring and analysing what they do so they can improve it.

Reproduced with special permission from LimeBridge – 'Making your business Fast + Simple™ for your customers' (Senior Executive Survey on How do customers get Fast + Simple experiences from companies like Amazon and what can you learn from that?) March 2005, www.limebridge.com

h. Use all the data they have and don't go looking for data they can't or don't use.

There is a range of best practice processes that we examined last year. In this 2005 report we have researched the return on investment that companies have been making from one particular best practice process that closes the loop for Amazon.com. We have also researched what companies are saying is stopping them closing the loop and what they think are their most important issues related to customers.

Extracts from the 2005 executive research are provided in the appendix and we expect to provide a further short paper shortly looking at these results in more depth.

Introduction

This white paper discusses the types of issues companies face in 2005 in trying to be Fast+Simple for their customers and gives best practice learning from companies who have excelled in 'closing the loop' across their organisations. It demonstrates how companies have been producing 300% return on investments by implementing a closed loop process called Skyline, originally developed at Amazon.com.

This white paper evidences the following argument:

- Customers want Fast+Simple experiences.
- 2004 research showed that the critical factor in delivering Fast+Simple experiences is closing the loop of 'customer/programmes/operations'.
- 2005 research shows boards are accountable for what customers want but the biggest barrier to being Fast+Simple is failure to act systematically as one organisation.

- Companies are trying ways to reduce cost and ways to improve customer satisfaction rather than addressing the systemic problem of closing the loop.
- Amazon.com is a great example of creating Fast+Simple experiences by closing the loop in a process called Skyline.
- A range of companies in the US, Europe, Australia and elsewhere are now reaping the rewards of implementing this best practice process.
- Applying the best practice processes for closing the loop brings differentiation AND cost advantage AND increased employee morale AND customer satisfaction.

Customers want Fast+Simple experiences

The competitive battle today is about delivering appealing products, quality services and making it easy for customers to do business with you – and so providing the reason for customers to want to stay with you. All too often, companies offer the opposite experience. Customers are frustrated by the dumb things that companies do and the poor response they receive in the name of 'Customer Service'.

Simply better

In their latest book *Simply Better* (HBS Press, 2004), Barwise and Meehan of London Business School offer a great deal of evidence for Limebridge's Fast+Simple approach. They strongly advocate the identification of what annoys customers about a category rather than focusing on unique brand benefits within the category. For example: Shell's work on providing clean toilets in petrol stations, Virgin addressing boredom on long flights. They strongly advocate simplicity rather than sophistication in a category. This means concentrating on the basics that customers want when they buy

Reproduced with special permission from LimeBridge – 'Making your business Fast + Simple™ for your customers' (Senior Executive Survey on How do customers get Fast + Simple experiences from companies like Amazon and what can you learn from that?) March 2005, www.limebridge.com

petrol rather than on the quality of the cappuccino served in a garage. 'Understanding the customers' priorities and ensuring that they were consistently satisfied on the basic attributes.....was challenging because the company had to introduce so many frontline employees to the approach'[1].

Go shop yourself

But companies continue to behave in ways that ensure customers shop elsewhere. According to one report, an estimated 84 percent of shoppers who go into computer and home entertainment shops leave empty-handed through frustration. The willingness of some staff in DIY and electrical stores to recommend a rival store rather than help the customer, costs an estimated £8bn in lost sales[2]. The most common replies to difficult questions were: 'Best advice I can give you is to go to xxx....'- in other words, to the competitor who is easy to do business with.

Winners listen and sense their customers for free

Companies that are able to listen and respond to what is important to their customers in an integrated way develop a strong competitive advantage. Not only are they able to remove negative customer noise, they are able to re-deploy resources to offer better service, to listen more effectively to the positive things customers are telling them and leverage this knowledge into new products or service innovation.

If you can leverage all the conversations your staff have with customers then, for example, a 100 FTE contact centre is investing

---

[1] Simply better: Winning and Keeping Customers by Delivering What Matters Most, Patrick Barwise and Sean Meehan, HBS Press, 2004.

[2] Quoted in John Lewis Gazette, 24 Jul 04 but sourced from British national newspaper.

circa 18,000 hours a month researching what customers want. How much would that cost if you had to pay for research companies to do that? How much is it worth if you can use the information quickly and effectively to drive your business?

This white paper discusses the types of issues companies face in 2005 in trying to be Fast+Simple and gives best practice learning from companies who have excelled by 'closing the loop' across their organisations, a process explained in the next section.

Limebridge's 2004 research showed the critical factor is closing the loop of customer, programmes and operations

The need to be systematic

In 2004 Budd, the Limebridge alliance partner in the United Kingdom, conducted research into the barriers to being Fast+Simple for customers. The top themes that emerged from Budd's Fast+Simple Survey in 2004[3] are given in the Table 7.1, below:

Table 7.1 Comparing themes from last year's Fast+Simple survey

Businesses admit they are not Fast+Simple	• 77% of businesses say they are not easy to do business with • Of these, 59% believe this is due to a lack of consistency across the business • 71% of companies do not gather the Voice of the Customer end to end across the business
Being systematic is critical to eliminating unwanted contacts	• Lack of resource and poor collaboration effort are blamed for not addressing the root cause of the problems end to end in 74% of all businesses • 52% of companies waste effort on activities that sporadically capture customer views and which are not fully acted on • Only 48% of companies address root causes

[3] For detailed findings see: Making your business Fast+Simple™ for your customers, Budd UK, 2004. Management summary can be obtained from info@limebridge.com.hk

Closing the loop

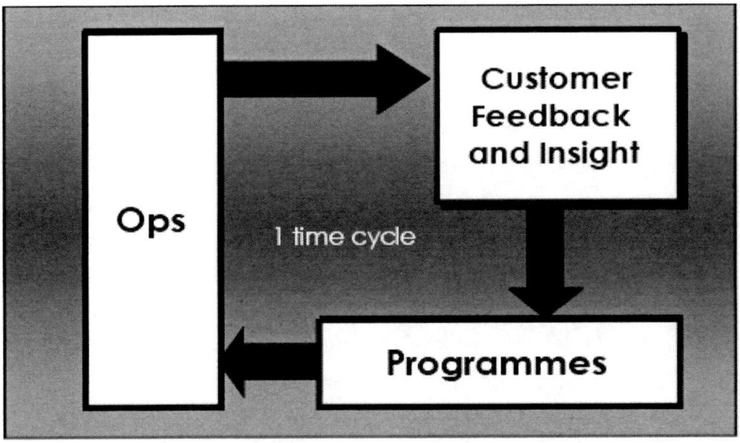

The critical success factor identified in being Fast+Simple for customers is the ability to think and act consistently across the business. The critical success factor is to 'close the loop' that encompasses customers, programmes (projects) and operations.

The weakest link

In 2004, Budd identified key failings in businesses at any stage in the loop were wiping out the effect of the good work done by other parts of the business – a phenomenon nicknamed 'the weakest link' of any zero multipliers (1 x 2 x 0 x4 x 5 x 6 x 7 =0). Failure in one link means you fail to improve for the customer. For example one financial services client was very good at surveying customers and understanding their needs, they were very good at making their operations more efficient, but they failed to target their projects at the issues that customers were telling them were most important to fix, negating the positive reactions they were creating elsewhere. Companies, who are good at closing the loop, are taking a systematic, holistic approach to the customer, business

Reproduced with special permission from LimeBridge – 'Making your business Fast + Simple™ for your customers' (Senior Executive Survey on How do customers get Fast + Simple experiences from companies like Amazon and what can you learn from that?) March 2005, www.limebridge.com

improvement programmes and their operational processes. They make sure they are effective at all steps in the loop.

The benefits of closing the loop

Companies that can remove causes of customer problems operate at better cost levels because they remove the unnecessary or 'dirty' work that causes customers to contact them in the first place. By removing the contact demand, they free up time to achieve excellence in customer service, to leverage cross selling opportunities and to motivate staff by listening to them and through great training and development. They free up time to identify product and service opportunities which customers suggest.

As we will see in this white paper the evidence for closing the loop shows very good returns on investment.

2005 research shows boards are accountable for what customers want but the biggest barrier to being Fast+Simple is failure to act as one organisation

Most companies are aware of the need to improve customer service and eliminate costly contacts. In a Limebridge survey of senior executives in February[4] 2005 senior executives demonstrate that companies want to be easy to do business with, to be Fast+Simple, but face hurdles in reaching that goal.

We're focusing on customers

Their most urgent customer-related issues stated for 2005 were:

- first time resolution and avoiding unnecessary follow on contact;

---

[4] Budd Fast+Simple Survey of Senior Executives, Jan-Feb, 2005.

Reproduced with special permission from LimeBridge – 'Making your business Fast + Simple™ for your customers' (Senior Executive Survey on How do customers get Fast + Simple experiences from companies like Amazon and what can you learn from that?) March 2005, www.limebridge.com

- containing costs of increasing contact volumes;
- increasing web-based self service;
- aligning KPIs to customer needs;
- improving customer satisfaction scores;
- consistency of service and response;
- service differentiation;
- retention of high value customers;
- keeping promises to the customer;
- demonstrating project ROI to top management.

The trend could be summarised by one executive's comment about his challenge: 'Turning an improved customer awareness attitude into actual improvements in service that customers can feel'.

The board members are accountable in 80% of cases

The 2005 research findings showed an increase to 80%, up from 44% in 2004, of companies were board members are accountable for improving customer satisfaction (see Figure A.1 in the Appendix). In practice, these are companies that are trying to make board accountability work, or have it working. This is backed up by the fact that 95% of respondents wanted to view contacts from the customer perspective.

We haven't got improvement processes working yet

However from the results it appears that this desire and accountability have yet to make their full operational impact on the business, as demonstrated in findings that show:

- 29% of companies say they are managing customers well across channels (2004 showed the same 29%);
- 57% say they have a good understanding or have got working why contacts occur (2004: 52%);
- 5% say they are good at applying continuous process to improving customer interactions, although another 35% are getting there.

From this we can see the trend of early adopters towards implementing good practice in identifying root causes of contact, but doing something about it – i.e. applying continuous process to address root causes – this is only just starting to be adopted.

In our view, there are no short cuts to understanding the root causes of customer-related problems across the business and orchestrating a coordinated response. There are no short cuts to implementing improvement processes that continually monitor and improve what the customer experiences. It takes detailed work and practical processes.

We're still getting the basics in place

In the 2005 survey, executives were asked what, in their view, was the biggest thing that stops the Fast+Simple experience being delivered to customers. The top 3 responses accounting for 64% were:

- Too many projects open and competing for resources
- Operational KPIs too internally focussed
- Not enough focus on Brilliant Basics.

This reflects the fact that most companies are BASIC i.e. they are working hard putting the basics in place. Definitions of BASIC,

Reproduced with special permission from LimeBridge – 'Making your business Fast + Simple™ for your customers' (Senior Executive Survey on How do customers get Fast + Simple experiences from companies like Amazon and what can you learn from that?) March 2005, www.limebridge.com

BRILLIANT BASICS and CLOSING THE LOOP are provided later in the chapter.

We can also conclude that companies where there is already a high degree of customer-centric management still find difficulty in applying that desire to the way they operate.

We think we're not ready to close the loop

The lowest scoring were:

- Good effort in one part of the business being wasted in another part because we're not systematic.
- Neither resource nor will to focus on cross departmental improvement activities.

This again demonstrates that many of the companies surveyed are not yet addressing the issues of closing the loop; they are not yet hitting the real barriers of doing this. Rather they are working hard to deliver basic service before they can start setting their aim higher.

The dichotomy is that if they closed the loop they would save enough money and create enough headroom and operational time to focus their efforts and put in brilliant basics too. The three stages are not exclusive.

Executives were also asked to identify the challenges of closing the loop between customer feedback and acting on that feedback and almost one third (31%) said that identifying root causes across the business was the top issue, closely followed by 29% saying that ensuring cross departmental collaboration was their top issue.

Conclusions: there's a gap between aspirations for customers and knowing how to fulfil them. So, we can conclude that:

Reproduced with special permission from LimeBridge – 'Making your business Fast + Simple™ for your customers' (Senior Executive Survey on How do customers get Fast + Simple experiences from companies like Amazon and what can you learn from that?) March 2005, www.limebridge.com

- Executives and boards are taking customer issues to the top of their agenda in the UK.
- They see the cross business issues they must address.
- Working on root cause of contacts has started well but processes to address the root causes, on a continual basis, are not in place.
- Executives are struggling to get beyond the operating basics and into the things which make a difference to the customer – the whole experience as underpinned by the improvement process and loop of customer experience/voice of customer/ programmes of change/operational delivery.

These conclusions are further confirmed by the survey's respondents' answers to which of 6 best practice processes would make the biggest difference to their business. The highest scoring was 'a process to continuously monitor why customers have to contact you and remove the cause of contact'.

Last but not least: People and performance

One final observation of note: Only 5% of executives chose the best practice process 'a process to maximise performance of people in your organisation'. Something you could read as an anomaly since people are probably the key driver of performance, of customer satisfaction, of first time resolution, of inconsistencies and of communicating with customers. Some of the results from the 2005 survey are extracted in the appendix.

Companies are running one off projects to reduce contact, reduce cost and improve customer satisfaction rather than managing their improvement initiatives systematically in closed loop processes.

As we can see, the demand is there to address root cause of contacts and close the loop. It sounds easy but being successful at it

Reproduced with special permission from LimeBridge – 'Making your business Fast + Simple™ for your customers' (Senior Executive Survey on How do customers get Fast + Simple experiences from companies like Amazon and what can you learn from that?) March 2005, www.limebridge.com

is demanding. Attempts to improve operational processes and increase customer satisfaction with 'one off' projects are rarely systematic in a continuous or cross-business way. They may fix something temporarily or, like squeezing the toothpaste, just move an issue elsewhere.

Partial answers that do not sustain the benefits

Technology has been tried and found wanting. Nearly half of new systems implementations suffer because adoption of the technology is not supported by corresponding change management initiatives[5]. For systems to be made effective, people must be made effective too[6].

Techniques such as Six Sigma[7] (which uses deficient diagrams and root cause analysis) or lean enterprise programmes deliver process improvements can help develop internal skills. Liam McGee, President of Bank of America Corp.'s consumer and small business division in the USA, for example, has brought in Six Sigma specialists to help turn around the 1,500 branches of FleetBoston's consumer banking business, which Bank of America acquired in April 2004. Specialists developed 'systems to generate reports on everything from customer satisfaction to sales productivity at each branch so district managers can quickly intervene at underperforming offices'. As a result, each Fleet branch employee has more than doubled the

---

[5] AMR research quoted in CFO Magazine, March 2003 indicated 47% of CRM implementations had failed in this way. Only 16% measurably improved the business.

[6] See: The Human Impact of IT Business: How to Avoid Diminishing Returns, Diane Morello, Gartner Group, 2005, www4.gartner.com.

[7] Six Sigma was developed by Motorola as a quality measure and production improvement program which focuses on the control of a process to a point of ± 6 (standard deviations) from a centreline or 3.4 defects per million items (or 99.9997%). Six Sigma has been applied by a variety of Fortune 500 companies including GE, DuPont, 3M, Bank of America, CitiBank and others in finance, health and education. See www.ge.com/sixsigma

signup of new products (savings accounts, credit cards), since the merger, from an average of 1.9 to 4.1[8].

The difficulty is that Six Sigma is optimised for manufacturing and not for service organisations leaving room for companies such as COPC[9] to provide more focused applications of such techniques. The other danger is forgetting to mix Six Sigma skills with contact management and customer relationship experience to avoid lots of analysis that leads up blind alleys.

Why cross functional projects fail

Attempts to implement change programmes or redesign organisational structures, so that the whole business behaves as one to the customer, are the graveyard of many an aspiring executive. These attempts have generally been failing in four ways:

- They only address issues within a single silo (e.g. within a channel, or within a segment, or within a product set) under the control of one executive who can be held accountable.
- The techniques used optimise operations within that span and although they can analyse more widely the solutions cannot be made to work cross functionally
- The cross-business projects remain the zone of the CEO where over complex analytical projects by consultants are forced into and onto the various operational divisions. These projects often end up being IT centric solutions because of vested interest of the consultants
- The measures on the business results remain valid for silos and stakeholders but not for the customer. Many boards are now measured on customer satisfaction, as we have seen in the 2005 survey, but without correlation to business impact and without linkage to the drivers of that satisfaction. Hence closed loop processes prove difficult to justify under old measures.

---

8 See article: BofA's Happy Surprise, Business Week, February 7, 2005, pages 42-43.

9 Customer Operations Performance Center.

Offshoring has proved that it cannot always reduce costs in the way managers anticipated, although companies like COPC has used Six Sigma improvement techniques to design certification for good practice in contact centres and improvement of client/vendor processes in offshore locations such as India. This in turn has driven UK outsourcers to challenge the way they improve processes for their clients.

Projects to improve customer interaction can often be fragmented, limited in focus, or carried out on a silo basis with little connection to other activities. To achieve continuous improvement requires senior executives to drive systematic processes, not just projects, on an ongoing basis, across the whole company, so that all roles and functions play a part in addressing root causes of customer frustration wherever they are to be found. And they need to do it again and again. The right people need to be made accountable for actions to remove root causes. This can be done if there is a reliable metric in place to measure and target those contact reasons providing the most pain to customers and cost to the organisation.

So what processes have been proven to work pragmatically in addressing customer demand, whilst increasing satisfaction to award winning levels? We have done research into 6 best in class processes from Amazon, Microsoft, Avis, GE and Virgin to produce processes which can be adopted by clients with equivalent issues.

- A process to identify root causes, costs and accountabilities and continually remove contact demand by addressing those root causes based on Amazon.
- A proactive complaints and top issues process to identify and prioritise root cause fixes and actions in large scale complex businesses based on Microsoft.

Reproduced with special permission from LimeBridge – 'Making your business Fast + Simple™ for your customers' (Senior Executive Survey on How do customers get Fast + Simple experiences from companies like Amazon and what can you learn from that?) March 2005, www.limebridge.com

- A process to treat different customers differently when they contact you and increase their satisfaction and profitability to the business based on Avis.
- A process that captures customer feedback and drives direct action back to those accountable for the experience whilst there's time to fix the customers issue and whilst coaching can be most effective based on GE.
- A process to maximise the performance of people in your organisation from recruitment through to their effect on customers based on Virgin.
- A process for continually optimising self service (IVR, web) take up by customers drawn from best practices at a number of businesses.

This white paper goes on to look in a little more detail how companies have been applying the process from Amazon.com and the returns they have been able to make.

Amazon.com is a great example of creating Fast+Simple experiences by closing the loop in a process called Skyline

An outstanding example of a company who has achieved continued service innovation, cost reduction and competitive advantage, whilst massively growing customer volumes is Amazon.com. In a way similar to Motorola, although with a totally different application, Amazon.com developed a process, which has become a strategic benchmark for service companies striving to become the best in terms of customer contact management. In Amazon's case 'zero defects' means elimination of all unnecessary customer contacts, or as Bill Price, former VP of Customer Service calls it 'the best service is no need for service'.

Dealing with growth and complexity

In 1999, Amazon.com had 10 million customers, to which it was adding nearly 900,000 customers per month during the holiday season. In Q4 the growth rate was double that of Q1 in the same year, straining both online and delivery services. The business increased rapidly in product offerings, geography, complexity and size. To be 'earth's most customer centric company' CEO and founder, Jeff Bezos, wanted to reduce the need for customers to contact them unnecessarily. In its early days, the major business costs related to the purchase and distribution costs. Once these were optimised the key driver of profitability was that of contacts per order. This single KPI of contacts per order was driven,

What Skyline Does

- Skyline is a systematic means of bringing the customer experience into the heart of the business. Skyline builds collaboration across all the departments and divisions of a business that cause customer contact and customer frustration. It helps you recognise that the direct customer contact areas (e.g. call centres, branches) are not, typically, the cause of most contacts and that the other areas (e.g. billing, marketing and credit) must be involved.
- It removes customer frustrations by helping you eliminate the root causes of unnecessary contact. Skyline assesses the contacts you have today from the customer perspective and thereby identifies those irritations. It identifies why these contacts occur and what can be done to prevent them.
- It shows you which operational improvements will have the biggest impact and so focuses decision making. Skyline quantifies the cost of contact today. This lets you scope and focus improvement investments, correctly.
- It tracks the impact of changes you make on a weekly basis so you quickly learn what works and doesn't Skyline is a continuous process and produces information each week. This allows you to track what is working and what isn't. This produces greater control of investment and results.
- It's a continuous closed loop improvement methodology that gives you cost reductions while improving service quality. Skyline is not a one off process to identify improvements. Once in place it lets you monitor the contacts you are having and drive change continuously.

Reproduced with special permission from LimeBridge – 'Making your business Fast + Simple™ for your customers' (Senior Executive Survey on How do customers get Fast + Simple experiences from companies like Amazon and what can you learn from that?) March 2005, www.limebridge.com

not by customer service, but by root cause factors in purchasing and distribution, in fact many parts of the business outside of customer service.

Stopping contacts and winning awards

Over the past five years, Amazon.com has achieved more than 20% reduction in contacts per order handled year on year, to become the highest scoring company on the American Customer Satisfaction Index (ASCI) at some 90% customer satisfaction. The award winning operational metrics and procedures used by Amazon to focus on the key driver of the costs and the effectiveness of selling, servicing and fulfilling what customers wanted, came to be known as Skyline.

'Everything in the company begins with "what's best for the customer"', says Bill Price, Amazon's first Global VP of customer service and co-founder of the LimeBridge global alliance of customer management specialists.

Whilst demonstrating massive savings in workload and reducing contact costs by 80%, Amazon has demonstrated retention and uplifts in revenue - a result of removing people's frustrations. To simplify things for customers Amazon had to address root causes for contact from across the business, not just in operations e.g. marketing and distribution 'owned' most root causes of why customers had to make contact.

Accountability for why customers make contact

At the time, Amazon had 300 email codes and around 50 codes for phone. These were reduced to 30 easy to remember integrated contact codes. This manageable number of codes was assigned to executives and project directors who were accountable for removing them. The whole team was able, on a weekly basis, to see

Reproduced with special permission from LimeBridge – 'Making your business Fast + Simple™ for your customers' (Senior Executive Survey on How do customers get Fast + Simple experiences from companies like Amazon and what can you learn from that?) March 2005, www.limebridge.com

the top customer contact reasons, and how much each reason was costing the business.

How Skyline works

- Key focus on metric of contact per order
- Project director and Board members are allocated specific reason codes and accountable for fast action to find and resolve root causes of customer problems
- Trend data per reason code is tracked over longer cycles
- Top to bottom involvement by whole organisation
- Agents' insights and customer feedback valued and acknowledged
- Allows you to continually represent the "voice of customer" from various existing operational and marketing sources

More than cost, Skyline is listening to and learning from the customer

Lots of executives have their own ideas but they can also learn from customers. Skyline was a new idea for them: that customer contacts can suggest new products and services.

According to Bill, Amazon were able to place more emphasis on the 'opportunity enlightenment of Skyline because of its culture, once it started to have a simplified way of measuring customer contact'. In fact, Skyline helped Amazon get its arms around both complaints abatement and opportunity enlightenment.

Two of the contact reason codes at Amazon were:

Customer feedback
Customers making contact to give their views on a subject or general feedback. Negative feedback covered many areas including:

- billing problems
- shipping problems

- backlog in distribution
- complaints and things to eliminate

Customer suggestions
Customers making contact to give positive feedback, new ideas, likes and dislikes with suggestions. Positive feedback included:

- opportunities for upscale ideas
- competitive intelligence
- don't like .... but prefer to get from you because.....

Very few companies engage with their customers in this way, especially via email. Email can be very powerful to quickly capture verbatim comments and suggestions which can be analysed subjectively to produce WOCAS reports – What Our Customers Are Saying – to inform the business. Today, using Unstructured Data Analysis (UDA) tools we can objectively identify the customers' ideas, quantify and present a broader picture of what large numbers of people are saying. It is even possible to extend this with leading edge tools for Unstructured Speech Analysis (USA) which capture not just what customers are saying on the phone but also how they are saying it.

More than cost, engaging your people

Skyline is a complete reporting package and feedback loop. It is a way to engage people in the organisation and change the orientation of company. It is imperative to close the loop – but do it with the front line staff in mind too. It is not just cost and customer benefit that should come from closing the loop.

It is critical to making reason coding work that front line staff engage and understand why they are coding calls by contact reason

Reproduced with special permission from LimeBridge – 'Making your business Fast + Simple™ for your customers' (Senior Executive Survey on How do customers get Fast + Simple experiences from companies like Amazon and what can you learn from that?) March 2005, www.limebridge.com

and what they can do with the opportunity. This is part of the bigger picture of:

- First time resolution of the customer's issue.
- Capitalising on the opportunity; be it for competitor intelligence, cross sell or educating a customer so they learn how to do something for themselves.
- Feedback to the agent of how they are coding and what got fixed as a result. If something that the agent coded well got fixed, there should be recognition for doing a good job.
- Changing the balance of metrics away from production times alone.

Together these things add up to a cultural shift when they are implemented. In Amazon, they recognised the agent contribution using:

- Major announcements at company meetings/ quarterly meetings
- Awards to agents if something good resulted from an agent's insight, making
- a big or small difference to the company
- Reinforcing the message again and again.

For management too there are benefits. The accountabilities and tracking stop contact centre managers feeling like victims: catching all the contact generated elsewhere, whilst budgets get pressured every year.

Reproduced with special permission from LimeBridge – 'Making your business Fast + Simple™ for your customers' (Senior Executive Survey on How do customers get Fast + Simple experiences from companies like Amazon and what can you learn from that?) March 2005, www.limebridge.com

A range of companies in North America, Europe and Asia are reaping the rewards of implementing this best practice process: Skyline

In January 2005, LimeBridge alliance members, Budd in the UK, Driva Solutions in the US LimeBridge Australia and Limebridge Hong Kong, reviewed organisations that have implemented Skyline. We found that they have delivered significant and simultaneous cost and service improvements. The benefits achieved and return on investment have been significant at the first level of direct cost avoided, before taking into account secondary effects on churn of customers and staff productivity and morale.

Substantial returns on investment

The results are demonstrated in the table below. Return on investment (ROI) can be quantified in these cases as 10-20 times initial set up costs. More than 300% returns have been made in less than one year when the Skyline processes are deployed.

Table 7.2 Skyline return on investment

Company	ROI	Comments
Large online retailer	200%	• 22% per year reduction in contacts per order • Estimated cost to achieve was <USD 4 million in programming/development plus USD 1.5 million logistics/fulfilment operations investment • Typical corporate IRR was >200%, equivalent to ~9 month payback
Fast-growing affinity marketing company	1000%	• After 18 months of improvements, and almost no project investment, the company reduced its customer service budget by 40% while delivering a simpler set of customer experiences • Virtually no incremental capital or operating expense required to achieve 50% reduction in CPS (contacts per subscriber) over first 18 months • After first year of Skyline implementation, Customer Service returned 40% of budget to the CFO to spend

Reproduced with special permission from LimeBridge – 'Making your business Fast + Simple™ for your customers' (Senior Executive Survey on How do customers get Fast + Simple experiences from companies like Amazon and what can you learn from that?) March 2005, www.limebridge.com

		on other departments
Large online bill payment company	300%	• Has kept Customer Service headcount flat over past 2 years while number of customers has more than doubled • >50% reduction in contacts per customer, saving tens of millions • Invested USD5 million in self-service automation +approx. USD2 million in other process improvements
Major bank subsidiary	300%	• 50% reduction in contact per customer ratio after one year, majority were points of frustration to customers
Major utility	300%	• 20% elimination of contacts • Reduced irritant contacts by 10% and repeat/hand off contacts by a further 10%

Source: LimeBridge (2005). Further case study information is available by contacting Limebridge HK

Applying the best practice processes for closing the loop brings differentiation AND cost advantage AND increased morale AND customer satisfaction

This white paper has summarised why customers want Fast+Simple experiences and why closing the loop of customer/programmes of change/operations is the key to doing it. It has illustrated one best practice process, Skyline, from Amazon which closes the loop and has been part of the reason they have won numerous awards for their customer service.

A step change in advantage by working with customers

One of the most striking differentiators about companies striving to win in competitive markets today is their ability to work with their customers rather than manage their customers. This step change has to be earned by first of all removing the frustrations that customers experience and then by freeing up agent time to listen to what customers are suggesting. Companies we see globally are at one of three stages of development:

- **BASIC:** Those that still need to put in place the basic operational processes which customers expect as a minimum. Often these companies lack clear leadership direction, have projects which do not address the real issues, gather voice of customer data but do nothing with it, fail to act on what their frontline staff suggest and have high cost operations which do not improve by being moved offshore or having technology layered on them.
- **BRILLIANT BASICS:** Those that have basic processes but need to operate them well and consistently – brilliant basics, first time resolution and reducing customer contact demand are symptoms. Cross functional collaborative projects still go to the back of the queue.
- **CLOSING THE LOOP:** Those that have brilliant basics and are now concentrating on service differentiation where it has commercial benefit – looking at correlations of retention and buying behaviours with very satisfied and dissatisfied customers. These companies have addressed or are addressing closing the loop.

What is evident is that this latter group, whilst few in number, show two order of magnitude advantages over the others (Tesco in the UK is one such example):

- Their customers and staff work with them to help them getter better still because they feel listened to, they feel the company is working to make things better for them, not just the shareholders.
- They are better on all four fronts: differentiation which drives revenues, cost which drives price advantage, staff morale which drives retention of knowledge and saves enormous costs and lastly very high customer satisfaction and delight which avoids churn and consequent effects on revenues. They have a systemic

Reproduced with special permission from LimeBridge – 'Making your business Fast + Simple™ for your customers' (Senior Executive Survey on How do customers get Fast + Simple experiences from companies like Amazon and what can you learn from that?) March 2005, www.limebridge.com

operating model which is optimised by closing the loop to provide Fast+Simple experiences to their customers.

A little self service test

So if you recognise the following symptoms then the Skyline process will be appropriate as a ready to run process supported by Limebridge:

- Customer service causes only 10% or less of customer contacts. Our research shows that 90% of the contacts handled by call centres are root caused elsewhere in the business but they're too hard to fix.
- The areas that cause 90% of contacts need an incentive to change. The areas that cause most unnecessary service contacts often have no visibility or accountability for them and do not pay for the contacts they cause. There needs to be a feedback loop on the impact these areas have on customers and customer contacts.
- The best service may be no service. Customers would prefer not to make many of the contacts they do today. Your customer satisfaction research may not tell you that the customer would have been even happier if they hadn't needed to call at all.
- Cost reduction, revenue and service should be achieved in parallel. Eliminating contact or deflecting it to self service should not be the only goal. The bigger challenge is ensuring you capitalize on remaining important contact with customers delivering quality interactions and creating revenue, retention or satisfaction opportunities.
- Customer contact reporting needs to reflect why, not what. Most contact coding and reporting reflects what the operators had to do, not why they had to do it. This makes it harder to understand

the customer's underlying motivation for contact and so whether the contact could have been prevented or dealt with differently.

- Customer satisfaction must measure how easy a company is to do business with. Many companies lack a 'killer metric' that reflects how easy they are to do business with. Fast+Simple companies track one meaningful metric religiously and have the ability to respond rapidly as it changes.

Further best practice processes which close the loop

Skyline is one of a series of best practice processes which Limebridge offers to its clients. These processes have been gathered from best practice across the world. Limebridge is a global alliance of top customer management practitioners in ten countries: Australia, China, France, Germany, India, Japan, Singapore, Sweden, United Kingdom, and United States.

Appendix A

This survey has looked at how well businesses across industries are achieving Fast+Simple experiences for their customers. The statistical data below comes from Budd's email survey conducted in January/February 2005. The survey involved CEO, board level and other senior executives, polled from Budd's own contact database, answering a short questionnaire taking approximately 5 minutes. 85% of respondents were located in the UK.

Q1. What are your top three, most urgent, customer related-issues for 2005?

Most companies are aware of the need to improve customer service and eliminate costly contacts. Findings demonstrate that companies want to be easy to do business with, to be Fast+Simple, but face hurdles in reaching that goal.

Their most urgent customer-related issues stated for 2005 were:

- first time resolution and avoiding unnecessary follow on contact;
- containing costs of increasing contact volumes;
- increasing web-based self service;
- aligning KPIs to customer needs;
- improving customer satisfaction scores;
- consistency of service and response;
- service differentiation;
- retention of high value customers;
- keeping promises to the customer;
- demonstrating project ROI to top management.

Reproduced with special permission from LimeBridge – 'Making your business Fast + Simple™ for your customers' (Senior Executive Survey on How do customers get Fast + Simple experiences from companies like Amazon and what can you learn from that?) March 2005, www.limebridge.com

Q2. How good are you are managing customer interaction?

In 80% of companies board members are accountable for improving customer satisfaction. In practice, these are companies that are trying to make it board accountability work, or have it working.

This is backed up by the fact that 95% of respondents wanted to view contacts from the customer perspective.

Figure A.1 80% of companies make board members accountable for improving customer satisfaction

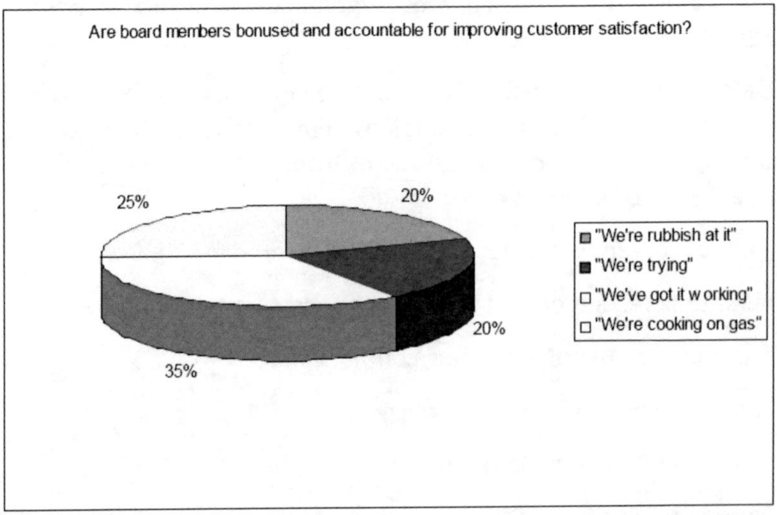

Source: Budd UK (2005)

Reproduced with special permission from LimeBridge – 'Making your business Fast + Simple™ for your customers' (Senior Executive Survey on How do customers get Fast + Simple experiences from companies like Amazon and what can you learn from that?) March 2005, www.limebridge.com

Figure A.2 95% want to view contacts from the customer perspective

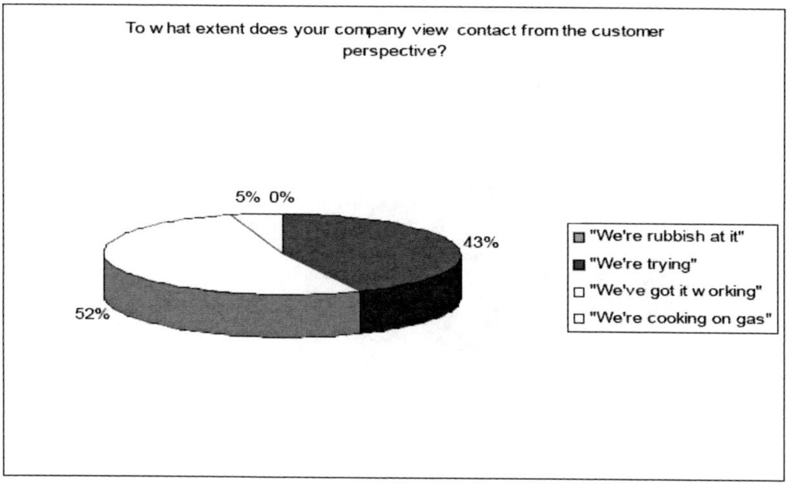

Source: Budd UK (2005)

We haven't got improvement processes working yet

Despite the results shown in Figures A.1 and A.2, it appears that board accountability has yet to make its full operational impact on the business, as demonstrated by findings in Figures A.3, A.4 and A.5 below that show:

- 29% of companies say they are managing customers well across channels;
- 57% say they have a good understanding or have got working why contacts occur;
- 5% say they are good at applying continuous process to improving customer interactions, although another 35% are getting there.

Reproduced with special permission from LimeBridge – 'Making your business Fast + Simple™ for your customers' (Senior Executive Survey on How do customers get Fast + Simple experiences from companies like Amazon and what can you learn from that?) March 2005, www.limebridge.com

Figure A.3 Only 29% can manage customer interactions across channels in their organisations

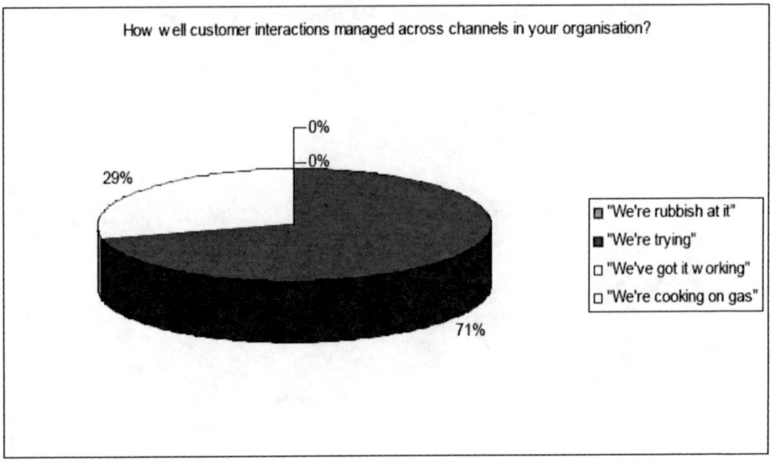

Source: Budd UK (2005)

Figure A.4 57% believe they have a good understanding or have got working WHY contacts occur

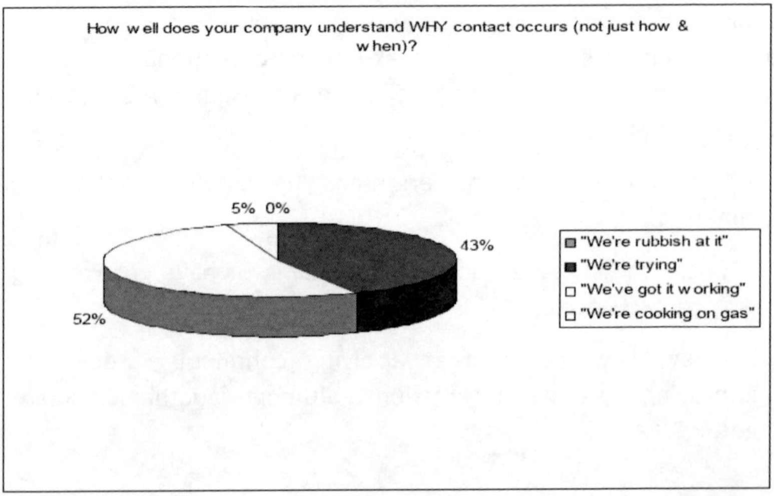

Reproduced with special permission from LimeBridge – 'Making your business Fast + Simple™ for your customers' (Senior Executive Survey on How do customers get Fast + Simple experiences from companies like Amazon and what can you learn from that?) March 2005, www.limebridge.com

Figure A.5 5% say they are good at continuous improvement focused on customer interactions; a further 35% have got it working to some extent

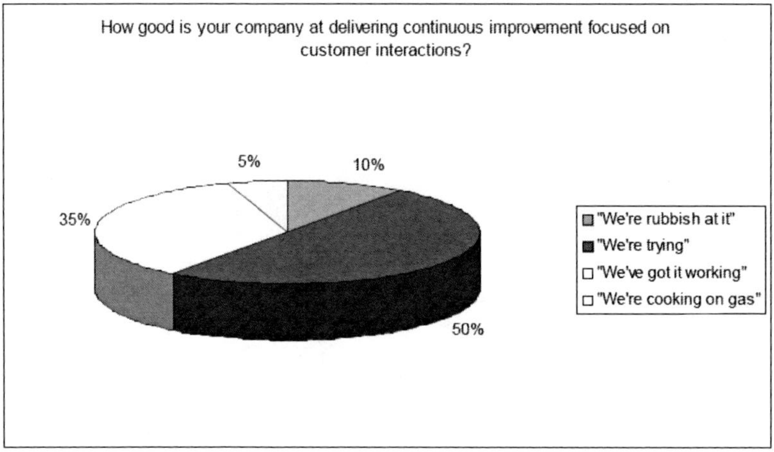

Source: Budd UK (2005)

From this we can see the trend of early adopters towards implementing good practice in identifying root causes of contact, but doing something about it – i.e. applying continuous process to address to root causes - this is only just starting to be adopted.

In Budd's view, there are no shortcuts to understanding the root causes of customer related problems across the business and orchestrating a coordinated response. There are no short cuts to implementing improvement processes that continually monitor and improve what the customer experiences. It takes detailed work and practical processes.

Q3. In your view, what is the single biggest thing in companies that stops a Fast+Simple interaction with a customer?

Findings show that companies are still getting the basics in place. The top 3 responses accounting for 64% were:

Reproduced with special permission from LimeBridge – 'Making your business Fast + Simple™ for your customers' (Senior Executive Survey on How do customers get Fast + Simple experiences from companies like Amazon and what can you learn from that?) March 2005, www.limebridge.com

- Too many projects open and competing for resources.
- Operational KPIs too internally focused.
- Not enough focus on brilliant basics.

This reflects the fact that most companies are BASIC i.e. they are working hard putting the basics in place.

We can also conclude that companies where there is already a high degree of customer-centric management still find difficulty in applying that desire to the way they operate.

Findings show that companies are not yet in a position to close the loop. The lowest scoring were:

- Good effort in one part of the business being wasted in another part because we're not systematic.
- Neither resource nor will to focus on cross departmental improvement activities.

Reproduced with special permission from LimeBridge – 'Making your business Fast + Simple™ for your customers' (Senior Executive Survey on How do customers get Fast + Simple experiences from companies like Amazon and what can you learn from that?) March 2005, www.limebridge.com

Figure A.6 Companies are still getting the basics in place

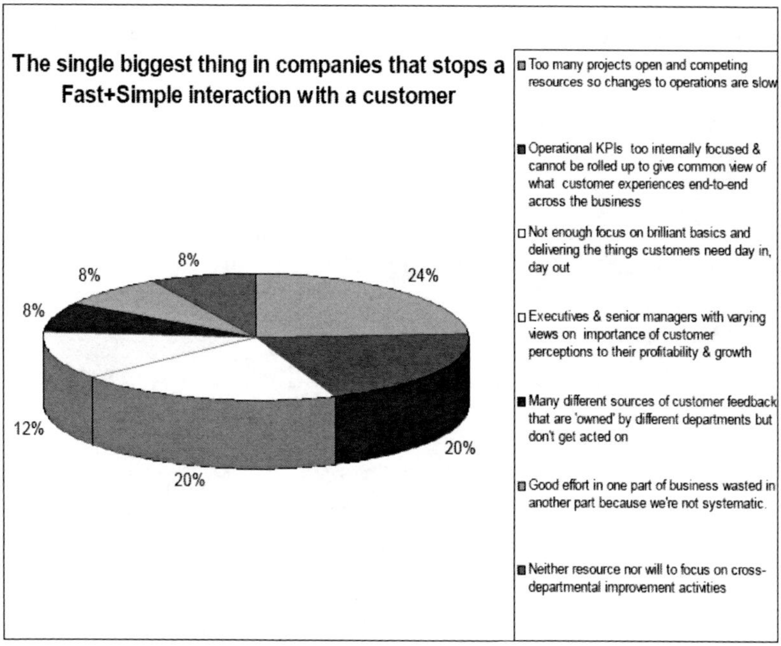

Source: Budd UK (2005)

This again demonstrates that many of the companies surveyed are not yet addressing the issues of closing the loop; they are not yet hitting the real barriers of doing this. Rather they are working hard to deliver basic service before they can start setting their aim higher.

The dichotomy is that if they closed the loop they would save enough money and create enough headroom and operational time to focus their efforts and put in brilliant basics too. The three stages are not exclusive.

Q4. In your organisation what is the greatest challenge in closing the loop between customer FEEDBACK from customers and CHANGES to the way you work with customers based on that feedback?

Executives were asked to identify the challenges of closing the loop between customer feedback and acting on that feedback and one third (31%) said that identifying root causes across the business was the top issue closely followed by 29% saying that ensuring cross departmental collaboration was their top issue.

Figure A.7 Lack of cross-business processes are providing a weak link in the loop

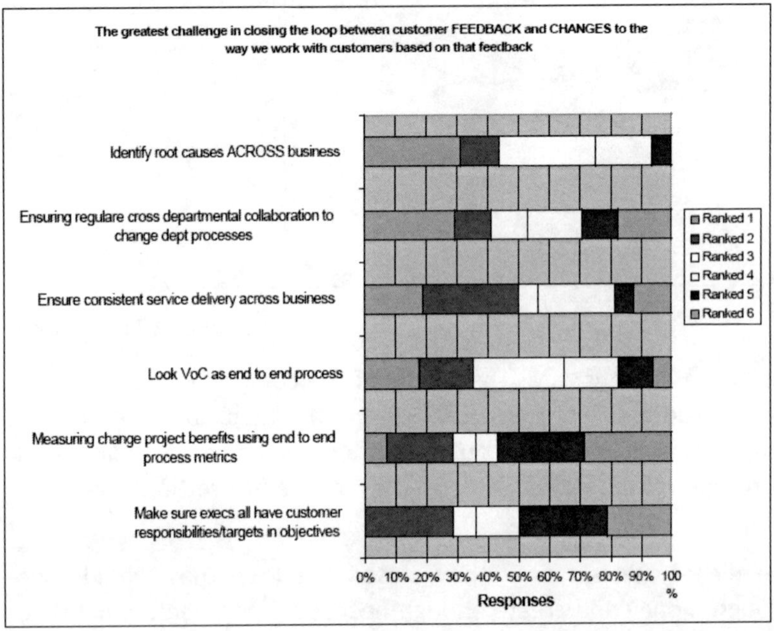

Source: Budd UK (2005)

From these findings, we conclude that there's a gap between aspirations for customers and knowing how to fulfil them:

Reproduced with special permission from LimeBridge – 'Making your business Fast + Simple™ for your customers' (Senior Executive Survey on How do customers get Fast + Simple experiences from companies like Amazon and what can you learn from that?) March 2005, www.limebridge.com

- Executives and boards are taking customer issues to the top of their agenda in the UK.
- They see the cross business issues they must address.
- Working on root cause of contacts has started well but processes to address the root causes, on a continual basis, are not in place.
- Executives are struggling to get beyond the operating basics and into the things which make a difference to the customer – the whole experience as underpinned by the improvement process and loop of customer experience/voice of customer/ programmes of change/operational delivery.

Q5. Which two best practice processes do you think would make the biggest difference to your business?

These conclusions are further confirmed by the survey's respondents' answers to which of six best practice processes would make the biggest difference to their business. The highest scoring was 'a process to continuously monitor why customers have to contact you and remove the cause of contact'.

Reproduced with special permission from LimeBridge – 'Making your business Fast + Simple™ for your customers' (Senior Executive Survey on How do customers get Fast + Simple experiences from companies like Amazon and what can you learn from that?) March 2005, www.limebridge.com

Figure A.8: Understanding the reason for customer contacts and finding ways to tier service response in relation to the value of the customer are priorities

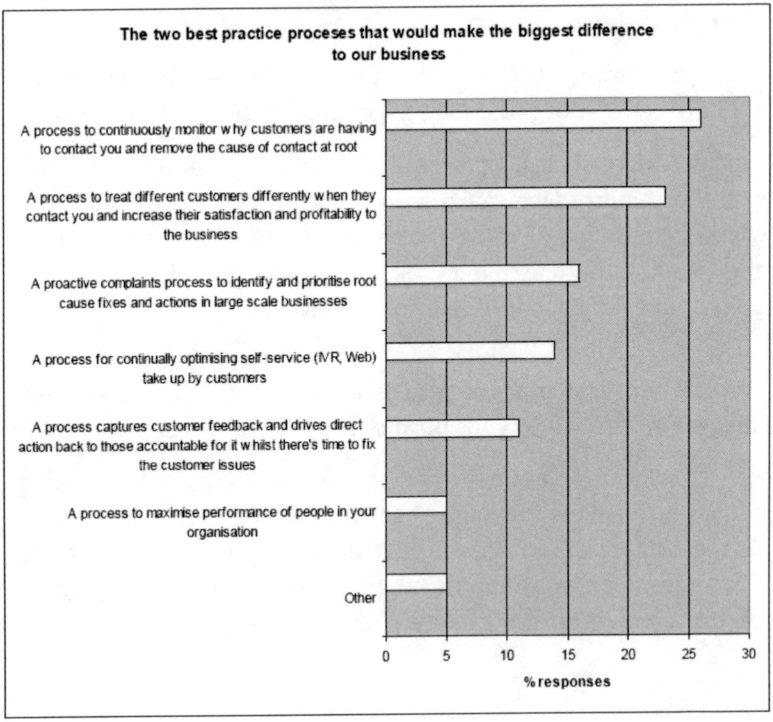

Source: Budd UK (2005)

We offer one final observation of note. Only 5% of executives chose the best practice process 'a process to maximise performance of people in your organisation'. Something you could read as an anomaly since people are a, if not the, key driver of performance, of customer satisfaction, of first time resolution, of inconsistencies and of communicating with customers.

Appendix B: Limebridge

Fast+Simple is the real differentiator

At Limebridge, we work on behalf of your customers to simplify things. We deliver practical, holistic programmes in contact centres and in customer management across your business. We help you to implement the common sense you would expect to see as a customer of your company.

We improve your effectiveness and enhance your customers' experiences. We help you to implement practical processes that reflect the most effective practice from around the world.

We can help you stretch your thinking with input from best practices in the UK and the major mature and emerging markets around the world.

We help you to implement the common sense things you would expect as a customer of your company, across your business units and in your contact centres. We help you to create a systematic operation that weeds out complexity and helps you to adapt faster to customer needs. The benefits in revenue, costs and customer satisfaction give you a triple win rather than a trade off.

Limebridge will help you achieve your goals to be Fast+Simple for your customers. We provide:

- Market leading expertise in operations and analytics.
- Innovative unstructured data analysis tools which read the data for voice of customer and root causes, not just word spotting.
- Prototyping and energising to validate Fast+Simple processes.
- Focus, coaching and skills to run best practice processes effectively.

Reproduced with special permission from LimeBridge – 'Making your business Fast + Simple™ for your customers' (Senior Executive Survey on How do customers get Fast + Simple experiences from companies like Amazon and what can you learn from that?) March 2005, www.limebridge.com

We know that every business is at a different stage of Fast+Simple development.

Internally, everyone has different needs - the board, the customer service director, marketing director or head of a business. Limebridge offers a range of services which together give you the ability to address your situation in the way that is most effective for you.

We will combine the right structured methods and tools from all our practice areas with innovative approaches that make our solution the best for you and your customers. For more information on Limebridge please go to www.limebridge.com

LimeBridge - Sharing best practice in many countries

The LimeBridge global alliance of customer management experts operates from many countries including: UK, France, Germany, Sweden, USA, India, China, Singapore, Japan and Australia.

LimeBridge shares best practice, methods and insights from the best operations on each continent. LimeBridge facilitates a user group, the Global Operations Council, representing over 100,000 seats from some of the largest client operations offshore.

LimeBridge also facilitates the Chief Customer Officer Forum championing the sharing of best practice amongst practitioners.

Index